AL DURA
Long Range Ballistic Myth

NIDRA POLLER

AL DURA
Long Range Ballistic Myth

*From the staged "death" of a Palestinian youth
to the real threat of an Iranian bomb*

authorship international

© Nidra Poller, 2014

All rights reserved. No part of this book may be reproduced in any form or by any means, electronic or mechanical, without written permission from the author except for the quotation of brief passages in reviews, articles or books.

Published by authorship international
Paris, France
authorshipintl@gmail.com

Cover illustration: Devis Grebu
Design: Aaron Levin

ISBN 9780-9887119-5-2

Contents

Foreword	1
Chapter 1	9
Excerpt: Notes from a Simple Citizen	10
Letter to the editor	13
Contre-expertise d'une mise-en-scène	13
Excerpt: Notes from a Simple Citizen	23
Holy Scolders	25
Blood Libel Intl.	28
Excerpt: Notes from a Simple Citizen	35
French Public TV and the Perpetuation of a Scandal	36
Chapter 2	41
Excerpts: Notes from a Simple Citizen	41
Myth, Fact, and the al-Dura Affair	44

The al Dura myth	58
Blame Israel Always	62
Chapter 3	65
Al-Dura: The Trial/Part One	65
Al-Dura: The Trial/Part Two	74
Al-Dura: The Trial/Part Three	76
Al-Dura Icon On Trial In France	87
Al Dura: The Verdict	90
Chapter 4	95
Al Dura: Second Trial	95
Sue Me Too Charlie Mon Vieux	96
Al Dura affair: France 2 wins by a decision	99
Trials: the Appeal	104
Stunning Turn of Events	106
It's official—Al Dura was staged	109
Israel's GPo says Al Dura report is a hoax	112
More on al Dura	114
The "death" of Mohamed al Dura comes back to life	115
Al Dura raw footage: a minute of truth	122
Al Dura raw footage: 27 minutes of what?	123
Al Dura: France 2 Cooks the Raw Footage	127
Al-Dura Raw Footage? It Doesn't Exist.	133
Chapter 5	137
The video shooting of Mohamed Al Dura: a long range ballistic myth	137
Chapter 6	165
Out damn spot	165

Al Dura trials and tribulations	168
Al Dura: Enderlin Loses. Civilization Wins!	172
Hear Ye Hear Ye Breaking News In The Al Dura Affair	173
Al Dura: A Hoax?	175
Guillaume Sans Conquête	179
Guillaume Again	182
Letter to Judge Trébucq	185
Al-Dura: The tide is turning	186
Chapter 7	189
Lethal Narratives	189
Un enfant est mort [a child is dead]	199
Enderlin, Charles. Un enfant est mort	203
A Retooled Libel	208
Chapter 8	215
The Muhammad al-Dura Hoax and Other Myths Revived	215
Attacking Israel with genocidal intentions	226
Memos to Cognitive War College	237
Debate between Pascale Boniface and Meïr Waintrater	241
Chapter 9	245
And Mohamed al Durah begat Mohamed Merah	245
French journalism drowns trying to save Charles Enderlin	249
Israeli government downs the al-Dura myth	252
The Al-Dura Blood Libel Affair:	255
Al Dura Show Trials End Badly	262
Afterword	267
From the staged "death" of a Palestinian youth to the real threat of an Iranian bomb	267

Foreword

In less than one minute an immense reality was created worldwide:

September 30, 2000, Netzarim Junction in the Gaza Strip. A man and a boy are "under fire from the Israeli position." They plead for mercy: "Jamal waves frantically..." but, "one more round of fire... the boy is dead, his father critically wounded." A France 2 cameraman was there. He filmed the incident. The station's Jerusalem correspondent, Charles Enderlin, rushed the video into his prime time newscast. A scoop!

The axis of current events tipped on that 52-second focal point. The failure of the Oslo peace process, initially attributed to Yasser Arafat's refusal to respond to the two-state solution offered at Camp David in July, abruptly fell on Israel's shoulders.

Atrocities committed against Israeli civilians were blamed on Israel, an outbreak of violent attacks on Jews, particularly in Europe, was blamed on Israel. The relentless campaign to destroy the Jewish state went into high velocity.

The "news report" that launched this concerted campaign was like the launch of a commercial product. Its impact was stupendous. Like a hard-hitting advertisement. The claims it made were no more authentic than the promises of love, beauty, prosperity and happiness carried by ads for cars, detergents, and skin creams.

Nothing happens in the video that was broadcast as the shooting in real time of two defenseless Palestinians by, of course, heartless Israeli soldiers. There is a total disconnect between the voiceover commentary and the image. This is not, as so often claimed, a case of a shocking image or even a doctored image. It is closer to mass hypnosis.

A man is crouched behind what looks like a barrel, in fact an upended concrete culvert. A youth is huddled behind him. They grimace in fear. There is a cloud of dust. The youth is stretched out at the man's feet holding his hand over his eyes. The man sits upright, bobbing his head. The tableau is framed by an arc of bullet holes, eight in all, that widely missed the target if, in fact, they were the target.

On the wall above their heads a blood-red graffiti screams: "What was taken with violence must be taken back with violence."

The question is, why were viewers convinced they had seen a fatal shooting? Why is their conviction so stubborn that no amount of evidence to the contrary can undo it? Why does the producer of the broadcast, a seasoned journalist, place his honor on the authenticity of this clumsy piece of play acting? Why does the French state protect the falsification with all the force of its institutions? Why does this affair that continues to enflame Arab-Muslim rage meet with indifference in the Western world?

Whatever may be said for or against the veracity of the 55-second al Dura scene (52 seconds broadcast plus 3 seconds edited out), no one can claim it actually shows the killing of the youth and the wounding of the man. Talal Abu Rahma, the cameraman who "captured" the scene, missed all the action. He was awarded prestigious prizes for this accomplishment. The wall that served as a backdrop missed every sign of damage from the high-power military weapons that purportedly fired at it for 45 minutes without interruption. The alleged attack on Mohamed and Jamal al Dura is inferred, insinuated, imagined but in no way demonstrated.

Al Dura demythifiers are compared to 9/11 conspiracy theorists that refuse to accept concrete evidence of the mass murder of close to 3,000 civilians, an act of war, a war crime. The al Dura scene was the furtive flash of a scribbled note. There is no way to believe in the reality of the "al Dura death scene" without swallowing the enveloping narrative that gave it substance... or inventing one's own story. But sophisticated viewers and professional commentators are under the illusion that they are judging by the video that was broadcast... and raw footage... that doesn't exist. If an incident is presented as a news report does that make it true? Of course not. It is the factuality of the event that makes it a news report. The basis for corroboration of the "al Dura death scene" was reversed: the incident was reported, so it happened. Even though nothing in the video shows it happening.

The burden of proof was lifted from the France 2 journalist and cameraman and dropped like a boulder on the chest of those who demonstrate its incongruity and refute the baseless accusation that Israeli soldiers deliberately killed a child and wounded his father. Heartless murders were in fact committed: In March 2001, a Palestinian sniper shot a Jewish baby, Shalhevet Paz, in the head and wounded her father who was pushing the stroller. One example among many.

Myth is ratified by belief. It is malleable, can be taken literally or figuratively, appreciated aesthetically, admired from a distance. News reporting must be based on verifiable facts. It can be sloppy, biased, incomplete, faulty...but it will always be subject to judgment based on the facts.

"The death of Mohamed al Dura" is a myth presented as a news report, challenged or defended as a news report, accepted or rejected as journalism. This is why essential details have been ignored or revised after the fact in order to make the myth palatable to different audiences. Talal Abu Rahma swore under oath that Israeli soldiers fired at the man and boy for 45 minutes without interruption. This detail is necessary for the myth of heartless cruelty but unacceptable to rational minds. For demythifiers it is proof that Talal and Jamal are lying and Charles Enderlin, who must know better, is covering for them.

That single fact is sufficient to disqualify the broadcast as a news report. Under normal circumstances it would have been withdrawn with a brief apology, and serious journalists would have been careful to avoid such glaring errors in the future. But it was presented as a news report and treated as a myth. The telltale 45 minutes were forgotten or trimmed down to a brief cross fire for Western consumption.

The death throes too horrible to show? When Charles Enderlin explained that he had edited out the death throes he was either deliberately lying or utterly incompetent. The last three seconds of footage that follow the words "the child is dead" are no more horrible, shocking, gory, or agonizing than the image of a youth lying on the grass in a public park. On another occasion the France 2 journalist claimed he had used the word "*agonie*" to encompass the entire 27-minute ordeal that he'd edited down to 52 seconds to fit into the broadcast format. But he knows the 27-minutes of al Dura footage don't exist, and he knows "*agonie*" is a precise term that means death throes.

A doctor at Shifa Hospital in Gaza cites, among Jamal al Dura's numerous wounds, a spliced femoral artery. If, as the cameraman swears, it took 20 minutes before an ambulance could evacuate the victims, Jamal would have bled to death before arriving at the hospital. The doctor was not giving a factual account of an incident that actually occurred, he was taking part in the creation of a myth for a higher cause.

Determined to defend the "killing of al Dura" myth, state-owned France Télévisions network and Jerusalem correspondent Charles Enderlin took some demythifiers to court! What explains their supreme confidence that judges would avoid questions of factuality and rule in their favor? Setting aside speculation on evil intentions or government influence on the court, it is apparent that the al Dura myth fits into a broader narrative that cannot be relinquished.

On a universal level, the al Dura myth functions as blood libel, unleashing genocidal violence against Jews. Within the specific canons of Islamic law it creates the circumstances under which Muslims are allowed to kill women and children or, more generally, civilians who have not lifted a hand against them: if "they" kill "our" children, the prohibition is lifted. And, geopolitically, the al Dura myth is the linchpin of what I call the lethal narrative of the Mideast conflict.

This is why it can't be subjected to normal standards of verification, why it can't be relinquished. Charles Enderlin, the facilitator, who carried the myth into the realm of news where it could accumulate extraordinary power, confirms this function albeit in a reverse formulation. He claims that certain people want to destroy his professional reputation because he contradicts official Israeli propaganda, namely "the demonization of Yasser Arafat, accused of rejecting the Palestinian state generously offered by Ehud Barak at Camp David in July 2000." [*Un enfant est mort*, p. 197]

The texts presented here in chronological order trace my itinerary on the routes of the al Dura affair, from my immediate reaction when the news was broadcast and, step by step, over a period of thirteen years of reflection and action in a sustained attempt to understand, clarify, and transmit. Though I am personally acquainted with many of those who are involved in the affair and have probably read everything written about it in French and English, my approach is synthetic not encyclopedic.

When al Dura debunkers are dismissed as conspiracy theory cranks, journalists and editors concerned with maintaining their credibility avoid the subject or treat it with worldly detachment. I have had the good fortune to work with courageous editors who trust my judgment and vouch for my reliability. Almost all the articles herein were published in print or online media, from the prestigious *Wall Street Journal* and *Commentary* to the lesser known *New English Review,* and including the *Middle East Quarterly,* the *National Post* (Canada), the *Jerusalem Post, Makor Rishon,* and many other internationally respected outlets.

The collection includes the only complete coverage of the al Dura trials (*Pajamas Media*), from the high profile libel suit brought by France Télévisions and Charles Enderlin against Philippe Karsenty to lesser known cases fought with the same goal of silencing critics. In the early days of the controversy, Neal Kozodoy had the foresight to publish the first in-depth article on the al Dura affair (*Commentary* September 2005), a milestone in this uphill climb.

Elsewhere, often limited to a 1,000-word format and obliged to recapitulate the affair for the hypothetical reader who would know nothing about it, I accepted this as a challenge to invent infinite variations on the hallmark introductory paragraph—September 30, 2000, Netzarim Junction in the Gaza Strip.... And I took pride in avoiding the clichés and inaccuracies that trip up so many commentators, whatever the gist of their arguments--the hail of bullets, fierce gun battle, the death of the child in his father's arms, captured in real time...

By reprinting the articles as they originally appeared I want to honestly convey the story as it unfolded in reality and in my mind. I have not retouched them to correct disparities in spelling of names or mistakes about the duration of the al Dura footage (not 65 or 59 but 55 seconds); they are part of the story. Though the family name of the alleged victims should be given as Dura or Durrah I have maintained "al Dura" because that is how they were introduced to the world and are consistently identified here in France.

Media-- with notable exceptions--have not been enthusiastic about following the ins and outs of the al Dura controversy: old news for some, obsessive repetition for others, and too prickly for most.

In fact, it is their subject as much as ours. The survival of democratic values is threatened today by underhanded manipulation of the media that reshapes the public mind by channeling lethal narratives—a form of warfare—through a system that is meant to inform and enlighten citizens of free societies. The al Dura report is the prime example of this use of a news broadcast to forge a hostile myth and entice citizens to embrace it as if it were for their own good. This is not propaganda. These are lethal weapons aimed at the heart of our civilization.

Re-reading this material as I prepared it for publication, I felt that any one of these texts, from the very first, is enough to destroy the al Dura myth. Not because I'm so brilliant but because the myth is so flimsy, it should blow away like a fleck of dust. But it doesn't.

These collected articles are the story of one person's relentless efforts to bring the affair to the public in the most truthful, clear, convincing form. Colleagues and allies have pursued the same goal in different ways with equal devotion. Drawing on decades of experience as a writer of fiction I composed countless variations in the telling of this tale and gratefully accepted the opportunity, when it arose, to report on a given development for several outlets.

Nothing is left out here, because it all belongs in the record and because the accumulation of repeated attempts to understand and convey is a faithful representation of the situation as it is, as we live it, with all it implies of constant pleading and, at the same time, a consistent effort at improvement.

Pushing beyond the absurd obstacles that obstruct the retraction of an unfounded broadcast that is a disgrace to the profession, we perceive the outlines of a global strategy within which the al Dura myth takes its rightful place. The opacity of this obstacle can be transformed to shed light on current manifestations of an ongoing conflict. This is the focus of the Afterword, composed in June-November 2013.

Whenever possible, within the limits of diverse editorial constraints, I have gone beyond journalism to bring this story to life with the depth and eloquence of literature. This is neither pretention, frivolous disregard for the facts, or superficial decoration. Literature is a belief in the power of the articulated word.

Chapter 1

[28-30 September 2000: The hysterical reaction to Ariel Sharon's visit to the Temple Mount, followed by the al Dura broadcast caused a radical shift in contemporary history. Instant repercussions in Israel and Europe have since spread throughout the world.
Intuitively, I set aside my literary project—a novel I had been composing in my mind— and opened a writer's notebook: Cahier d'une honnête citoyenne. Writing in French, reaching out to my adopted country, I used my literary skills to chronicle the dramatic story unfolding before my eyes.
This led eventually to publication of excerpts and, gradually, to something akin to journalism. After publishing alternatively in French and English for several years, I reluctantly chose to abandon French and take advantage of the greater opportunities offered by English-language media.
The English version of the chronicle, Notes from a Simple Citizen, will be published in the spring of 2014.]

EXCERPT: NOTES FROM A SIMPLE CITIZEN
October 2000

... And it is still going on.

So how did they manage in the space of a few short days to turn the Jews into child killers? What is this public opinion that can make gentleman's agreements with Algerians who slit the throats of women and children, isn't bothered by the rise to power of a Chechnya-beating Putin, takes its own good time to get Milosevic, Karadzic, Mladic behind bars, accepts a whitewash of crimes in Rwanda but cannot bear the sight of big bad Israel persecuting those poor little Palestinians? Hubert Védrine runs into the arms of the new providential leader Kostunica, who's hiding Milosevic behind his back, but it's Ariel Sharon, "the butcher of Lebanon" (Radio France Internationale), who stands for absolute Evil!

How does it happen? How did the press, the state and, consequently, French public opinion gullibly swallow this propaganda treat—so blatant it couldn't fool a 2nd grader—and start spitting out anti-Jewish garbage we thought we'd never hear again? Trashing Jews, burning down synagogues, attacking Jews in the street, shouting "death to the Jews"?

The past few days [end of November 2000] there has been a sort of embarrassed semi-silence. As if the press, practically forced to face the truth, has decided that the less said the better. Which is probably true, but we're not going to leave it at that. The harm is done. Now we have to undo it.

On the cover of *Paris Match*: "THIS WAR THAT KILLS CHILDREN"

Baby Sarah is in our face, plastered all up and down the city on big ads for this week's *Paris Match*. "Killed by a Jewish colonist." Accusation. Machination. And then the truth comes out: the child was accidentally shot by her father, who belongs to the Tanzim. Does *Paris Match* admit the mistake? No. *Paris Match* does its own investigation, which boils down to going back and asking the father if by chance he didn't kill his daughter...accidentally of course. No, no, the father says, there's no doubt, it was a Jewish colonist. And you think Monsieur Genestar is going to trust an official Israeli investigation? You're joking! Shortly afterward a *Paris Match* journalist is wounded. Caught in the crossfire? No sir, deliberately targeted by an Israeli soldier. As you can clearly see, this "war" that kills children will not forgive the honest journalists who told it to the world.

Anyway, who exactly is "this war"? It's Israel = the Jews = Jews kill children. Pretext for so many pogroms. The Jews kill Christian children and use their blood to make matzot.

Therefore on this festival the Jews, sufficiently hated for their religion, their wealth, and the debts due to them, were entirely in the hands of their enemies, who could easily bring about their destruction by spreading the report of such a child-murder, perhaps even secretly putting a bloody infant's corpse in the house of a Jew thus accused. Then there would be an attack by night on the Jews at their prayers, where there was murder, plunder, and baptism; and great miracles wrought by the dead child aforesaid, whom the Church eventually canonized.

(Heinrich Heine, "The Rabbi of Bacherach" Jewish Stories and Hebrew Melodies, *Markus Weiner Publishing, Inc, NY. 1987, pp. 22-23, translated by C. G. Leland)*

This war that kills children... The images do not speak for themselves, they say what they are told to say. Though a few of the most blatant errors have been belatedly recognized, no critical reexamination of the Al Aqsa Intifida images within the broader context of Palestinian propaganda has been undertaken. Without this propaganda campaign it would not be possible to accuse Israel (= the Jews) of attacks against civilians, savagery, massacres, crimes.

One single act of savagery was in fact perpetrated, filmed, and broadcast worldwide: the massacre of two Israeli reservists by a Palestinian mob in Ramallah. But these unbearable images of unforgivable barbarity have little weight in a dirty war that doesn't even try to hide its methods. It looks like the formula still holds good: the bigger the lie, the better it works.

How can the truth reply to propaganda? The truth is complex, it speaks with a human voice, it requires intellectual effort from listeners/viewers. Propaganda is intoxicating. It demands blood money. In fact I wonder if what looks like a clumsy failure to hide methods might not be essential to this kind of propaganda. It appeals to the lowest, most ignoble human impulses; so it has to give a wink now and then to show it's ready to stoop to the worst.

Let's go back to the death of Mohamad al Dirah.
According to his uncle Ziad, Jamal [the father] had no problem passing

by Netzarim. A crowd of Palestinian demonstrators, who couldn't go to Jerusalem, had gathered on the side of the road in front of the colony to protest against the visit of rightist Israeli leader Ariel Sharon to *l'esplanade des Mosquées* the day before. However, on their way back in the collective taxi the driver stopped a bit short of Netzarim because the shooting had started. He [Jamal] wanted to continue on foot across the area where the agitation was going on, and get to the camp on the other side. But there was this shooting.

("Mohamad, simple child of Gaza," Gilles Paris, <u>le Monde,</u> 11 October 2000)

Now the dead child is the Al Aqsa Intifada mascot. First they denied, swore on the heads of the Palestinian children, declared, proclaimed, shouted and screamed that they do not put children on the front lines of their anti-Israeli "demonstrations." These Palestinian denials were relayed by the French press with the appropriate profound conviction and complete disregard for the reality clearly visible in illustrated news magazines and TV reports: Palestinian children are there, in the front lines, when Jewish soldiers and civilians are attacked.

Gradually the discourse changes. Yes, the children are there and proud to be there. They want to die for Jerusalem and nothing and no one could keep them from fighting the glorious fight *jusqu'au bout*. So, first the death of children is used to prove the savagery of the Jews who seek them out on their way to school, in their mother's arms, in their peaceful homes. And then the child martyrs become proof of the determination of the Palestinians to fight for their land.

The images show savage mobs and the text speaks of kind souls asking for bread and freedom. All those Davids armed with slingshots facing up to the Israeli Goliath. How's that for expropriation? They take our very name. David/ Judaism/ Jerusalem becomes David/ Palestinian/ Jerusalem and, ultimate nastiness, the Goliath label is torn from the ancient *philistim* and stuck on the Jews. The reality of those crowds is another story. As we saw in Ramallah, the poor little stone-throwers can kill a man with greater savagery than a wild beast.

LETTER TO THE EDITOR
11/03/00 - Published in the <u>International Herald Tribune</u>
Response to: Who Will Protect Palestine's Children? by Jumana Odeh, dateline Ramallah, West Bank, <u>International Herald Tribune</u> 27 October 2000.

Under cover of a heartfelt plea for protection for Palestinian children, Dr. Jumana Odeh adds one more stone to the concerted campaign to convince the world that Israelis are child killers. Indeed, who will protect Palestine's children if their own people send them into battle and, as if that weren't enough, kill them a second time by using their deaths as an incitement to murderous hatred!

Mohammed Durra was not killed "in cold blood," he was caught in a cross-fire. And Sarrah "not yet two years old" was not "killed by an Israeli settler," she was shot accidentally in a tragic domestic accident. By her own people.

No, Israelis are not child-killers. Jews do not rejoice in the death of children, even when those children are throwing stones at them, even when those stone-throwing children are fronting for heavily armed men.

It will be a long long time before any plea arising from Ramallah can speak "to all those who still believe in humanity." When the propaganda smoke screen has dissipated the truth will stand, indelible: a heinous crime was committed against two Israeli men in Ramallah and the savagery unleashed there will turn against its perpetrators a hundredfold.

CONTRE-EXPERTISE D'UNE MISE-EN-SCÈNE
[The publication of the first book-length exposé of the al Dura hoax—Contre-expertise d'une mise-en-scène by Gérard Huber © éditions Raphaël Paris 2003—was ignored by French media, as could be expected. Out of the blue, I contacted David Kupelian of World Net Daily, who immediately replied. We decided to work together to bring Huber's book to the attention of a large English-speaking audience. Drawing on my chapter-by-chapter summaries (page numbers in parentheses) reprinted below, as well as his own sources, Kupelian brought the affair to the attention of a wide audience online and in a special issue of WND's print magazine, Whistleblower.]

Synopsis

N.B. the tone of the book is consistently sober, calm, decent, fair-minded. The author expresses no hatred, clearly states that he is not accusing anyone of manipulation. He does not claim to have the whole truth but he does convincingly show that the commonly accepted version of the death of Mohamed Al Dura simply cannot not stand up under meticulous examination. The author has no axe to grind, no hidden agenda, no scores to settle. And there lies the strength of his *contre-expertise*.

Prologue

Gérard Huber cites and comments on *Muhammad*, the Mahmoud Darwich poem that tells the tale of Mohamed Al-Dura murdered in cold blood by Israeli soldiers. The myth of the innocent child killed by the evil enemy. Rightfully shocked by the powerful—and unjustified—accusation conveyed in the poem, Huber nevertheless ends the prologue on a note of hope:
"Let us only hope that beyond the diametrically opposed conclusions that separate us, the poet and the writer will go back one day to restored confidence in free thought, the hunger for truth, and the protection of children." (15)

Introduction

Announces the purpose of the book: to examine the incident of the death of Mohamed Al-Dura as reported by France 2 and broadcast all around the world.

The emotional impact of the incident was so great that blatant discrepancies went unnoticed by both professionals and ordinary viewers: the image does not correspond to the commentary, does not show what it is said to represent. A team of journalists, including Huber and Stéphane Juffa, editor in chief of Metula News Agency, started to investigate. They studied the testimony of French-Israeli journalist Charles Enderlin, cameraman Talal Abou Rahmé, the boy's father Jamal Al Dura, taking note of discrepancies, inconsistencies, contradictions. They viewed rushes [outtakes] filmed by other accredited cameramen present at the time of the incident.

The method of investigation is rigorous, as explained here (25):

"Let there be no misunderstanding. We do not claim that a child named Mohamed Al Dura did not die in the Palestinian Territories that day or before. And we do not claim that this child is still alive today; because we have not done an investigation on this point, we cannot know. We think simply that:

"(1) an investigation should be able to establish the truth beyond all reasonable doubt; and no such investigation has been made.

"(2) the body of the child shown on the screen [in the France 2 report] cannot be that of a child mortally wounded by high-speed bullets."

The book reads like a scholarly mystery story but the suspense does not lie in the search for the criminal--as in a whodunit--but rather in the search for the <u>absence</u> of evidence that belies the accusation of crime. Where is the blood? Professionals and nonprofessionals alike were informally questioned; no one remarked the absence of blood. Once this absence is pointed out, all agreed that the absence of blood is a crucial issue.

In mystery stories the sequence of events at the crime scene is reconstructed by deduction from the evidence; in this case a cameraman just happened to be there when the incident occurred. The chances were slim...

Chapter 1-Anatomy of the France 2 commentary

French-Israeli journalist Charles Enderlin narrated the incident as it was shown on TV, giving the impression that he was a direct witness (45):

"Three o'clock. The situation suddenly changed at the Netzarim settlement in the Gaza Strip. The Palestinians are shooting live bullets, the Israelis fire back. Ambulance drivers, journalists and simple passersby are caught in the crossfire.

"Here Jamal and his son Mohamed are the target of gunfire from the Israeli positions. Mohamed is twelve years old, his father tries to protect him. He waves his hand..."

"But a new round of fire bursts out. Mohamed is dead, his father seriously wounded. A Palestinian policeman and an ambulance driver also lost their lives during this battle."

Here Enderlin clearly accuses the Israelis. Two years later in <u>The Shattered Dream</u> he changes his testimony. Neither version stands up to examination.

Huber dissects Enderlin's commentary sentence by sentence; he will come back to this in Chapter 4 where we see that the journalist and the cameraman deny they had ever accused the Israelis of deliberately or accidentally killing the boy.

Testifying under oath on 3 October 2000 before the Palestinian Center for Human Rights Talal Abou Rahmé describes the murder of Mohammed Jamal Al-Durreh and the wounds inflicted on his father Jamal Al-Durreh, both hit by gunfire from the Israeli occupation forces. The cameraman describes the incident with a wealth of detail and places it within a timeframe that largely exceeds the scope of the famous TV report. In fact he had started filming incidents at Netzarim junction at 7AM that day. His testimony is closely examined by Huber. It is full of holes.

Several weeks later Enderlin, explaining how he decided to put the report on the air without delay, mentions that he was in Ramallah when it happened. But in the broadcast he is shown as if he were on the scene.

Concluding his testimony on the incident, Talal Abou Rahmé asserts (61):

"I can affirm that the fire that hit little Mohamed and his father Jamal came from the abovementioned Israeli outpost because it was the only place from which it was possible to hit them. This is why, logically and naturally, and from my long experience acquired covering vigorous incidents and violent confrontations, and my ability to distinguish the noise produced by gunfire, I can confirm that the child was killed and his father was wounded intentionally in cold blood by the Israeli army."

In subsequent interviews, the cameraman changes his story. He says the cloud of dust made it impossible to film the precise moment when the boy was fatally shot. But Enderlin claims that he has footage of the boy's death throes, which he edited out because they were too terrible to show.

Chapter 2-From the dossiers to the Esther Schapira report

Within hours after the incident was broadcast all over the world, intense emotional reactions blocked what might have been a rational analysis of the images and commentary. In France the *Comité Solidarité avec la Palestine* published the full text of Talal Abou Rahmé's testimony before the Palestinian human rights commission.

The Israeli army, preoccupied with military problems as the Intifada exploded, and not really aware of the propaganda impact of the Mohamed Al Dura story, handled the whole thing clumsily. The France 2 journalist and cameraman continue to give their versions of the event, constantly adding new details, modifying, contradicting themselves but all of this hinges on small details which, given the emotional and propaganda impact, go unnoticed.

Huber gives an account of the army investigation, its problems and weaknesses.

The Esther Schapira documentary [*Three Bullets and a Dead Child*] leads Huber and his colleagues to again question the entire sequence of events. Something is awry but they do not yet know exactly what. They write articles about the affair, and ask France 2 to air the Schapira film. The response is totally negative: France 2's position is that they have nothing to hide, nothing to show, nothing to explain, nothing to answer. No French TV station will air the Schapira film.

Huber analyzes negative evaluations of the Schapira film by Israeli historian Tom Segev and French journalist Denis Sieffert. The latter, after giving his account of the incident and clearly claiming that the child was killed by gunfire from the Israeli position, goes on to demolish the distinguished philosopher Alain Finkelkraut and sociologist Jacques Tarnero for daring to question the veracity of the France 2 report:

"The France 2 images went around the world. The death of the boy became the symbol of the second Intifada.... Nearly two years after the facts, Finkelkraut and Tarnero, speaking to a pre-convinced audience, dare to claim that a counter-investigation has established that the fire came from Palestinians. Without the shadow of a contradictor and blissfully ignoring what has been said and written on the subject, they still accuse France 2 of hiding the truth from TV viewers...France 2's Jerusalem correspondent Charles Enderlin has repeatedly pointed out that the document broadcast by the ARD was made by the Israeli army and offered to all television stations. But Finkelkraut and Tarnero...don't seem to see anything wrong with showing TV viewers a document from a military source...."

Chapter 3-Deconstruction of a Legend
"...public opinion was immediately convinced that the Israelis were

guilty. And whatever the Israelis subsequently asserted in an attempt to exonerate themselves and place the blame on the Palestinians turned against them, trapping them in a logic of disavowal that added to their guilt." (127)

At each stage in the investigation Huber has to fight against a strong temptation to drop the whole thing and let the legend carry on with its own momentum. He has reached this point once again when someone puts him in touch with Nahum Shahaf, the expert who had led the first investigation, with Doriel, and then parted company with him. Shahaf firmly believes that the death scene is a fiction. Huber decides to pursue the investigation: if Shahaf's theory is truly convincing then he'll pursue to the very end. If not he'll go no further.

Huber reflects on the difference between a crackpot theory—T. Meyssan debunking the 9/11 attacks—and Shahaf's investigation into the Mohamed Al-Dura affair. The crackpot goes to all ends to ignore massive convincing evidence which stands the test of examination by rational minds, whereas Shahaf is struggling to bring to light massive evidence that has been ignored. There were other cameramen at Netzarim Junction when the boy's death scene was filmed. They have extensive footage of events that took place that day. Why didn't any of them film the death of Mohamed Al-Dura?

The legend took on its own life.

"The legend developed first in the form of a sanctifying myth organized around the father's media tours in the Arab-Muslim world, and spread by the systematic teaching of hatred of Israelis in Palestinian schools where children were taught to say: 'The Israelis killed our friend. Shame on them.' The Mohamed death scene was dramatized and played in schools and camps with all the children joining in.

"Then the legend was enriched with theological-political content that had nothing to do with the event: just-cause suicide as an arm of destruction against the enemy." (136)

There are extensive references to Shahaf's rushes in a July 2002 article by Amnon Lord in which the question of who killed Mohamed Al Dura is raised once more. Lord describes incongruous scenes where battles, injuries, and ambulance evacuations take place in the presence of laughing onlookers, and makeshift movie directors do retakes of botched scenes. Gérard Huber decides to introduce Shahaf to Stéphane

Juffa, editor-in-chief of Metula News Agency.

As the evidence mounts, the author asks himself how is it possible that this event which has stirred the entire world could be an imposture. He resolves to pursue the investigation but refuses the word "imposture." No matter how convincing is the Shahaf interview, it will not be enough to clinch the argument. There has to be more.

Other evidence does come forth. This time from France 2. 30 September 2002: cameraman Talal About Rahmé sends a fax to France 2 reversing his previous testimony: (158)
"To France 2 Jerusalem, from Talal Abu Rahma, Gaza: 'I never said to the Palestinian Human Rights Organisation in Gaza that the Israeli soldiers killed willfully or knowingly Mohamed al Dura, and wounded his father. All I always said in all the interviews I gave is that from where I was, I saw the shooting coming from the Israel position.' Signed, Talal Abu Rahma. Private message."

However, Charles Enderlin does not mention this crucial detail the next day (1 October 2002) when he is interviewed for *Proche-orient info* by the agency's director Elisabeth Schemla. Loyally defending her colleague against people "who want to change the way journalists cover the conflict," she does make two critical remarks (160-1):
"I find that your report on the 8 PM France 2 newscast on the night of the incident includes two points that can be contested but have nothing to do with what we've been hearing since then. First, it would have been more cautious in your on-the-spot commentary to say that it was impossible in the crossfire to attribute responsibility for the boy's death to one of the two parties. Second, given the dramatic importance of the images it would have been better to show the whole film, so that the public would have been able to take note that already--on the second day of this Intifada-- Palestinian children and youths were flanked by armed Palestinians who were shooting. But let me add, so that everything will be clear, that I myself wrote that 'the entire video footage shot by France 2's Gaza correspondent Talal Abu Rahmé, who has become a star of Palestinian nationalism, hardly leaves room for doubt: it is most improbable that in the shootout, given the shooting angles, Palestinian gunfire could have killed Mohamed Al-Dura.'"
When E. Schemla asks Enderlin why he didn't cooperate with the investigation he dismisses the whole thing by discrediting Shahaf under the

pretense that Shahaf claimed to have proof that Ygal Amir did not kill Prime Minister Rabin. Enderlin gives his own version of the Mohamed Al Dura story in vivid detail. It becomes obvious that other cameramen were present during or just before the incident. If they left, why did the father and son remain behind the barrel? (167)

"'My answer is that they were paralyzed with fear.' In other words fear kept them from fleeing but the other cameramen were able to run away except of course for Talal Abu Rahmé who was peacefully shooting the scene of the child's death but couldn't go to his rescue because it would expose him and his crew to the Israeli gunfire. I [Huber] found this explanation totally incoherent!"

And what about the Schapira film? Enderlin discredits Schapira with one swipe on the grounds that the Israeli soldiers she says she interviewed have obviously Jewish names. Enderlin says all the soldiers in the outpost were Druze. In fact it has been proven that there were 20 Jewish soldiers and 5 Druze at the outpost.

The next day, 2 October 2002, Schemla interviews France 2 News Director Olivier Mazerolle. Mazerolle does not reveal the radical change in the cameraman's testimony, dismisses the Schapira film as bringing nothing new, denies there is any reason to investigate the affair and subsequently refuses Huber's request to view the France 2 rushes.

9 October 2002, Metula News Agency publishes an article by a contributing Palestinian journalist Sami El Soudi (info# 010910/2 "Nous sommes des êtres humains adultes!")

El Soudi deplores the way Westerners lap up shoddy Palestinian propaganda.
"I have had the opportunity in previous articles to speak out against the false friends of Palestinians living in liberal democracies. I asked that they stop encouraging the propaganda buffoonery orchestrated and managed by the corrupt leaders who govern us and take us each day deeper into a strategic impasse.
"....
"Almost all Palestinian directors take part more or less voluntarily in these war commissions, under the official pretext that we should use all possible means, including trickery and fabulation, to fight against the tanks and airplanes the enemy has and we don't.
"I didn't take part in the specific investigation related to the A-Dura

affair ...but you should know that our official press reported 300 wounded and dead at Netzarim junction the day when Mohammad was supposedly killed.

"....

"Most of the cameramen there were Palestinians.... They willingly took part in the masquerade, filming fictional scenes, believing they were doing it out of patriotism. When a scene was well done the onlookers laughed and applauded. Of course there are hours and hours of footage shot that day and I fear, for the image of my people, that they have been recuperated by Nahum Shahaf and his team of investigators, and these things I'm talking about will soon be showing on screens in America and Europe."

El Soudi mentions that for the first week the Palestinian press called the dead boy "Rami," but finally followed the Western media precedent and called him Mohammad.

At this point in the investigation there is only one road to follow—to the rushes. Juffa and Huber set off to see what Shahaf has to show.

Conclusion

"1. The hypothesis of the mise-en-scène of the death of the Palestinian child is verified on three levels:" (215)

Commentary: France 2 has never publicly corrected the testimony of Talal Abou Rahmé though he has since retracted his original claim that he was sure it was the Israelis who shot the child,

Image: the Palestinians made their own version of the film which has been circulating ever since: they added an Israeli soldier who is clearly visible as he stands a few meters from the child and fires at him point blank.

Fiction: Palestinians produced and directed a fiction film and passed it off as a reality.

"2. The mise-en-scène of the child's death opened a new era in the war of images. "Will we be able to bring it to an end?" (217)

Charles Enderlin defends himself by saying that he shows violent images because the reality is violent, he is only showing things as they happen. In fact he is showing them as they do <u>not</u> happen. Enderlin admits that television coverage may influence public opinion but denies that it can influence the course of events.

3. The Palestinians staged the scene of the child's death, the Israelis did not realize the danger involved. They should have acted immediately, while there was still some communication with Palestinian security forces, to deconstruct the fiction, and both sides should have worked to prevent this propaganda strategy from placing children at the center of the conflict.

The Mohamed Al-Dura death scene became a case study in journalistic ethics at the *Centre de Formation et de Perfectionnement des Journalistes* [Journalism School]. However the study accepted the fiction as a reality; no attention was given to the numerous anomalies and discrepancies pointed out here.

Shortly thereafter, France 2 drew up a Code of conduct for news coverage. Theoretically this should have led to a reexamination of the Mohamed Al-Dura affair and, to begin with, a public retraction of the accusation of murder against the Israelis. According to the Code, Charles Enderlin should not have posed as anchorman when in fact he was not on the scene, and the news should not have been sent to the four corners of the world when no one had taken time to verify it. The Code stands, the rectifications have never come forth. (227)

"The new elements that figure in this book should lead France 2 to understand that though it is out of the question to force a journalist to reveal the origin of information given in his reportage, protection of sources cannot apply to a reportage in which fiction is presented as reality.

"Will application of the Code lead France 2 to open a debate on the reality or fiction of the death of the Palestinian child named Mohamed Al Dura?

Epilogue

Sums up the position of the author at the term of his investigation: The death scene was staged by Palestinians, filmed by a Palestinian cameraman, authorized by a France 2 journalist, and used as a crucial element in the Intifada image strategy. (231-2)

"But if that is fiction, where is the truth?
"The truth is, first of all, that the child shown on the screen is not dead. He plays dead."

The badly wounded corpse of a child was shown by doctors at the

Shifa hospital in Gaza; the child was dead, but he is not the child seen in the famous TV newscast. A child was buried as a martyr. The same child seen in the Gaza hospital or another one? No way of knowing. (233)

"...to this day no one has been able to demonstrate with proof that the child we saw on the screen was killed or that he was killed that day, like that (without bleeding), there."

Deeply buried in the heart of this drama is the sacrifice of the son of Abraham as narrated with significant variations in the traditions of Judaism, Christianity, and Islam (234).

"The intention, whether by desire or failing to interpret desire, is the murder of the son but the act is his preservation and protection.

"So we must listen to both discourses, the discourse of illusion and the discourse of reality, if we want to restore its full meaning to this fiction.

"This presupposes freeing ourselves from the yoke of the 'society of spectacle,' and forgoing surrender to the almighty power of illusion which, because it attributes a definitively fictive statute to all that exists, turns falsehood into truth."

Appendix

The text of the Amnesty International Report on the Al Duras published in London in December 2001: the report follows Talal Abou Rahmé's original narrative of the events with the claim that the child was killed by Israeli gunfire. An Amnesty expert who visited the scene on the 10th of October 2000 concluded that the child was killed by Israeli gunfire. The IDF claim that the child was caught in a crossfire is mentioned and implicitly dismissed.

EXCERPT: NOTES FROM A SIMPLE CITIZEN
July 2003 *"Let's be friends"*

The CRIF website sends readers directly and with no commentary to a long article by Christophe Ayad (*Libération* 3 July 2003) on Al-Rowwad, a Palestinian children's theater troupe currently on tour in France. Ayad reports, among other *misérabilismes*, the real life stories of these children of the camps. Wou'oud: Israeli soldiers stormed into her house, set up an explosive charge to break through the wall into the adjoining house; her mother was injured, the soldiers would not let them call for help, her mother died. Khaled is Palestine's best dancer of *dabké*, "a rural dance where they tap their feet on their beloved soil." Mohamed: loves to play soccer and fight with the soldiers. And Ayad adds for good measure the conclusions of a study by a Gaza psychiatrist: "Most Palestinian children idealize the model of the kamikaze [French misnomer for *shahid*] the only one capable, in their eyes, of avenging the flouted dignity of their fathers, condemned to unemployment, humiliated at checkpoints, helpless to protect their families from attack." Abdel Fattah Abou Sourour, founder of Al-Rowwad, describes the desperate conditions in the camp that lies at the feet of the "colony of Gilo." Using culture as an arm of resistance, Abou Sourour is determined to save the children, for they are the future of Palestine. The children worked for three years on their play, presented as a series of tableaux that tell the history of their parents and grandparents.

And Ayad appreciates: "The passage where they lampoon the absurd litany of aborted peace plans is hilarious. The one where four of them 'play' at being Israeli soldiers at a checkpoint with sadistic realism is chilling." And what strikes the children of the camps about France? Wou'oud notices the changeable weather and, "Oh yes, there aren't any Jews here." Abdel corrects the impression, "There aren't any soldiers. It's not the same thing."

Why in the world would the CRIF post this article? And not even mention the excellent Metula News Agency article (*Un jeu d'enfants palestiniens, quelque part entre la culture et la culture de la haine* [Palestinian child play, somewhere between culture and the culture of hatred] info # 010606/3) by Gérard Huber, author of *Contre-expertise d'une mise en scène*, the investigation into the simulated murder of Mohamed Al Dura.

Huber does not ride roughshod over the frail Palestinian "refugee" children as they bask in the spotlight of Ayad's partisan praise. But he does, precisely and intelligently, expose the instrumentalization of the Mohamed Al Dura myth, in connection with their French tour. If the purpose of such cultural activity is to save the children from a dead end *shahid* future, it should not be presented under the patronage of the poster boy whose simulated murder was the starting gun for this never ending massacre of innocents. By displacing the responsibility for their culture of murderous martyrdom onto the Jewish victims, the Palestinians lock themselves into the impossibility of honest self-critical examination and healing transformation. And the introduction to the children's Passion play clearly establishes a connection between their suffering at the hands of the Israeli "occupation," and the sufferings of French Jews during the German occupation.

Without getting into the narrow streets of French Jewish community politics, and without accusing anyone of dastardly motives, I must say that the failure to post Huber's article, at the very least side by side with the *Libération* rave review, was not an oversight. What exactly is the deal? Isn't it let's be friends, we the Jews of France, and you the powers that be, will exchange visits, handshakes, moving speeches and you'll post policemen in front of the synagogues—sometimes—and in exchange we won't make waves or call you to account on any of the preceding.

HOLY SCOLDERS

3/08/04 French journalists miss the story in their own backyard.

Two days after the murderous attack against the Number 14 bus in Jerusalem, and smack in the middle of the "off the wall" deliberations of the International Court at the Hague, France's public channel France 2 broadcast one of those investigative panoramas of Israel that we watch with understandable trepidation. It is all so familiar, and still it hurts — as the same nerve is hit, and the same insidious message is transmitted to an all-too-credulous audience.

The February 24 episode of *l'Oeil sur la Planète* opened with France's favorite talking heads— Israel's soul-searching, breast-baring holy scolders, always on call when it comes to scourging their country and countrymen. It's not as if their message brings any new tidings; we've heard it all before. Avrum Burg can get space in <u>Le Monde</u> at the drop of an eyelid, the refuzniks are invited to speak to hot-headed Muslim kids in the *banlieues*, any Israeli who has a word to say against the government of Ariel Sharon, the doings of Tsahal, the awful stubbornness of the "colonists," the dangers of theocracy, or the shabby treatment of Arab Israelis is welcomed by the French media.

There is nothing inherently evil in soul-searching, even in wartime; it may well be motivated by the highest Jewish values and the difficulties of respecting them in a beleaguered Jewish state. There is always room for honest debate about ethical values within a community that, at least theoretically, respects them. But why, if they are so intelligent and so ethical, do the holy scolders line up to confess our sins to a tacky French journalist *cum curé*?

Do they have any idea how ridiculous they look as they pour out the secrets of their true Zionist hearts to Thierry Thuiller, who drools as he gathers the salt to rub into Israeli wounds? Egged on and flattered, *monsieur* the-Conscience-of-Israel accuses the army of atrocities, the "colonists" of indecent settlement, the government of failure to comply with peace plans, the ultra-orthodox of oppression and draft dodging, and Israelis in general of deep-seated imperfections and indelible stains.

Who exactly are you talking to, *monsieur la-Conscience-de-Ton-Peuple*? Beyond the nervous little journalist hopping around like Jiminy Cricket lies a French audience that is kept on intravenous anti-Zionism. Do they live by the higher values you profess and demand? Do they expect their compatriots to be kind to widows and orphans — if the cost of kindness comes out of their own pockets? At the price of their own lives?

You are speaking to France, a wannabe world power jockeying for paternalistic leverage in the European Union and drugged on the fantasy of being the leader of the Arab world. You are tour guides for a nation that looks down its nose at *yeshiva bochers* rocking back and forth while their fathers and mothers are fruitful and multiplying; a nation that cuddles up to a poor Cohen who can't marry his divorced beloved because of the stupid rules of the nasty rabbis; a nation that scowls at the armored cars taking Jews in and out of their shamefully neat and pretty neighborhoods provocatively nestled in Palestinian lands.

Israel is its own worst enemy, because the real enemy is kept out of the picture. So Daniel Bensimon can tut-tut about all the money spent on the military that could be better used elsewhere. He sounds so reasonable — and it's not just because he's wearing a turtleneck sweater. Compared to the modern offices of <u>*Haaretz*</u>, the Judean hills look as old as Methuselah and the wild men who live there — the one who shows the reporter a little archeological site attesting to ancient Jewish presence, the other who refers to the biblical promise — are made to look like prehistoric atavisms. Even the good-looking young ladies and men dancing in a Tel Aviv nightclub on Friday night are turned into a reproach against the comical throwback dressed in black, blowing his horn to close a Jerusalem market before *shabat*.

All of this might seem like slim fare hardly worth 15 minutes of indignation. But wait until you hear the punch line. The pearl in the oyster, the gold nugget buried in this take-a-look-at-this-and-that stroll: Israeli soldiers kill Palestinian kids for fun.

The sequence takes place near "the wall." Which is, in reality, a fence, seen from a distance in the background. In the foreground, a formidable Tsahal-watcher named Yvonne Mansbach explains to Thierry Thuiller that some Palestinian kids were horsing around near the barrier. The soldiers said "we're going to have a good time," ran over to the fence and, without even firing a warning shot, killed three Palestinian kids. This is supposed to be happening in real time. Yvonne Mansbach makes a phone call. She says she reported the incident to the army spokesman, and he asked if the kids had done something to the fence, and she replied, "What does that have to do with it, is kicking the fence punishable by death?"

The army spokesman appears deaf to ethical entreaty. The French journalist hears the testimony and draws the logical conclusion: Israelis know this kind of thing is happening, they approve, and it doesn't even get a line in a newspaper.

This is the France 2 that brought us the Mohamed Al-Dura "death" scene, the blood libel that kicked off these long years of murder and maiming of Israeli civilians. That day, September 30, 2000, at Netzarim junction, France 2 stringer Tala Abu Rahma was in the right place at the right time. Thanks to his too-good-to-be-true scoop, the whole world was fed the Jews-are-child-killers story. The repercussions are global and enduring.

Riding on the credibility of the poster boy — a France 2/PA production — a jumpy little journalist can blithely claim that IDF soldiers just killed three Palestinian kids. He doesn't even have to ask his cameraman to zoom in on the scene or run over and film the bleeding corpses before they are rushed off for a Hamas funeral.

Muslims can beat up Jews in French streets and schools, burn synagogues and kosher butcher shops, without stinging the French conscience. They provoke a shrug of the shoulders, a solemn official declaration — France is not an anti-Semitic country — and a low mumble: What can you expect, when they kill Palestinian children for fun! Palestinians can kill and maim Israelis by the thousands, and a blasé French public yawns and mumbles: What can you expect, they build a wall and then use it as an excuse to kill Palestinian children for fun!

I have a suggestion: Instead of explaining *kashrut* to a ham hock, the Israeli holy scolders should come over here and make a film about France, its ills and misdeeds, its failings and disappointments, its untroubled conscience that takes a handful of NGOs for G-d's gift to the world, its Salafist mosques and anti-Semitic comics, its pacifism funded by Saddam's oil money, its anti-Americanism fed by bitter jealousy, its Pravda press and defenseless borders...

But don't expect the special report to be aired on French television. Holy scolders are not kosher if they turn their scorn on France.

— *National Review Online*

BLOOD LIBEL INTL.
Gérard Huber and Nidra Poller

How many times over how many centuries have Jews been killed by murderous mobs inflamed by the accusation of blood libel? Christian children who had died of natural causes were held up for the crowd to see, and then the real blood flowed, Jewish blood. The pogroms are a matter of historical fact. And the Christian children murdered by Jews? How many of these accusations were based on the truth? We can fairly reply without further research: none.

Then how are we to explain the indelible quality of the Mohamed Al-Dura international blood libel accusation? And how can we dare to underestimate its power to motivate a new type of worldwide pogrom, a new wave of jihad against the Jews? A jihad that, if it is not stopped in its tracks, could put the Shoah to shame! Irony of ironies, people who have taken the pains to study and analyze all available evidence and present the results of this research for public scrutiny are labeled "revisionists."

Let us put it simply: at the dawn of the 21st century, television audiences in the entire world were convinced by a crudely concocted fictional death scene instantly transformed into the founding myth of the so-called Al Aqsa Intifada. Global village indeed! Global shtetl, in fact.

One is hard put to know where to begin. An avalanche of questions hurtles down the sharp peak from myth to reality, carrying millions in its wake: they would rather be buried than face such immense doubt. They would prefer to believe there is no way of knowing the truth than withdraw the emotional investment provoked by their initial reaction to the scene. They do not want to wade through the factual evidence, picking over small details, comparing conflicting testimony, discerning discrepancies; they will not dare to stand up against a mountain of belief.

The child "died in his father's arms." So what if the image contradicts the belief induced by the France 2 journalist's voiceover commentary? He died in the arms of his father who tried frantically to shelter him. It would seem heartless to point out that the image shows no such thing. Clearly visible details contradict features discernible only to the believing eye: the blood soaked t-shirt, the fatal moment captured live, the father's frantic appeals—in the wrong direction—to stop the shooting. Even before examining discrepancies in testimony by people directly involved in the incident, we must admit that the emblematic image imprinted on the collective mind contradicts the myth it sustains.

The death—real or fictional—of Mohamed Al-Dura is an accusation against Israel, against the Jews.

If the truth could be chosen, if one could choose the truth in the Al-Dura affair, what would be the best truth? That the "death scene" displayed before the eyes of the world is a fiction and the child, as seen in the film, was not shot and killed. It doesn't matter if we cannot find him and bring him back to take a bow on the world stage, offering catharsis, ushering in a new era of peace and harmony. The human best truth is that this child was not killed before our eyes, was not killed at all.

If, as it would seem, the organizers of the "intifada" or more precisely the latest phase in the ongoing jihad against Israel, created and distributed the myth of the child murdered in cold blood by Israeli soldiers, that can be repaired. If all's fair in love and war, meaning all is unfair, peace can be pieced together. If the child is dead, the loss is irreparable. If he is alive, that's good news.

Why does this possible good news provoke reactions shading from disdainful skepticism to vicious hostility? The refined intelligence searches for truth without arbitrarily excluding potentially valid hypotheses. Honest research is impossible when alternative hypotheses are previously hooked up to ideological poles erected at opposite extremes like goals on a football field. The truth lies ahead on a road that cannot be traced in advance. It isn't a football disputed by two teams.

For what could be broadly described as the Arab/Muslim/anti-Zionist team the truth is undeniable: Mohamed Al-Dura was killed in cold blood by brutal Israeli soldiers. And in fact the role of the soldier implied in the soft version distributed worldwide is made explicit in the hard version peddled to this day in the Muslim world: the image of an Israeli soldier aiming at the Palestinian boy is spliced into the Al Dura scene. Western viewers who have never seen Palestinian propaganda films will be surprised to discover how similar they are to the Al Dura broadcast: same crude style, same amateur acting, same slipshod directing. According to the football game version of the truth the position defended in *Contre-expertise*—the death scene is a fiction—is necessarily at the opposite extreme from the hard version—the child was killed in cold blood by Israeli soldiers. Two extremes to be avoided by the discerning mind.

Which leaves us in the crossfire. *The child was killed by accident, by Palestinian gunmen?* If this is the truth, it's worthless. *No one knows what really happened, there is no way of ever knowing?* Again, worthless. Mohamed Al Dura cannot be the founding myth of the "intifada" unless he was deliberately killed by Israeli soldiers.

This explains, at least partially, the ambiguity entertained by those who brought the myth into the world and those who need it to sustain a movement, which is not finished but only just begun.

We must not forget that the Al-Dura image is a Palestinian creation backed up by French credibility. According to the news report spread around the world with the speed of light, a French cameraman filmed the incident (which he claims lasted 45 minutes) as the child was felled by Israeli bullets. In the reportage offered free of charge to all the world's television, the cameraman's evidence is corroborated by a voiceover from the France 2 Jerusalem correspondent Charles Enderlin speaking as if he were on the spot (he was in Ramallah). In fact the "French" cameraman is a Palestinian stringer named Talal Abu Rahma. His sworn testimony presented to the Palestine Human Rights Commission is still available on sites such as *solidarité-palestine.org* where his detailed account of the incident is posted under the headline "Mohammed Al-Durreh was murdered deliberately, in cold blood." Abu Rahma's extensive description of the events is illustrated with the famous pictures of father & son crouched behind the concrete "barrel," and authenticated by his credentials as an experienced journalist working for France2 and CNN. His unambiguous assertion that the shots that killed the boy and wounded his father could only have come from the Israeli position stands as gospel truth for millions who would never believe a word that could contradict it, not even when the contradiction is written and signed by the very same Talal Abu Rahma in a fax addressed to the France 2 Jerusalem news desk on 28 September 2002: "I never said to the Palestinian Human Rights organization in Gaza that the Israeli soldiers killed willfully or knowingly Mohamed Al Dura, and wounded his father...."

As James Fallows observed in his Atlantic Monthly (June 2003) article, *Who shot Mohamed Al-Dura*? the same image is functioning on radically different levels in different regions of the international community.

So where does the French public stand on this continuum? Curiously enough, this French society that prides itself on the finesse of its *cinéma d'auteur* while demeaning lowbrow glitzy Hollywood products has swallowed the Al Dura film with uncritical candor. In an obvious attempt to deflect attention from the French peacenik foreign policy fiasco, America bashing took to gasps and tut tuts over the biased American media manipulated by a dictatorial warmongering government. French media, you understand, would never stoop so low. In a world of sordid self-interest and backroom deals, France has elected itself to a permanent seat on the higher plane. Did France not show its valor in opposing the heartless war machine of the *hyperpuissance*? Does France not stand, alone if necessary, for a just solution to the Middle East crisis?

There is no Mohamed Al Dura affair in France! It is an open and shut case. Charles Enderlin, the journalist who brought the Mohamed Al Dura image to the world's screens, always has the last word in the French press. Interviewed by the lightweight weekend magazine VSD (N° 1344: 52) after he was awarded the Peabody prize for the English language version of Le Rêve brisé, Charles Enderlin was asked:

VSD: How did you feel when you were accused of misinformation on the death of Mohamed al-Dura before the cameras on 30 September 2000?

Charles Enderlin: It's defamation propagated by extreme right organizations that pretend the scene was staged. The Israeli army never investigated. We suggested they contact us to get the rushes, but no request was presented to our legal service. Since that time France 2 and I have filed 4 lawsuits in Paris.

(See menapress.com info # 012905 for a full reply to the above)

None of the alleged lawsuits ever reached Gérard Huber or any other person involved in this investigation!

When the subject was raised in whispers on a television program called *Campus, Libération* journalist Hatzfeld* shrugged it off with "*nous assumons le dérapage*," which freely translated means okay it was a fiction film, so what? We might call this media *libertinisme*. Everyone's doing it so what's the big deal?

Maybe so. But it is legitimate to ask why the Al Dura affair is such a big deal in the United States? David Kupelian's in-depth investigation (*Whistleblower* March 2003) and the abridged version posted on WorldNetDaily circulated widely. Fallows' *Atlantic Monthly* piece has attracted attention in all quarters. It is reasonable to expect that TV stations unwittingly involved in broadcasting the myth will come into the fray. And, further, one can ask whether French-speaking people have been given a chance to decide for themselves, since the issue has never been openly treated in the French media and, we might add, not even in French Jewish media. *Contre-expertise*, a serious, solidly documented study of the Al-Dura case, published in January 2003, has met with dismissive silence. Total refusal to consider the evidence and respond to the arguments is coupled with a pernicious smear campaign against the author Gérard Huber—labeled "right wing extremist"—and assorted supportive individuals, associations, and news agencies bunched together in an anonymous mass and accused of being unconditional supporters of Sharon, Likud fellow travelers, dangerous members of the Betar, etc.

There is no need for a conspiracy against those who suggest that the Al Dura story is weighted with too many discrepancies to float undisturbed in the upper atmosphere of journalistic reliability; the defensive reaction draws on ingrained attitudes and habits of thought. The reaction of contemptuous silence is eating away at the French media culture and making serious inroads into French democracy. Because of course the Al-Dura affair is not an isolated incident; it is an essential element in a troubling climate of antisemitism cloaked in antizionism. The distress of French Jewry is no secret to anyone...but the French. In the same way that the media cannot dare to ask if Mohamed Al Dura is alive and well and living somewhere, French society cannot ask what French Jews are complaining about. And this is leading to ever more complicated contortions and variations on the theme of "don't we have the right to criticize the government of Ariel Sharon without being accused of antisemitism?" Of course the answer is yes. But the corollary is not heard: if criticism supposedly directed against the Israeli government is constantly translated into acts of aggression against French Jews is this not evidence of the underlying antisemitism that motivates this "criticism"?

The false accusation of ritual murder has led to the real murder and mutilation of thousands of victims...with no real end in sight. Israeli children murdered in their beds, homes, streets, schools, playgrounds, cars, restaurants. Palestinian children killed accidentally in actions aimed at terrorists embedded in the population; children foolishly throwing stones at soldiers and tanks and taking the fire directed at killers hiding behind them; children roped into blowing themselves up in terrorist bombings; a whole generation of the living dead, children with no model but suicide, no hope, no future. Demystifying the Al Dura myth could help to roll back this culture of suicide.

Whatever provisions might be made and eventually respected in this road map or that peace process, no plan for reconciliation and peaceful coexistence between Israel and Palestine—between Jews and Muslims-- can succeed if it does not include an end to the incitement to murder Jews. Which is more degrading? To pursue the incitement and make peace impossible, or to renounce jihad and build new relations based on mutual respect? It takes courage to dismantle the emblematic myth of this "Intifada," but we believe that the hope generated by such a gesture is no less crucial than the hope of political autonomy.

In today's "we are not anti-Semitic" France, Jews are called to task from morning to night, from right to left, from a vulgar-to-sophisticated wide spectrum of commentators, and summoned to answer for a century's hit parade of crimes attributed to the "Hebrew state": genocide, apartheid, occupation, colonialism, crimes against humanity, war crimes.

Certainly the death of Mohamed Al-Dura is in the top ten of this hit parade. It is the knot that holds together the intricate enterprise of delegitimization of Israel, denied the right of self-defense against attacks perpetrated with the ultimate aim of extermination. It is the beginning, or the fake beginning, of this "intifada." The "provocation of Sharon's visit to the Temple Mount" has already been deflated. The Al Dura myth will not resist much longer. This leaves the atrocious murder of two Israeli reservists in a Ramallah police station as the real first bloody horror of this conflict.

In questioning the authenticity of the claim that a Palestinian child was killed in cold blood—or by accident—by Israeli soldiers—or Palestinian gunmen—at the Netzarim crossing on 30 September 2000 we are not seeking to whitewash Israel, to save face, to cover crimes in order to have a free hand to pursue a criminal project. We are simply showing that the image of the "death scene" does not stand up to unbiased examination. Then why should it be left standing?

Flashback:

Dateline Gaza, 11 October 2000, 11 days after the alleged death of the Palestinian child and one day before the bloody mob murder of two Israeli reservists in Ramallah: *Le Monde,* France's newspaper of record, publishes a full-page article signed Gilles Paris—*Mohamad, a simple child from Gaza.* A tour de force of narrative journalism studded with endless details of local color that place the reader in the heart of the tragedy —the stairway, the metal door, chirping birds in cages, plastic chairs for condolence visitors. The child in the article is named Mohamad El Dirah, the woman identified as his mother is known today as his stepmother, the shoulder injury sustained by her husband Jamal in the France 2 news report has turned into an unspecified injury that will cause him to limp for the rest of his life. The mother comments "I know that martyrdom is the best way to die but I doubt that it will change anything....when it comes to international negotiations."

The Gilles Paris article, twisted with wilful bias stitched into every word and dripping in gooey pathos that curdles into anti-Israeli poison, is a stunning demonstration of the confused and contradictory gospels built up around the Al Dura legend and glibly presented as factual reporting. Why quibble about the discrepancies when the point is that Mohamad, "the martyr of Al Aqsa....an ordinary child who loved birds..." is dead.

But what if he isn't dead? If the death scene is a fiction film then where did the *Monde* journalist draw such vivid details for his human interest story? How did he pump such convincing authenticity into these tales embroidered on a myth?

Mohamad's older brother Iyad remembers a marvellous trip to Jaffa with their father, the only time he and Mohamad had ever left Gaza. Compared to Gaza, Jaffa is a "paradise." Iyad would love go there again. But, writes Gilles Paris, "he will never go to Tel Aviv. 'Because there are many Jews there and it's the Jews who killed my brother,' says Iyad calmly." And Gilles Paris adds, as if the words fell from heaven, "It's perfectly clear."

[1] For example the "rape" scene reproduced in Pierre Rehov's Contre-Champs video *Israel and the War of Images*. Palestinians dressed as Israeli soldiers rape a Palestinian woman and slit her husband's throat. The scene is so grotesque that it is limited to domestic distribution. But French journalist Sara Daniel made the no less grotesque claim in a *Nouvel Observateur* article that Israeli soldiers deliberately rape Palestinian women so they will fall victim to honor killings.

* [Hatzfeld would again demonstrate his elastic notion of truth with the publication in 2011 of a pretentious novel, *Où en est la Nuit*, in which he invents a grotesquely unreal Ethiopian long-distance champion for the express purpose of heaping scorn on the authentic champion Haile Gebrselassie.]

—*Makor Rishon June 2004 (Hebrew translation)*
Israel Hasbara Committee & Atlas Shrugs June 2006

EXCERPT: NOTES FROM A SIMPLE CITIZEN
July 2, 2004

I didn't know anything about Karen Armstrong, Eastern Christians, or replacement theology when I opened this notebook with a reaction to her op-ed about sharing Jerusalem. I didn't know, when I wrote the letter published in the International Herald Tribune, that Mohamed Al Dura was not killed in a crossfire, he was killed in a Pallywood fiction film. And so there is a wrapping up of sorts when France 2's I-know-everything-about-Israel reporter Charles Enderlin, the same Enderlin who turned a two-bit Palestinian propaganda film into a 21st century blood libel, makes his last stand on the security barrier. Enderlin is a phenomenon and a half. There are all kinds of ways to manipulate the facts. He does it with a hallmark voice and delivery system reeking with latter day saintliness. Where did the prophets go after the end of prophecy? They went to the Jerusalem desk of France 2. No matter what the subject, Enderlin's voice condemns Israel. If Israel handed out Ramadan baskets to every last Muslim in the disputed territories, Enderlin would report it as an affront, a crafty maneuver, a heavy-handed interference in the lives of noble Palestinians, a too little too late and too much too soon.

These days Enderlin's on the fence, exposing Israel's crimes. An Arab from East Jerusalem who is working on the security fence is captured live as he discovers that his home has been destroyed by Israeli government forces. Before our eyes he phones his boss and says he doesn't want to work for him anymore. Who could blame him? Why was his house demolished? We see him with a thick file of official papers. Repeated requests for authorization. Post-construction. The house was built without authorization. Is that any reason to destroy it? Can't I build a house in that lovely little square on boulevard Saint Germain, or why not in the middle of Place des Vosges. Doesn't a man have an inalienable right to build a house wherever he wants, however he wants, and all the more so if he's an Arab living in East Jerusalem? Enderlin leaves no doubt. His voice is judge, jury, and jailor. Israel once again is thrown in jail. Clang! End of reportage. A few days later it's a Palestinian crying because the Israeli fence is going to cut him off from his olive trees. Might as well cut off his head. In fact, beheading is more common these days than separating peasants from their olive groves, but you wouldn't know it because Charles Enderlin is there to replace an old guy named Solomon. The olive trees belong to the man who is crying. And if you're not impressed, listen to this: his olive trees are 200 years-old.

You might think that separating a man from his olive grove, even if he's owned it for 200 years, is not as serious as shooting a 12 year-old Palestinian boy in cold blood, but think again. The sins of Israel are all the same size, infinite, and punishable by the same sentence: extermination. It can be meted out anywhere. Against Israeli civilians, of course, but also against the tombs of Jewish soldiers killed defending France against the Nazis, against *yeshiva bochers* in the streets of Paris and its *banlieue*, against synagogues, Jewish day schools, torah scrolls, wherever.

FRENCH PUBLIC TV AND THE PERPETUATION OF A SCANDAL
November 26, 2004

The United Nations should have thought of this one. They wouldn't have to work so hard at spinning the oil-for-food scam investigation. There wouldn't be any investigation at all. You just ask the public prosecutor to sue anyone who dares to question the integrity of U.N. officials. And it's shut their mouth and business as usual.

That's what is happening in France as the Mohamed Al Dura scandal finally hits the mainstream press. French public television channel

France 2 is suing, or threatening to sue, anyone who questions the integrity of its journalists. And questioning the truth of one of the most unsubstantiated news reports ever to hit the screen is considered questioning the integrity of the journalists who produced it. Even if the whole thing was a fake. It was reported, so it has to be true. Something like the Koran. You don't question it.

It all started on September 30, 2000, at Netzarim Junction in the Gaza Strip. The Al Aqsa Intifada was a gleam in its Abu's eye, President Clinton was trying to piece together the shreds of the Camp David negotiations, and a Palestinian stringer working for French public TV channel France 2 just happened to capture the scoop of the Middle East conflict: the death in real time of a 12-year-old Palestinian boy, targeted by heartless Israeli soldiers who shot at him for 45 minutes until they managed to mangle his father and kill the boy.

Mohamed Al Dura became the poster boy *shahid*, spurring an unprecedented wave of atrocities against Israeli civilians while an unhealthy swath of public opinion sat on the sidelines and applauded the brave Palestinian desperados.

The Al Dura legend is a story that deserves to be covered in full.

But it is urgent to put a few salient details on the table today, because the current outbreak of articles, interviews, chats, and forums may soon wash up on American shores —most likely in a rehash of the mishmash of misreporting poured out in the past two weeks. Agence France-Presse, *Le Monde*, le *Nouvel Observateur*, *Télérama* and all the little ducklings that follow in their tracks have been clucking and cackling something terrible.

And all of this noise is being made to protect France 2 from the wily foxes who could eat it up alive. Vindictive anger is aimed straight at Metula News Agency, a prickly French-language Israeli news service operating up in the Metula hills overlooking Lebanon, with an excellent track record and particular tenacity in denouncing the Al Dura blood libel. But Metula is not alone in asking for the truth.

While many reasonable people in the Western world have forgotten the Al Dura image, it is indelibly engraved in the Arab mind —template of accusations of Israeli cruelty; an icon of Palestinian innocence. Osama bin Laden rallied jihadis to his cause in a pre-9/11 recruitment tape that includes a long passage on Mohamed Al Dura. Many Arab language TV stations open the day's programs with an Al Dura cameo in a corner of the screen.

Daniel Pearl's murderers pasted an Al Dura sticker on the video of the journalist's beheading.

Now, France 2 news director Arlette Chabot is giving interviews all up and down the town, pouring into the ears and microphones of naive journalists who haven't done their homework a flood of explanations that would be laughable if they were not so utterly dismaying.

The sheer number of factual errors published in the French press on this subject is mind boggling. And yet it's not the worst of the story. The real problem is that the idea that one should judge the case on the facts is banished as if it were too evil to even be considered in private.

Did it happen? Did Israeli soldiers fire for 45 minutes at a man and a boy crouched behind a concrete culvert? Where was the Israeli position? Were the man and boy in the range of Israeli gunfire? Was the boy shot dead and the man seriously wounded? What was happening that day at Netzarim junction? Are the witnesses reliable? The Palestinian stringer, Talal Abu Rahmeh, declared under oath that the Israelis shot the man and boy intentionally, in cold blood. France 2 Jerusalem correspondent Charles Enderlin, who was in Ramallah when the incident took place, clearly stated in the voiceover commentary that the man and boy were targeted by gunfire coming from the Israeli position. The father, Jamal Al Dura, says he was shot in the hand, the arm, and the leg (by high-power military rifles), and his elbow and pelvis were crushed. He claims that a bullet ripped through his son's stomach and came out through his back.

Mr. Abu Rahmeh says he filmed the scene for 27 minutes. He says the boy bled for 15 or 20 minutes. Well, there's no blood on the victims, no blood on the ground. And the 27 minutes of footage turn out to be under three minutes.

These and a hundred other precise allegations are duly recorded and analyzed. I have studied massive documentation, screened dozens of hours of visuals. The conclusions of every single honest investigation of this case are the same: there is no convincing evidence that the incident took place. The eyewitness testimony is incoherent and unsubstantiated by verifiable evidence, the filmed "news report" does not show anything that could corroborate the drastic allegations.

Which leaves us with a news report of an incident that never happened.

Or, if it did happen, it happened out of range of the journalist's camera, in the absence of eyewitnesses, under conditions that no one has ever hinted at or even elucidated. In short, something was reported without a shred of proof. And when the veracity of the report is questioned, the questioners are slandered and the incoherent unsubstantiated evidence is reshuffled and dealt out again as proof of the proof. And the entire French press corps, Jewish press included, seems to be buying it.

What do you do when the facts of the matter are judged on the basis of total ignorance of the facts?

This is done to the point that they illustrate their articles with this penultimate frame of the news report, where we see the father just a few seconds before his son is felled with a single bullet, marking the end of the incident. Look at the man's arm. According to his testimony, he has been shot in the hand, the forearm, the shoulder, and the leg. His elbow and pelvis are shattered.

Much has been said about the wily power of images to shape ideas. The Al Dura case will one day be recognized as a demonstration of the power of words to convince our eyes that a pale nothing is the image of a stunning reality. Death captured live.

Maybe France 2 will bring it off on its home turf where the press is above suspicion. Can they bring it off worldwide? The unforgettable Al Dura death scene was given free of charge to all the press that would have it. Bob Simon did a memorable "60 Minutes" in September 2000, based on the Al Dura martyrdom and dozens of lesser Netzarim junction fabrications.

Someone might get the idea to check the facts in a safe place where you don't get sued for questioning the accuracy of a news report.

Unless, of course, France 2 plans to take the issue to the International Court of Justice at The Hague.

— *New York Sun*

Chapter 2

EXCERPTS: NOTES FROM A SIMPLE CITIZEN

7/27/05 But first, a brief report on some inside information that sheds light and perhaps, even more so, darkness on all that is said in this notebook. The scene takes place in the garden of a home not far from Mont Valérien where the Nazis executed more than 1,000 *résistants*. A birthday party. Over a glass of champagne, one of the guests lines up four prominent women and sweetly shoots them down with a volley of gossip {*it's gossip, that's why I can't name names.*} It goes more or less like this:

Do you know why (the online news magazine) ---------- shut down? The ----- ------ ------ withdrew its financial backing, furious because ----- -- ------ wanted 100,000 euros to do a report they requested, on the undergoing negotiations between Hamas and the European Union. They pulled the plug on her! Well, what really happened is that the couple ----- - ------ exploded. -------- started writing strongly anti-Chirac editorials, ----- was still writing pro-Chirac but it wasn't enough to calm the pro-Chirac French financiers, they backed out. ------- was having an affair with ~~~~~~ ~~~~~~, cheating on ~~~~~~~~ and, what's more, with ~~~~~~, who was going with (~~~~~~). Shortly afterward, ~~~~~~ was appointed Minister of (-- ~~~~~~ ~~~~).

In the space of one glass of champagne we go from a supposedly scrupulous unbiased source of information on the Middle East to the cabinet of Dominique de Villepin, with a leapfrog over the head of the news director of state-owned France 2 who has been handling the spin on the Al Dura affair. At other dinner tables in other gardens in Paris and in the provinces and even in the far flung vacation spots where this cardboard elite is drinking, partying, and switching partners, similar tidbits are served with the champagne. No, France is not a banana republic, it is a royal farce.

Driving home with a friend after the party and then, after she drops me off in the middle of the scrunge at Place Clichy where I take a cab the rest of the way home, past the Opéra in all its splendor, down quiet summer streets between rows of Hausmanian architecture, balconies, mansard roofs, giant *porte cochères* where carriages no longer drive into paved courtyards, I see Paris as the best preserved ruins in the world. The architectural glories stand firm, the aristocracy that created them, that ruled from them, is gone forever. The plebes have moved into the palaces, the masses stumble in constant confusion, the barbarians have seeped in through the cracks, the servant girls are frolicking with the master or the mistress or each other, according to their tastes, butcher's apprentices jump out of state limousines and into gold embossed offices, and the journalists dutifully cover for them. Talk to any journalist off record, he'll describe the mess. Not only the mess, but the pettiness of it all. But you mustn't quote him, mustn't say anything that could identify her. Why? So they can keep their jobs.

Has it occurred to any of them that if one or two or six or eight started to tell the truth, they could all tell the truth? No, it does not occur to them.

They all know that France 2, in collusion with a Palestinian cameraman working for Al Aqsa brigades or Islamic Jihad or both or all of the local jihadis, fabricated a news report about Mohamed Al Dura, the Palestinian boy "killed by Israeli soldiers." This kicked off the intifada, primed the *shahid* pump that poured death and destruction on Israelis for four years, now reduced to a trickle by Israeli action, but ready to go full force again. And rapidly spreading in Europe. By now, all French journalists know that the Al Dura news report was a crude fabrication. They know that France 2 Jerusalem correspondent Charles Enderlin knows that it is a fabrication. I think he knew from the very beginning. They think that if they come out and say it, they will lose their jobs. They don't understand that by their silence they have lost their jobs. They are not journalists, they are courtesans.

8/10/05 One day, I asked the technician to show me what was in the data base. He opened the files one after the other. A wealth of images we had not exploited. Finally the project took shape in my mind. He translated the Hebrew. TV interviews, documentaries. I had it! A carefully constructed video argument, a sequence of images that proved our point, realities that spoke for themselves. I replaced the heavy discourse of the earlier versions with these new elements. But cautiously. My collaborator was back in the States but I could feel him looking over my shoulder. And I wanted to be fair to him too. So I conserved elements that seriously bothered me, heavy elements that dragged down the whole document. And so much material that he had borrowed from others. Not to mention the inextricable problems that arose with investigators who had, willingly or unwillingly, provided the material in the data base. Under false pretenses, they said.

A few days before I left Israel, the whole thing exploded. My collaborator, who considered himself producer, director and all the rest, wanted an implementer who would make his video work, without changing anything. He was furious with me because I innovated. For me it was only normal, for him it was high treason.

And we were such good friends, we had such a fantastic intellectual complicity. I've tried to keep the friendship alive. He has too. But it's touch and go. It took me months to get my professional life back on track. And that absolutely worthy, not to say urgent, project was lying undigested in my mind. How could I abandon it?

A lovely summer evening. When I closed the shutters at midnight the sky was clear dark blue, and the street was empty. Paris is a ghost town in August. I didn't even go out for a stroll this evening, I spent the whole evening re-organizing my files on the Al Dura affair. Glancing at papers here and there as I went, asking myself for the thousandth time if I could be wrong. What if it's not a fake? Could I have been misled by the investigators? Shahaf, Juffa, Huber? But Rosenzweig is an old grisly retired *Monde* reporter, and he believes it's a fake. I don't think I'm mistaken. But I ask myself every day. Just to make sure.

They don't feel free, so they don't feel pinched. They can tell you privately that they know the Al Dura news report is a fake. But they won't come out and say it publicly, they won't write it in an article, they won't quote someone who says it. Why? Because it's not true that it's false? No. Because they don't want to lose their jobs.

8/12/05 Does this explain why they can portray jihad murderers as freedom fighters? Because they don't know what freedom is? And they don't have any sense of responsibility.

8/18/05 Our reporting [on the Gaza withdrawal] here is coming from the same Enderlin who brought us the Al Dura fiction. And his sidekick Talal is just the other side of the line, doing his thing.

Today, France 2 invited PA spokeswoman Leila Shahid to explain the ins and outs of the liberation of Gaza. Talal's report had shown Palestinians who want to reclaim their land that was requisitioned during the intifada (they always mention it as if the Israelis started it) to create a no man's land between the Palestinian villages and the Jewish neighborhoods that they call colonies.

Later, they asked Leila if the farmers were going to get their land back. She said, "Yes, if they have proper deeds... which would be true of 3% of the land now occupied by Israelis. 97% of that land is *dominial*." She didn't use the term "*dominial*," she said it was public lands.

So there you go about Israelis stealing land from Mohamed and Bashir and Hassan. Just more Palestinian fairy tales.

MYTH, FACT, AND THE AL-DURA AFFAIR
September 2005

This past June, Wafa Samir al-Bis, an aspiring twenty-one-year-old *shahida*, or "martyr," was apprehended by Israeli guards at the Erez checkpoint in Gaza and found to be carrying 20 pounds of explosives in her underwear. The young woman intended to make a last trip to the

Soroka Medical Center in Be'er Sheva, where she had been receiving medical treatment for severe burns incurred in a domestic accident. Her goal this time was to blow herself up and kill as many young people as possible. Asked why she was aiming specifically at children, she replied that she wanted to retaliate for the death of Muhammad al-Dura.

Wafa Samir al-Bis is but one in a long line of *shahids* and would-be *shahids* inspired by the image of a twelve-year-old Palestinian boy whose death scene was broadcast worldwide at the very onset of the so-called al-Aqsa *intifada* that broke out in September 2000. Televised images of the boy, reportedly killed by Israeli soldiers, instantly ignited anti-Israel and anti-Jewish passions all over the world, provoking a wave of violence from the lynching of two Israeli reservists in Ramallah to synagogue burnings in France. In the ensuing years, the story of Muhammad al-Dura has attained near-mythic stature in the Arab and Muslim world. In the West, though its essence is largely forgotten, it has fired the political imagination of many who accept it as emblematic proof of Israeli culpability for the outbreak of the armed conflict and even for Palestinian "martyrdom operations" against Israel's civilian population.

The killing of Muhammad al-Dura is not the only long-lived accusation against Israel in the last five years. Another tale of atrocity, perhaps even better known, is the Jenin "massacre." In the spring of 2002, the Israeli army moved into that West Bank city to wipe out a nest of terrorists responsible for a particularly intense sequence of murder and mayhem. Immediately, Palestinian sources claimed a figure of 5,000 dead (later reduced to a more modest 500) and an entire "refugee camp" bulldozed to rubble. By the time the truth emerged—Palestinians themselves finally confirmed a total of 56 dead, most of them in armed combat, and aerial views demonstrated the pinpoint nature of the Israeli operation—the damage had been done. Still today the Jenin "massacre" endures, out of reach of rational refutation.

But at least there is reliable information on what really happened in Jenin. That is not the case with the death scene of Muhammad al-Dura.

The background can be quickly summarized. In the summer of 2000, even before Yasir Arafat brought down the final curtain on the Oslo "peace process" by rejecting an American-brokered deal at Camp David, reports were circulating of a Palestinian military buildup. The first act of war was the murder of an Israeli soldier by his Palestinian partner on a joint patrol. But this was dismissed as a mere fluke. Instead, the spark that ignited the *intifada* was alleged to be Ariel Sharon's September 28 visit to the Temple Mount, Judaism's most sacred site and also the home of a number of Muslim shrines, including the al-Aqsa mosque.

The next day, September 29, the eve of Rosh Hashanah, riots broke out as Palestinians exiting from Friday prayers in the mosque overran a police post and hurled paving stones, conveniently stockpiled nearby, onto the heads of Jewish worshippers at the Western Wall below. On September 30, Marwan Barghouti, the West Bank leader of Arafat's Fatah organization, asserted that he could not and would not restrain further expressions of Palestinian protest.

It was later on that same day that a cameraman for France-2, a channel of the state-owned French television network, captured the death of a twelve-year-old Palestinian boy, allegedly shot in front of his helpless father by Israeli soldiers in the Gaza Strip. A news report, dramatically narrated by France-2's Jerusalem correspondent, was instantly aired and was offered free of charge to the world's media.

The effect was immediate, electrifying, and global. Overnight, Muhammad al-Dura became the poster child of the incipient Palestinian "struggle" against Israeli "occupation" and a potent symbol of the genocidal intentions of Israel's government. A doctored photomontage was soon produced for Arab-Muslim viewers, featuring an imported image of an Israeli soldier apparently shooting the boy at close range.

That the death of Muhammad al-Dura was the real emotional pretext for the ensuing avalanche of Palestinian violence—and a far more potent trigger than Sharon's "provocative" visit to the Temple Mount—is attested by the immediate and widespread dissemination of his story and of the *pietà*-like image of his body lying at his father's feet. Streets, squares, and schools have since been named for the young Islamic *shahid*. His death scene has been replicated on murals, posters, and postage stamps, even making an iconic appearance in the video of Daniel Pearl's beheading. His story, perhaps the single most powerful force behind the Palestinian cult of child sacrifice over the last years, has been dramatized in spots on Palestinian television urging others to follow in his path, retold in a recruitment video for al Qaeda, and immortalized in epic verse by the Palestinian poet Mahmoud Darwish.

But is it true? Although serious doubts were immediately raised about the veracity of the France-2 news report, they were swept aside by the emotions it provoked and by the flare of violence in the last months of 2000. France-2 indignantly turned down all requests to investigate or even to help others investigate by releasing outtakes. To this day, many people believe that even to raise a doubt about the authenticity of the report is tantamount to denying the reality of the 9/11 attacks on New York City.

But let us begin at the beginning, with France-2's prize-winning scoop, aired just hours after the incident.

Here is what viewers saw and heard: a few seconds of rioting somewhere on the West Bank, followed by a vague scene of armed men at Netzarim junction, a crossroads in the Gaza Strip. A jeep comes down the road. A single shot rings out, and a man in uniform at the open door of the jeep falls or jumps to the ground, clutching his right leg. An ambulance pulls up, stops on the far side of the road. The man is dragged across the ground, placed on a stretcher with his weight resting on his wounded right leg, and loaded into the ambulance. Charles Enderlin, France-2's correspondent announces in an eyewitness-style voiceover:

"Three PM at Netzarim junction in the Gaza Strip. A dramatic turn of events. The Palestinians shot live ammunition, the Israelis replied. Ambulance drivers, bystanders, journalists are caught in the crossfire."

Now the camera focuses on a man and a boy crouched behind a concrete barrel or culvert, their faces contorted in fear. Enderlin: "Here Jamal al-Dura and his son are targets of gunfire from Israeli positions." The camera pans to a nearby Israeli outpost. The father waves with his right hand in the direction of the Israeli position. The father is hunched behind the barrel, the boy nestled against his back. Enderlin:

"Muhammad is twelve years old. His father tries to protect him. He waves. But another round of fire bursts out. Muhammad is dead, and his father grievously wounded."

During the 55-second sequence, two shots have hit a concrete-block wall that stands like a backdrop for the scene, landing far afield of the father and son. Other bullet holes, similarly off-target, can be seen in the wall as well. The father shields the boy; the father's arm is clearly visible, perpendicular to the ground. Guttural cries are heard, adding to the feeling of panic. The last round of gunfire kicks up a cloud of dust, obscuring the man and boy. When the dust clears, the boy is stretched out at his father's feet; the father bobs his head as if groggy.

And that was it. As Enderlin would later explain, the reason France-2's scoop was offered free to the world was that the producers did not want to earn a profit from so tragic an incident. Only the terrible moments of the child's death throes, he added, had been edited out, being "too unbearable." The film sequence itself, attributed at first to a "France-2 cameraman," was subsequently identified as the work of the station's Palestinian stringer, Talal Abu Rahmeh. By then, the full authority and reputation of France-2 itself had been indelibly stamped on the footage.

Within days, an elaborate narrative was being disseminated to flesh out the elusive details of the 55-second video. On October 3, 2000, testifying under oath before the Palestinian Center for Human Rights, the cameraman Talal Abu Rahmeh alleged that Israeli soldiers had intentionally, in cold blood, murdered the boy and wounded the father. Abu Rahmeh's testimony was precise and vivid. There had been, he said, a five-minute exchange of fire between Palestinian policemen and Israeli soldiers. This was followed by fully 45 minutes of gunfire coming exclusively from the Israeli position and aimed directly at the man and the boy crouching desperately behind a concrete barrel. According to the cameraman, he had captured on film a total of 27 minutes of this fusillade, risking his own life in the process. As an experienced war photographer, he could attest without hesitation that the Israeli outpost was the only position from which the boy and the man could be hit.

This amplified version of the incident, with slight but significant variations and a wealth of human-interest details, then took on a life of its own, being repeated and embellished in numerous background stories, special reports, and interviews about the tragic fate of the "simple boy from Gaza, who loved birds." In one of these narratives, Jamal and Muhammad were said to have left the El Bureij refugee camp early on the morning of September 30 to visit a used-car market. Finding the market closed, they headed home in a communal taxi, arriving at Netzarim junction shortly before midday. The taxi was blocked by a raging gun battle, so Jamal decided to go the rest of the way on foot. In an interview on Israeli television, Jamal said that upon entering the crossing he found the firing so heavy that he took refuge behind an upended concrete culvert, where he and his son were pinned down for the 45 minutes of relentless gunfire aimed deliberately at them from the Israeli position. He waved to the soldiers, who could see he was an innocent civilian trapped there with a boy; they shot him in the hand. He tried to protect his son with his arm, but they shot him in the arm and shoulder. He tried to protect him with his leg, but they shot him in the leg, smashing his pelvis. The tragic outcome was described for a BBC documentary by Talal Abu Rahmeh: Jamal tried to call for help on his cellphone, asking someone to get the soldiers to stop shooting, or to send an ambulance. The ambulance driver was shot dead. The soldiers kept on shooting until they killed Muhammad, who died either instantly from a fatal wound to the stomach or, in another version, bled to death for 15 to 20 minutes because no ambulance could get through to evacuate him.

In the following weeks, journalists like Suzanne Goldenberg in the (London) *Guardian*, Gilles Paris in *Le Monde*, and dozens of others would write about this incident as if they themselves had been at Netzarim junction on the fatal day.

The Al-Dura story was so immediately and so deeply harmful to Israel that no matter what government officials might say or do, they only seemed to make matters worse. Enderlin has stated that, before airing the report, he called the IDF spokesman to inform him of the breaking news and to caution him against shirking Israeli responsibility. The soldiers in the fort, however, had reported nothing remotely resembling what Enderlin described, for the simple reason that they had seen nothing. And yet, the first official Israeli statement on the incident included an apology for the death of the boy and a promise to investigate. It took a few days before the IDF concluded that, given the shooting angle from the Israeli position, the man and boy could not have been hit by IDF gunfire. This was treated as adding insult to injury.

Other objections were dismissed with similar contempt. Early on, for example, it was pointed out that the 55-second video did not show any of the normal signs consistent with wounds from high-power bullets. There was no blood on the victims' clothes, on the wall, or on the ground. Their postures appeared wholly voluntary, with no sign of shock or trauma. As for Abu Rahmeh's claim of a 45-minute free-for-all, experts in ballistics concurred that automatic rifles fired uninterruptedly for that length of time would reduce their victims to shreds, and the concrete block wall behind them to rubble. Nor did such behavior accord with what one knew about the ethics, discipline, and skill of IDF soldiers.

Early doubters of the received version included the French documentary filmmaker Pierre Rehov, who sued France-2 for spreading false information; the case was thrown out of French court. Nahum Shahaf, an Israeli physicist who led the first official IDF investigation, has been studying the incident ever since, accumulating one of the most exhaustive film libraries on the subject. Metula News Agency (MENA), an Israel-based, French-language service, likewise undertook a lengthy and still ongoing investigation. Esther Schapira, a German television producer who went to Israel convinced of IDF guilt, came away with a film exposing the contradictions and discrepancies of the France-2 news report; she was convinced that the boy had been killed by Palestinians. In a June 2003 article in the *Atlantic*, the American journalist James Fallows concluded that Muhammad al-Dura "was not shot by the Israeli soldiers who were known to be involved in the day's fighting," but also that we would never know who killed him.

Was Muhammad al-Dura shot by Israelis? By Palestinians? Perhaps not shot at all? Most attempts to develop a cogent counter-scenario have fallen victim to the tangle of conflicting details and the sheer accumulation of minutiae. Though it is almost impossible to say anything meaningful about the 55-second filmed news report to someone who knows little or nothing about the elaborate surrounding narrative, it is extremely difficult to get beyond the emotions elicited by the visual image to a critical examination of that narrative. Even "corrective" articles regularly commit factual errors about everything from the chronology of the *intifada* to the layout of Netzarim junction, ignore anomalies in the eyewitness accounts, or are oblivious to the absence of corroborating evidence. Finally, and fundamentally, every effort to reproduce the event dispassionately butts up against quite understandable resistance from those who cling to the packaged version.

But we do have extensive evidence of what was occurring at Netzarim junction on September 30, 2000. More than a dozen cameramen were at the junction filming the action that day. They were all Palestinian, but they were working for Reuters, AP, NHK, France-2, and other prestigious networks. Aside from Abu Rahmeh's footage, brief excerpts from what they shot have appeared in news broadcasts. But hours of outtakes also exist, and their eloquence is astounding. I cannot claim they show everything that happened, but enough raw footage exists to substantiate what follows.

Netzarim junction is a simple intersection where one road leads (or, following Israel's disengagement, will have led) to the Jewish settlement of Netzarim and another to the Palestinian village of El Bureij. A rudimentary Israeli outpost stands on the road to the settlement—a small fortress of blind slabs with a few tiny gunslits surmounted by a fragile lookout cage. Otherwise, Palestinian police and civilians circulated freely throughout the area on the day in question. They occupied a pair of three-story apartment buildings, known as "The Twins," that overlooked the outpost and that housed the families of Palestinian policemen assigned to joint patrols under the Oslo agreement. Palestinians also held another building, an abandoned factory, that towered over the Israeli position. In addition, they operated from a mound of sandy earth directly facing the al-Duras and known because of its shape as "the pita," and, down the road a bit toward El Bureij, from a cluster of what look like concrete bunkers.

On all the outtakes I saw, only one exchange of gunfire takes place: a brief outburst from the bunkers and a responding series of shots, ostensibly from the Israeli position. As for the death scene, it was filmed in front of a concrete-block wall abutting a makeshift building, opposite the pita but situated at an angle that made the al-Duras' barrel inaccessible to gunfire from the Israeli outpost.

In one version of his story, Talal Abu Rahmeh went to Netzarim junction at seven in the morning on a hunch that the children would be out demonstrating "because it was a school day," and he knew they demonstrated on school days. In another version, he ran over to the junction at 3 PM, after someone called his office to inform him that there were fierce battles going on. The outtakes show he was there from early morning. Apparently, a dozen of his colleagues had the same intuition; they too can be seen in the raw footage.

The Reuters, AP, and France-2 outtakes that I viewed show two totally different and easily identifiable types of activity at Netzarim junction: real, *intifada-style* attacks, and crudely falsified battle scenes. Both the real and the fake scenes are played out against a background of normal civilian activity at a busy crossroads. In the "reality" zone, excited children and angry young men hurl rocks and Molotov cocktails at the Israeli outpost while *shababs* ("youths") standing on the roof of the Twins throw burning tires down onto the caged lookout; this goes on seemingly for hours, without provoking the slightest military reaction from Israeli soldiers.

At the same time, in the "theatrical" zone, Palestinian stringers sporting prestigious logos on their vests and cameras are seen filming battle scenes staged behind the abandoned factory, well out of range of Israeli gunfire. The "wounded" sail through the air like modern dancers and then suddenly collapse. Cameramen jockey with hysterical youths who pounce on the "casualties," pushing and shoving, howling *Allahu akhbar!*, clumsily grabbing the "injured," pushing away the rare ambulance attendant in a pale green polyester jacket in order to shove, twist, haul, and dump the "victims" into UN and Red Crescent ambulances that pull up on a second's notice and careen back down the road again, sirens screaming. In one shot we recognize Talal Abu Rahmeh in his France-2 vest, filming a staged casualty scene. (Students in a special course at the Israeli Military Academy, who had access to this raw footage, tagged and tracked the amateur actors as they went through their day, playing multiple roles. The injured and dead jump up, dust themselves off, play at offensive combat; casualties evacuated by ambulance are later seen loading a fellow actor into an ambulance or smiling with satisfaction as the ambulance door slams shut.)

Split seconds of these ludicrous vignettes would later appear in newscasts and special reports; the husk, the raw footage that would reveal the fakery, had been removed, leaving the kernel rich in anti-Israel nutrients. Such staged scenes showed up, for example, in a dramatic CBS *60 Minutes* special report on Netzarim crossing—a place "now known," intoned Bob Simon, echoing Palestinian sources, "as Martyr's Junction."

The al-Dura death scene was filmed right in the middle of these falsified incidents. It can be localized and situated. In one section of Reuters footage we see the man and the boy crouched behind the upended culvert as a jeep drives slowly up the road, stops in firing range of the Israeli position that is clearly visible in the near distance, makes a U-turn, drives in the opposite direction, stops short of the barrel/culvert, and helps perform the clearly faked evacuation of a man wounded in the right leg, as also shown in the France-2 news report. In fact, two ambulances stand for a long moment no more than fifteen feet from the al-Duras. There is no evidence of armed combat in their vicinity. No sound of gunfire. Men run down the road, passing in front of the al-Duras. No one is hit.

Nobody who was present at the junction that day has ever corroborated Abu Rahmeh's testimony, though he claims that several children huddled around him for protection as he filmed, and voices—of grown men—were recorded by the microphone attached to his camera. None of the other cameramen working at the junction that day filmed the al-Duras during their alleged ordeal under Israeli fire (though the pair can be discerned on one occasion, inadvertently captured in the background in an uneventful stretch of Reuters outtakes).

I also viewed a copy of the satellite feed transmitted by Abu Rahmeh late in the afternoon of September 30. In addition to the 55 seconds aired that evening, it includes a final image of the boy who would be described afterward as "killed instantly by a shot to the stomach": in it he is seen shifting position, propping himself up on his elbow, shading his eyes with his hand, rolling over on his stomach, covering his eyes.

In addition, I saw outtakes from an interview in which Abu Rahmeh tells how he discovered the boy's identity. Leaving the junction at around 4:30 PM, he bumped into a colleague and showed him the images he had just filmed. The other journalist, by chance a relative of Jamal al-Dura, supplied the names of the victims. Mourners in the massive funeral procession, allegedly held before sundown that very day, carried Muhammad al-Dura posters. Where and when were they printed?

It is no easy task to challenge the integrity of a powerful broadcaster in France, where the state-owned media operate with limited independence and no real competition. Charles Enderlin's prestige and the dominant position of *France Télévisions* were enough to discredit the most diligent early analysts. To this day, Enderlin (a French Jew who became an Israeli citizen some 20 years ago and has served in the Israeli army) refuses to reply to questions about the accuracy of the news report and its enveloping narrative; responding with ad-hominem counterattacks, he threatens to sue his detractors for libel.

More than normal journalistic pride may be involved here. Enderlin's news report was consistent with his stated overall view of the Middle East conflict. In his 2003 book, *Shattered Dreams*, he places the blame for Oslo's failure squarely on Israeli prime minister Ehud Barak and U.S. President Bill Clinton, effectively absolving the Palestinians of responsibility. The same interpretation is, of course, shared by virtually the entire French intellectual and political elite, and endorsed by influential print media like *Le Monde, Le Monde Diplomatique, Le Nouvel Observateur,* and *Télérama*.

Still, in 2004, as the *intifada* slowed and its mythology faded, the al-Dura story, too, began to break down. Charles Enderlin and the French media gradually backed away from their initial assertion as to the origin of the fatal bullets, leaving the incident in a limbo where the Palestinians could continue to accuse Israel of murdering the boy in cold blood while the French let it be understood that he was killed in a crossfire. Then, at the end of October 2004, something happened that would have broken the logjam if the French media were truly free, which they are not.

Luc Rosenzweig, a retired *Le Monde* journalist who had doubted the veracity of the al-Dura news report from the first, completed an investigative article in which he formally accused France-2 of an "almost perfect media crime." His essay was scheduled to appear in the mainstream newsweekly *l'Express* on the fourth anniversary of the *intifada*. But the magazine's editorial director, Denis Jeambar, decided to delay publication in order to double-check Rosenzweig's facts.

Given his position, Jeambar was able to arrange a meeting with France-2's news director. He was accompanied there by Rosenzweig and Daniel Leconte, a prize-winning TV producer. Asking simple questions about Abu Rahmeh's satellite feed, the trio got shocking answers. They requested the 27 minutes of raw footage showing the al-Duras pinned down by Israeli gunfire; they were shown a half-hour of fake battle scenes similar to those described above. They asked why there were no pictures of Israeli soldiers aiming at the al-Duras; they were told that on this point the cameraman had retracted his testimony, given "under pressure" to the Palestinian Center for Human Rights. They asked to speak to the cameraman, then said to be undergoing medical treatment in Paris; they were told he did not speak French and that his English was too rudimentary (patently untrue). They asked to see the scene of the child's death throes, professedly edited out by Charles Enderlin because it was "too unbearable"; they were told that no such images existed. They in turn produced pictures of a dead child, identified as Muhammad al-Dura, who had been admitted to Gaza's Schifa hospital at noon or 1 PM on September 30, several hours before the alleged incident occurred; his face did not match that of the boy in the shooting scene, his wounds did not match the eyewitness descriptions. They were told that the channel's forensic specialists would look into the matter.

At this point, Jeambar, perhaps thinking that the whole affair had become too hot to handle, reneged on his commitment to publish Rosenzweig's exposé. Seizing the initiative, Metula News Agency immediately leaked a report of the meeting and, at a press conference in Paris, reiterated its case for the al-Dura death scene as an outright falsification. Thereupon France-2, threatening legal action against anyone daring to question the integrity of its journalists, launched a spin operation: it sent Abu Rahmeh to Gaza to film Jamal al-Dura's scars and showed the resulting footage at a press conference from which all known skeptics were excluded. Articles appeared defending Charles Enderlin and denouncing Metula News Agency; most of them were incongruously illustrated with an image from the original news report clearly showing Jamal's bare arm—perfectly intact—a few short seconds before the round of gunfire that ended the scene.

But the bubble of tolerance protecting the French media had begun to stretch and tear. Three months after their October 2004 meeting with France-2, Denis Jeambar and Daniel Leconte came forward with their side of the story. The gist of their essay, published in *Le Figaro* after being rejected by *Le Monde*, confirmed the MENA release while chastising both Rosenzweig and MENA for jumping to the unwarranted conclusion that the death scene had been staged. Jeambar and Leconte also enjoined France-2 to make a full disclosure, withdraw its unjustified accusations, and recognize the incalculably damaging effects of its report in inciting violence and blackening Israel's name.

The very next day, Enderlin responded with an article in *Le Figaro* suggesting that his distinguished colleagues join him in a sort of gentleman's agreement to lay the affair to rest. His broadcast may have been hasty, he wrote, but it was justified on the grounds that the public had to know the truth, because so many children were being killed. He should have said, "were *going* to be killed," because Muhammad al-Dura, as his father proudly proclaimed, was the first *shahid*, and Enderlin's broadcast itself was instrumental in much of what followed. But, more than four years later, Enderlin was still trying to defend his report as an accurate reflection of the situation on the ground.

Whatever his intentions, the result for Enderlin was disappointing. Indignantly defending their integrity, Jeambar and Leconte took him to task for having compromised his own. As Jeambar stiffly noted, journalists are supposed to report on what happens, not on what might have happened. Or, one could add, might not have happened.

So, is there now general agreement on the truth about the al-Dura affair?

Interviewed on a French-Jewish radio station in the thick of the controversy, Jeambar and Leconte described their sense of astonishment upon discovering the staged battle scenes. And yet, by the end of the interview, they were assuring themselves and their audience that the death of Muhammad al-Dura was *not* staged, that the father's injuries were authentic, that the Metula News Agency had exaggerated, and that the poor child must have been killed in a crossfire.

This notion of a death by crossfire is the *deus ex machina* of the al-Dura controversy. I have heard it a hundred times, and once used it myself. It is invoked in order to save reasonable people from even contemplating the possibility of a fabrication. But it is a figment of the imagination. The sole eyewitnesses—the cameraman and the surviving victim, Jamal al-Dura—have described 45 minutes of uninterrupted shooting from one direction only.

And what does the filmed news report show? The answer is staring us in the face, cinched by the collapse of France-2's four-year concealment of its lack of evidence. As even Charles Enderlin has tacitly admitted, the al-Dura report was not some brief excerpt from a longer stretch of filmed reality but a scene with no depth, no duration, no origin, and no continuation. The 45 minutes? Gone. Abu Rahmeh's 27 minutes? Gone, too. We are left with approximately a single minute of Jamal and Muhammad al-Dura filmed in continuous time.

In that minute, the two crouch behind an upended culvert and contort their faces in fear. Guttural screams are heard, but they do not come from the man or the boy; they come from men standing within range of the France-2 cameraman's microphone. Jamal bobs his head. Muhammad stretches out at his father's feet. Then, in the brief portion that was carefully edited out but that can be seen in the outtakes, the boy changes position several times, using voluntary muscles that only living people can activate.

During the 55-second sequence we see two bullets hitting the wall, which is already pockmarked with a number of other bullet holes nowhere near father and child. A cloud of dust obscures the last few frames. There is no sign or sound of a crossfire. There are no death throes.

The rest, as we say in French, is literature. There can be no further attempts to reconstruct the incident by adding to those 55 seconds since, as France-2 has now revealed, there *is* no additional footage.

But now look again at the Reuters outtakes. A jeep drives up a road, turns, goes down the other side, takes part in a battle scene. An ambulance pulls up, a "wounded" man is dragged across the road, placed on a stretcher, loaded into the ambulance, the ambulance drives away. Men run from position A to position B. Children toss Molotov cocktails at the IDF fortress. There is much laughter and cheering from the "audience," clusters of cheerful young men watching the show. All this time, traffic trundles through the intersection, schoolchildren go by with their bookbags, a fashionably dressed woman talks on her cellphone and chats and jokes with cameramen who stand nonchalantly with their backs to the Israeli position. Things are moving, the energy level is high, the *shababs* are fearless. Palestinian policemen mingle in the crowd, occasionally shoot a few rounds into the air, join in the battle scenes, get "wounded" and come back for more. Children set fire to tires; you can almost smell the rubber burning. The France-2 cameraman, Abu Rahmeh, is there, too, clearly visible, in the heat of the action, filming ambulance evacuations of fake casualties in large patches of real time. Familiar, retrievable, believable.

Where then did the story, the enveloping narrative, come from? Where did all those prestigious journalists get the background information they developed with such evident sincerity in their reports? There is only one source: Talal Abu Rahmeh. The story told by Jamal, bandaged in a hospital room, dovetailed with Abu Rahmeh's story.

Enderlin religiously confirmed it. Everyone else repeats it.

Charles Enderlin constantly reaffirms his confidence in the professional competence and honesty of Abu Rahmeh—they have been working together for years—and systematically reiterates the dramatic facts of the al-Dura incident just as he heard them from his trusted cameraman. Where else could the story have come from? Though Enderlin narrated the incident as if he were on the spot, he has made no secret of the fact that he was in Ramallah on September 30, covering Marwan Barghouti's press conference. His account of the dramatic phone calls he received from Abu Rahmeh is part of the fleshed-out narrative. According to Enderlin, the cameraman phoned to say that he was caught in a shooting zone and that his life was in danger. He asked the France-2 correspondent to look after his family if the worst should befall him. The two men called each other several more times, the photographer describing the scene of the man and the boy trapped, the father repeatedly wounded, his hand, his shoulder, his elbow, his hip. The child's horrible death. Somewhere around 5:30 PM, the cameraman transmitted the satellite feed that would be edited into the famous news report narrated by Charles Enderlin.

How long did it take Enderlin, a seasoned journalist, to realize that his cameraman was lying, and that there were no additional images, no 45 minutes and no 27 minutes, to confirm the scene Abu Rahmeh said he had filmed? How long did it take France-2 officials to realize they had made a mistake in trusting the word of Enderlin? As long as the burden of proof rested on France-2's challengers, it was relatively easy to quibble over details. Now that the event has been reduced to its 55 inconclusive seconds, one must ask a different question. What was the role of the government-owned French television network, which is to say the French government itself, in devising, implementing, and spreading this atrocious calumny, whose repercussions are with us to this day?

—Commentary, September 2005
Vol. 120, No. 2

THE AL DURA MYTH

"In the first year of the Intifada, 581 Palestinians and 34 Israelis were killed. This was because the IDF ... is the least moral [army] in the world. I want to remind the entire world that saw how the boy Mu-

hammad al-Dura was killed while the soldiers sat and laughed."
-- West Bank Tanzim chief Marwan Barghouti in the closing arguments of his Israeli terrorism trial in 2003.

Five years ago last Friday, on Sept. 30, 2000, the now-famous Muhammad al-Dura death scene flashed on the world's television screens for the first time, instantly creating a powerful icon of Palestinian suffering. Viewers were stunned at the sight of a man and a boy cringing in fear, allegedly targeted by Israeli gunfire, captured on film by a French cameraman. In the flash of a minute, their tragic fate was announced by France 2 correspondent Charles Enderlin: "One more round of gunfire, Muhammad is dead, his father critically wounded."

The news report was distributed to the international media free of charge by the state-owned French channel. Viewers felt as if they could enter into the very heart of the Arab-Israeli conflict and seize its essence. The image of the 12-year-old Palestinian boy killed by Israeli soldiers — or so viewers were told — was given unprecedented exposure. Muhammad al-Dura became the poster boy of the al-Aqsa Intifada, inspiring a Palestinian death cult, and provoking murderous hatred of Israelis and Jews in the Arab and Muslim world.

But what really happened at Netzarim Junction in the Gaza Strip on Sept. 30, 2000? Close examination of available evidence shows that the al-Dura death scene was deliberately fabricated, and that this fabrication fits into a broader strategy of violent confrontation masked as resistance.

The France 2 cameraman who filed the news report, Palestinian stringer Talal Abu Rahmeh, is the unique source of the accepted al-Dura media narrative; Jamal al-Dura, identified as the boy's father, has lent credibility to the cameraman's account by repeating it in his own words. Countless journalists have assimilated and retold the story without noticing the telltale signs of fabrication.

Here's how Talal Abu Rahmeh, who has worked with Charles Enderlin for 15 years, explains the incident: Jamal and Muhammad al-Dura were pinned down for 45 minutes by Israeli gunfire aimed directly at them. The father was wounded repeatedly. The boy was shot in the stomach and died instantly or, in another version from the same source, bled to death for 15 to 20 minutes. An ambulance was sent to evacuate the victims, but the driver was killed by Israeli soldiers.

In sworn testimony and countless interviews, Abu Rahmeh claims to have filmed 27 minutes of the al-Dura's lengthy ordeal, which began with a five-minute exchange of fire between Israeli soldiers and Palestinian policemen, followed by 45-minutes of fire coming only from the Israeli position. He said that the al-Duras were clearly visible from the Israeli outpost, which was directly facing them. The cameraman testified under oath that the Israeli outpost was the only position from which the boy and the man could be hit.

Human interest details provided by Jamal, his wife (subsequently identified as Muhammad's stepmother) and other family members were eagerly collected by journalists and retold. This material has created a mythical Netzarim Junction connected to a mythical day in the life of the al-Duras, which in turn serves as a platform for the mythical death of Muhammad al-Dura.

But we now have evidence that contradicts this myth.

More than a dozen Palestinian stringers working for major networks and agencies were present at Netzarim Junction that day, yet the al-Dura death scene was filmed by only one cameraman: Talal Abu Rahmeh.

Extensive raw footage from the other cameramen has been obtained and analyzed by European, American and Israeli investigators. From that footage, we can see that Palestinians, far from being pinned down by Israeli fire, ran unobstructed throughout Netzarim Junction on the day of the incident. They occupied a cluster of bunkers and two large buildings that towered over the single Israeli outpost; they had free run of the streets, the fields and a mound of earth known as the "pita," directly opposite the wall where the al-Duras were filmed. The IDF soldiers stayed inside their rudimentary fortress, kitty corner from the al-Duras, who are shown hiding behind an upended concrete culvert at an oblique angle to the Israelis. Ballistics experts testify that the "targets" could not have been hit from such an angle.

Looking again at the famous image of the al-Duras huddled against the concrete wall, we see that it is intact. Military gunfire sustained for 45 minutes would have reduced much of it to rubble.

As the story goes, Jamal and the boy were on their way back to their home in al-Bureij when the taxi they were riding in had to stop short of the junction because of heavy gunfire; Jamal decided to go the rest of the way on foot. But Israeli soldiers saw them and started shooting. He and the boy took refuge behind the culvert, where they remained while the soldiers shot at them for three quarters of an hour. Jamal was wounded in the hand and the leg, his pelvis and shoulder were smashed. The Israelis didn't stop shooting until they had killed the boy.

In a BBC documentary filmed shortly after the incident, a wounded and grieving Jamal says that he looked at the boy, saw the bullet come out through his back, and knew he was dead, a shahid (martyr).

But raw footage filmed at the time shows an entirely different reality. Normal traffic trundles through the intersection, large crowds of young men fearlessly attack the Israeli position, throwing rocks, Molotov cocktails and burning tires. Bystanders laugh and applaud. Tellingly, groups of Palestinian men, some dressed in military uniforms, can be seen staging fake battle scenes, complete with ambulance evacuations — in an area out of range of Israeli gunfire.

The al-Dura death scene is totally disconnected from this reality. Contrary to Talal Abu Rahmeh's claims, it is not a 55-second excerpt from a 45-minute incident excerpted, in turn, from a day in the life of the al-Duras; it is a 55-second film that bears the hallmarks of artifice.

Though France 2 officials admitted in private that the Palestinians fake battle scenes, injuries and ambulance evacuations, they insisted that the al-Dura scene was authentic. They also claimed to have conclusive evidence to substantiate the news report. Then, in the autumn of 2004, current France 2 news director Arlette Chabot admitted publicly that the 27-minutes of outtakes showing Israeli soldiers shooting at the al-Duras do not exist. And the five seconds of death throes edited out because, according to Charles Enderlin, they were too horrible to show, do not exist either. The 45-minutes of Israeli gunfire aimed at the al-Duras disappear too; France 2 officials unashamedly affirmed that Talal Abu Rahmeh had testified under duress. He had withdrawn his testimony in secret.

Knowing that the 55-second film is not an excerpt but the totality of the al-Dura incident, we can go back to the news report, remove the voiceover commentary and see what really happened.

There is no hail of bullets: Two bullets hit the wall, off target. Jamal is not wounded: his pelvis bears his weight; his arm is pressed against the boy in an incongruous gesture of protection. No bullets hit Muhammad al-Dura. Jamal had said that he looked at his son and knew he was a shahid; yet at no point in the 55-second film does he look at the boy.

We are left with a baseless news report that is kept afloat because the state-owned French television channel that produced it has backed off, but refuses to release a clear-cut retraction. And so Israelis still stand accused as child-killers.

Many people are still asking: Who killed Muhammad al-Dura? But the real question is how many innocent people have been killed or maimed because the media broadcast an unsubstantiated "news report" that enflamed deep-seated hatreds in the Arab-Muslim world, and turned sophisticated 21st-century viewers into gullible villagers ready to swallow the latest blood libel and condone a shameful wave of terroristic reprisals against Israeli Jews.

— *National Post, Canada*

BLAME ISRAEL ALWAYS
Why are Western journalists so credulous of Palestinian sources?
Summer 2006

No one knows exactly how seven members of the Ghalia family died June 9 on a Gaza Strip beach. There are no impartial observers in the area. Since last year's Israeli withdrawal and Hamas's recent electoral victory, Western media rely almost entirely—and with surprising gullibility—on Palestinian sources for information.

Here's how the Palestinian version of the story goes. Unsuspecting Palestinian families were picnicking on al-Sudaniya beach on a Friday afternoon, the Muslim Sabbath. Suddenly, an Israeli gunboat started shelling the beach. Before the panic-stricken victims could escape, a shell landed right in the middle of the Ghalia family picnic, instantly killing the father, one of his wives, and five of his children, including a baby and a toddler, and injuring others present.

Eleven-year-old Huda Ghalia was in the water when the shell hit. A camera captured her as she ran across the sand and found the carnage. Her tears rent the heart, and her message was surprisingly articulate: she called for the world in general, and Muslims especially, to witness the evil that Israelis had done.

While Hamas shouted that the Israeli gunboat had deliberately aimed at the hapless family, Western media outlets toned the charges down a notch: it was an accident, but a vicious one that never would have happened if the evil Israelis were not blasting at a public beach.

Hamas announced that it would break a 16-month "truce" and launch an all-out offensive against the Zionist enemy. Palestinian Authority president Mahmoud Abbas joined in, and UN secretary general Kofi Annan added his outrage to the flood of hatred whipped up in the wake of Huda's tears.

Two days after the incident, though, ample information, leaked to and posted on reputable websites, suggested that the Palestinian-supplied video "proving" Israel's responsibility for the deaths and injuries had been manipulated—a shot of an Israeli Defense Forces gunboat, filmed earlier that day, spliced in to give the impression that it was firing directly at the beach, the scene of Huda finding her father's body apparently staged. Data on the six shells fired from an Israeli gunboat that afternoon showed that the soldiers had aimed at a Qassam rocket-launching site at least 800 feet from the sunbathers. And so on.

But even after the IDF made the results of its investigation public at a press conference at the Defense Ministry in Tel Aviv, Western journalists maintained a climate of artificial doubt—balancing, even overshadowing, the government report with a reiteration of the Hamas narrative, now dressed up in pseudoscientific trappings supplied by a Human Rights Watch "expert," Mark Garlasco.

Why is a lone investigator, working for a nongovernmental organization, more reliable than General Meir Kalifi's investigating commission? What impartial agency has verified the data presented by Human Rights Watch and its self-designated expert? Hamas has an agenda. HRW has an agenda. But what is the agenda of the free press in our own democratic countries?

Rational examination of the evidence shifts the burden of doubt to the Hamas (and HRW) version of the incident. Israeli officials have now released ample details to support their conclusions. Hospital reports testify that one of the wounded had shrapnel removed by Palestinian doctors before her transfer to an Israeli hospital—medically inexplicable treatment that might have been about getting rid of any proof that Palestinian ordnance had caused the explosion. Close scrutiny of outtakes from the original video reveals a mixture of staging and real-time filming. Interviewed by Süddeutsche Zeitung, the Palestinian cameraman who filmed the explosion delivers a garbled story that unravels under questioning.

All of this recalls the al-Dura affair. On September 30, 2000, the Jerusalem correspondent of the France 2 public television network, Charles Enderlin, reported the shooting of 12-year-old Mohamed al-Dura at Netzarim Crossing in the Gaza Strip, the "target of gunfire coming from the Israeli positions." The accusation triggered a wave of attacks on Jews in Israel and worldwide. The 55-second al-Dura video, "proving" Israeli guilt in that incident and featured in an Osama bin Laden recruiting tape, was also doctored, with an archived image of an Israeli soldier spliced into the Arab-Muslim version, making it look as though he was firing point-blank at the boy. Here, too, the Western media treated Palestinian sources credulously. (Fittingly, correspondent Enderlin has weighed in on the Gaza beach video, too, applying to it an absurd "two sides to every story" logic: no one can know what really happened; it's up to public opinion to decide.)

Do Western journalists think that Israel is always guilty in principle, if not in fact? If so, perhaps they should openly join ranks with the "militants" they portray as national liberators.

— *City Journal*

Chapter 3

AL-DURA: THE TRIAL/PART ONE
September 13, 2006

The commemoration of 9/11 was the occasion, here in France, for another round of shameful Bush bashing. Jumping on the just-released Senate report, the media triumphantly announced that there was no connection between Saddam Hussein and Al Qaeda before 9/11. The Report must have included all sorts of information, much of it contradictory to orthodox French anti-Americanism, but it was not deemed worthy of interest. The accusation stands: Bush deliberately lied in order to make illegal war on Iraq for his own personal reasons and *voilà* the disaster that ensued.

No such accusation has ever been brought against state-owned French television channel France 2, purveyor of the al-Dura death scene that triggered a new phase of jihad against Israel and a gigantic wave of violence against Jews worldwide.

Compared to the unjustified "Bush lied" slander, the demonstration that France 2 lied should be a pushover. On the contrary, it has been an uphill fight for six years. Six years during which the state-owned television network (*France Télévisions*), the media control agency (*CSA*), and French media all across the spectrum have refused to respect the basic rules of journalistic ethics. The simple re-examination of a questionable news report, with disclosure of all available evidence, would have settled the affair in the space of a few days. Instead of which it festers and spreads and poisons the atmosphere. It should be added that little help was forthcoming from Israeli officials or from the organized Jewish community in France or the United States.

People who have been struggling to discover and make known the truth about the al-Dura affair—I count myself among them—have often been shunned and dismissed. But they have made significant progress, and none of them have given up.

Charles Enderlin, the France 2 Jerusalem correspondent who produced the al-Dura news report in collaboration with Palestinian stringer Talal Abu Rahmeh, has used a strategy of intimidation and indignation to ward off independent investigation of the affair. But the protective mechanism began to falter in the autumn of 2004 when current news director Arlette Chabot was instructed to allow three reputable mainstream journalists—Luc Rosenzweig, Denis Jeambar and Daniel Leconte—to view the ace in the hole evidence that would convince them of the authenticity of the report.

Leaks on that groundbreaking preview of the famous al-Dura outtakes made their way into high profile media, including the WSJ, IHT and, later, Commentary Magazine, LA Times, Reader's Digest, and Fox News, etc. France 2 launched an aggressive spin operation, whipping up the same old arguments to prove the same old story and adding for good measure a lawsuit against X, X being anyone who would question the authenticity of the al-Dura report. Far from being intimidated, some of the potentially accused Xs forged ahead. The first of three subsequently individualized Xs —Philippe Karsenty, founding director of the online media watch enterprise Media-Ratings— will be judged for public defamation of the honor and reputation of an "individual," namely France 2, Arlette Chabot, and Charles Enderlin. To avoid a lengthy digression on the French legal system, let us just accept as given that a holy trinity composed of the TV channel and two of its employees can be treated as an individual for the purpose of pleading the case against Karsenty. On the other hand it is easy to see the advantage of standing as a private party whose honor has been sullied rather than appearing as media professionals expected to hold to certain standards.

The same questions come to mind at every step of this simple-complicated imbroglio: do the plaintiffs know they are lying, do they think they are telling the truth, do they realize that the evidence would hang them in any honest trial, are they counting on a fail proof system of *omerta* to sustain the falsification?

The trial will take place in the august halls of the Tribunal de Grande Instance in Paris on the 14th of September 2006. Philippe Karsenty stands accused of casting dishonor on the reputation of the plaintiffs by suggesting, in a brief article published by Media-Ratings on 22 November 2004: "Arlette Chabot and Charles Enderlin should be immediately dismissed." The sober factual article, devoid of inflammatory language and personal attacks, politely accepts the challenge inherent in the lawsuit against X and expresses the readiness of Media-Ratings to defend in court as it defends on its site the claim that the al-Dura news report is a staged scene. It should be mentioned that Karsenty has been sued three times in the short life of Media Ratings, simply for doing what media watch organizations do. The media are quick to remind critics that error is human but apparently in France a media watch organization isn't even free to express itself when it is not mistaken. The incriminated article is based on concrete details that have led serious analysts to conclude that the al-Dura death scene cannot possibly represent the shooting, wounding, and killing described in Enderlin's voice off commentary and elaborated in a stock narrative indiscriminately repeated ever since the incident allegedly occurred.

French society has never examined the implications of the news report that served as the founding myth of a Palestinian war against Israel, the so-called "Al Aqsa Intifada," enflamed in September 2000 by the "death" of Mohamed al-Dura and the wounding of his father Jamal, "targets," according to Charles Enderlin, "of gunfire from the Israeli positions." Debate has been stifled by the defensive reaction of Enderlin, his hierarchy and, apparently, the government itself. It is significant that in the absence of debate the myth will be "judged" in the narrow confines of a lawsuit, within the strictures of legal language and rules of evidence.

How could France 2 have taken the risk of losing the lawsuits against Philippe Karsenty and, at a later date, Pierre Lurçat and Charles Gouz?

Did they single out three supposedly soft targets with the intention of silencing all those who are actively engaged in dismantling the myth, and discrediting them in the eyes of clear-minded people who are slowly discovering that the al-Dura news report is a fake?

Within minutes of the September 30 2000 broadcast astute observers saw that something was awry. Different people in different places for a variety of reasons noted disparities between the image and the commentary. Something was fishy about this scoop that just happened to pop up when needed. Today, six years later, a significant body of documentation confirms that initial intuition. In fact, everyone seems to agree on the prevalence of staged news, but few are willing to draw the logical conclusion. They sideswipe the question. The three French journalists who saw Talal Abu Rahmeh's outtakes have discredited the al-Dura news report and rejected Enderlin's attempts to justify it as "corresponding to the general situation." A doctoral candidate at the Institute of Political Studies (IEP) in Paris declared, in a thinly veiled apology for Enderlin published two days before the trial:

As for claims that Hizbullah and the Palestinians "stage scenes," even if they are all confirmed it won't change the fact that 4000 Palestinians and 1300 Lebanese, most of them civilians, have been felled by Israeli gunfire in the past six years...(Arnaud l'Enfant. "Israel and the media," La Libre belgique, Sept. 12 2006)

Many journalists who are unashamedly hostile to Israel admit that the Palestinians produce falsified news but they find nothing to deplore in this practice—it's simply propaganda, and everyone does it. One France 2 official acknowledged in the presence of news director Arlette Chabot, whose honor is allegedly sullied by Philippe Karsenty, that the Palestinians regularly enact fake battle scenes, some of which are reported as news in Western media.

All of these people freely admit that some, much, or even most of the material contained in the 27-minute video shot by Talal Abu Rahmeh at Netzarim Junction in the Gaza Strip on that fatal day are in fact staged scenes. (French journalists admit in private that the al-Dura scene, too, was staged; they say everyone knows it, no one will ever admit it publicly, this sort of revelation is totally and absolutely impossible in France, and besides it's an old story and no one is interested.)

For four years Enderlin claimed to have absolute proof of the authenticity of the al-Dura report in the form of 27-minutes of footage, the golden outtakes, which he refused to make available for independent investigation. When Rosenzweig, Jeambar, and Leconte described, in articles and radio interviews, what they had seen, the golden outtakes were reduced, by reverse alchemy, to dross.

Enter the phlogiston theory of media integrity: the al-Dura outtakes are effectively composed of 27-minutes of staged scenes and one nugget of reality, a bit less than one minute by the clock, the "death" of Mohamed al Dura, the truth of which must not be contested. And there is no limit to the coercion, contortions, inventions, and distortions added to that skimpy minute of phlogiston-reality to make it hold.

Talal Abu Rahmeh was captured by another Palestinian stringer, working for Reuters, who shows him filming a staged scene. Common sense would reason that the France 2 cameraman knowingly filmed staged scenes at Netzarim Junction on 30 September 2000 and handed them over to his employers without any warning that they might be harmful to the health of media integrity. Given that the al-Dura death scene also seems, at first glance, to be staged, and further investigation by a variety of experts confirms that suspicion, it would be reasonable to conclude that the incident did not occur in any verifiable form that could qualify as appropriate material for a news report.

It is humanly impossible to <u>prove</u> that it did not occur.

Within, then, the realm of the possible it appears that Talal Abu Rahmeh is devious or unreliable, his immediate superior Charles Enderlin is complicit or incompetent, and news director Arlette Chabot is either ignorant or following orders from her superiors. Common sense would dictate that devious, complicit, and/or incompetent journalists should be fired.

Instead, we have a trial, an ordeal for the accused who must spend untold thousands of euros to defend himself against extravagant accusations brought by an alliance of individual journalists and a television network who are, in reality, the state. Obviously such a state of affairs precludes the slightest whimper of media watch. And what do the media do when no one is watching?

At the time when the lawsuits were brought against Karsenty, Lurçat, and Gouz, there was little reason to hope they would attract international attention. Nothing—not the initial investigation, not articles in known, unknown, and/or prestigious publications, not the lectures, meetings, books, videos, websites, letters, demonstrations, revelations—nothing had pierced the invisible wall that separated the truly fascinating documentation of a monumental hoax—with extremely grave and widespread repercussions—from the wall of indifference and confusion that blocked every attempt to bring the case to light and obtain some form of justice.

Ah, but reality is stronger than any theory, and phlogiston stands as the symbol of imposed ignorance in the face of troubling evidence. The July –August Hizbullah war against Israel brought a windfall of staged news. From Pallywood to Hizbollywood with its cohort of fauxtography the blogosphere rapidly produced a wealth of documentation on a phenomenon that replicates everything we had observed in the al-Dura case. But this time, the results were immediate. Reuters dismissed fauxtographer Adnan Hajj and withdrew his photos from their archives. The information leaped from blogs to mainstream. CNN journalist Anderson Cooper admitted he had been manipulated by Hizbullah handlers. The *NY Times* wriggled out of its false pieta with a lame excuse, but lame is better than nothing. Pristine cuddly toys among the ruins; Green Helmet bouncing dead kids in the air; rescue workers becoming, by turns, bereaved fathers, distressed neighbors, and Hizbullah operatives; a grieving old lady performing in front of several different ruined homesteads, all of them 100% civilian, all of them hers, all of them source of unbearable sorrow; a wounded ambulance driver miraculously cured; press cars hit by missiles and resisting better than a Merkva tank... all of this and more available for analyses that yield a coherent picture of something beyond propaganda—a weapon, a type of warfare that I call "lethal narratives."

The difference between Gaza and Hizbullah strongholds in Lebanon is that Western journalists circulated in semi-freedom in the latter, at their own risk in the former, as attested by the kidnapping and forced conversion of Fox journalists Centanni and Wiig. The al-Dura story remains trapped in a gilded French cage six years after the fact; Hizbullah falsifications are out in the open and resulting in a few, admittedly hesitant and partial, changes in Western media practices.

We observe striking similarities between the different theaters of staged war-zone scenes.

The staged scenes are incredibly crude. No offense meant to those who have skillfully dissected them but, they are so big they hit you in the eye at first glance. Which, strangely enough, has served to protect them from detection. A series of logical reversals lead observers to conclude that the fake is so fake it must be real, that no one would dare to make such an obvious fake, and those who describe the fake must be a bit unhinged, or have an axe to grind, because if the thing were such a fake, everyone would know it.

The scenes obscenely violate the sanctity of life: real dead bodies are dragged in to serve as props on the site of a real false bombing, live people are presented as dead, corpses are set out in macabre displays of blood and gore without a shred of evidence as to where and how they died or were killed, bloodied bodies of small children are handled like meat on the hook, and this mishmash of a stew is served with the hysterical cries and breast beating of fake real false genuine mourners. When challenged, this collective gore is carved up into neat portions of rebuttal: yes, this or that scene was in fact staged, but so many have died, such terrible suffering, how can you be so cold-hearted as to pick over the corpses trying to see which ones are really dead.

Ambulances, press cars, convoys of fleeing villagers, refugees huddled in schools, mosques, convents are repeatedly attacked...by Tsahal or by Hizbullah film directors? No one seems to care. The news reports are churned out and broadcast. The burden of proof is not in the image, not in the witness, but in the purpose served: do they illustrate the cruel inhumanity of Israelis? Yes? Then they are valid.

The technicolor accusations—Jenin massacre, Gaza Beach massacre, Qana massacre—gradually fall apart in the light of rational analysis and fade away when no longer sustainable, only to reappear when necessary, reconstituted, recycled, cleansed of the still unanswered legitimate questions about their validity. The narrative and the image are effaced but the effects are eternal

A new kind of journalistic "ethics" has shifted the burden of proof from the originating source of the report to the challenger, placing the latter in the impossible position of proving that something did not occur.

In the al-Dura affair this has led to a counter-productive emphasis on the icon: the man and the boy up against the wall, cringing in fear, targeted, wounded... How many millions of words have been composed to describe the anomalies, incoherence, aberrations, contradictions, oddities, technicalities, absurdities of the scene and how many words, on the side of the myth's defenders, to describe the circumstances, attempts to alert, to protect, the anguish, ordeal, suffering, the hail of bullets, the terrible wounds, the frantic waving, the fatal outcome? Whether in defense of the authenticity of the scene or in analysis of the discrepancies, the words overflow a thousand times the timeframe of the incident. Few of us are experts in ballistics, forensic pathology, or physics but we all know approximately how much drama can fit into a minute. Try this experiment: take the most minimal description of the ordeal, as told by Jamal al-Dura, and read it out while watching the 55-second broadcast.

No evidence has ever been produced to sustain the claim that Israeli soldiers shot at the man and the boy for 45 minutes; the claim was made by Abu Rahmeh, repeated by Jamal al-Dura, and echoed by journalists near and far. Later, the 45 minutes were discretely set aside without ever being retracted, and boiled down to the 27 "al-Dura" minutes allegedly filmed. In November 2004 the 27 minutes were reduced to roughly 24 minutes of staged scenes, and 3 minutes of doubtful material, including 1 minute of the al-Dura scene.

Here on earth, in the absence of an omniscient deity, all hypothetical portions of the drama are relegated to vain suppositions, leaving us with approximately one minute of filmed reality, real or fake. And yet every account of the incident describes fifty times more gestures than could ever be crammed into one minute of human time, no matter how intense it might be!

Through the looking glass:

Now it is time to look at the case from the other side of the looking glass, here in France. Your ordinary French person knows nothing about staged scenes in Hizbulland. He might have read something about a Reuters photographer who got fired because he used photoshop to retouch the smoke from a bombing scene in Beirut, and most probably he would file that incident under the heading "heartless employers," and never give it a second thought. He was told that Beirut was in ruins, Lebanon was destroyed, Israel was engaged in an offensive against Lebanon, the international community was pleading for a humanitarian ceasefire, but could not be heard because the war criminal states of America and Israel, with the backing of poodle Blair, were intent on pursuing the destruction of the beautiful land of Lebanon just because two soldiers had been captured. A small minority of web surfers may have visited the English-language blogosphere and discovered the extensive revelations about faked news; an even smaller minority would have been informed by Jewish media in France or French language news agencies from Israel (Guysen, Metula News Agency) but, for all intents and purposes we can assume that French public opinion has not been exposed to the mass of information on cheating news from questionable Lebanese sources. I wonder if the judges who are going to hear the Karsenty case know about fauxtography, child corpse fashion shows, vehicles that hardly dent when hit by missiles, and all the rest. My guess is no. And how about Charles Enderlin, Arlette Chabot, and their colleagues at France Télévisions? Could they possibly be uninformed? Or not recognize the similarities?

A vicious article by Pierre Veilletet and Robert Ménard, respectively president and general secretary of *Reporteurs sans frontières* (Reporters without Borders) accusing Tsahal of deliberately targeting the media ("Tsahal traite les medias en ennemis," *Le Monde*, 4 September) begins this way:

Gaza, August 27th. Two Israeli missiles hit a Reuters press car. One of the journalists is seriously wounded. NGOs protest. Tsahal replies: They "shouldn't have been there."

France's newspaper of record accuses the Israeli army of deliberately firing at journalists and destroying media property (including the Al Manar studios). France's state-owned television network produces, broadcasts, and distributes worldwide a blood libel against Israel. A cameraman employed by France 2 films staged news. And somehow French society can accommodate all of these attitudes and practices. But when a media watch site calls for the dismissal of those responsible for producing, broadcasting, and defending a falsified news report that accuses Israeli soldiers of the cold blooded murder of a Palestinian child, the director is sued for defamation, for sullying the honor of the plaintiffs.

How will this case be pleaded, tried, and judged in a French court?

[Stay tuned for Al Dura: The Trial / Part Two]

— Trial coverage
September 2006-January 2008
PJ Media unless otherwise indicated

AL-DURA: THE TRIAL/PART TWO
September 13, 2006

Flash:

Here are my first impressions of the trial. A proper account will follow tomorrow.

The trial was beautiful, the Palais de justice is beautiful with its aspiring architecture and gilded gates, it was a beautiful late summer evening in mid-September as we walked out of the Courthouse at 8:30 PM, exhausted and relieved. Richard Landes and I danced out of there singing Vive la France.

The trial was almost the opposite of what I expected. I thought the issue was going to get laminated in legalese, evaporated in ennui, entangled, garbled, swallowed up under the high ceilings of the 17th *Correctionel* Chamber of the Tribunal de Grande Instance. No, it was a genuine debate conducted in a civilized manner by intelligent responsible citizens aware of the importance of every word they uttered. except, of course, for the Plaintiff, France 2-Chabot-Enderlin, who apparently thought they could flitter through the court with the same arguments and the same methods they have been using for the past six years to cover up the cover up.

The presiding judge and his two associates (I'll get the details straight tomorrow) were human, humane, attentive. Especially the judge. He listened attentively, smiled, put people at ease, engaged in no silly manners or intimidating attitudes. The prosecutor, was bright, forceful, and forthright. Her name is Madame Halimi-Selam (more on that later). If the judge follows her appreciation of the case, Karsenty will win. He is free to ignore her interpretations and recommendations but I don't think he will.

I can't save this anecdote for tomorrow: a journalist from Le Figaro said to a photographer sitting near him in the press box—"the prosecutor looked at the case that way because she's Jewish." I'll find out his name tomorrow and tell you a bit more about him.

There were not many journalists in the courtroom, not many people in the audience...they don't know what they missed.

It was a beautiful trial. It was held in an atmosphere of respect for justice. Karesenty's lawyers presented solid arguments and four sincere witnesses. The al-Dura affair, which is so difficult and complicated, was presented in such a way that an outsider could follow the arguments. My impression is that the judge started out with what I would call the James Fallows approach, a middle ground position safely installed in the reasonable zone. It is too radical to suggest that the Israelis killed the boy in cold blood, it is too extreme to suggest that the whole thing was a shoddy hoax, so it has to be that he was killed in a crossfire. Never mind that there is no crossfire in the death scene as filmed. So what's so reasonable about dragging in all that ammunition and gunfire when in fact it is nowhere to be seen. It is easier to see the hoax than the crossfire.

I think the judge was surprised to hear four different witnesses explain in four different ways how, as a result of extensive investigation and/or analysis they arrived at the conclusion that it was, in all probability, a hoax.

A judge who is not willing to learn stiffens when his position is challenged. And uses his power to stifle dissent. This judge listened. You could see in his eyes, in the expression on his face, that he was taking everything into consideration. Independently of the details of this particular case, whenever a lone individual is accused by an imposing national organism like France Télévisions, it is frightening. The court can take sides, can add its weight to the weight of the accusation, and crush the individual. Today, to my great surprise, I felt that I was in the presence of a commitment to justice.

Is it because this court hears so many cases involving freedom of speech, press freedom... Is there something of the dignity of literature at work? I'll have to attend other trials to find out.

The court was divorced... I should say the court was above the atmosphere that reigns in French society today, in the media, in politics. That's why I was so surprised. I felt like I was in the presence of a certain French decency that is hardly manifest anywhere else these days.

Next big surprise: the paucity of France 2's arguments. Their lawyer, a slim racy woman with long thick white hair that she constantly coiffed and uncoiffed, ruffled, caressed, raised, lowered, and twisted with obvious pride, was seated about 2 meters away from me. I watched her working quite feverishly, shuffling papers, attaching post-its, scribbling notes, consulting with a colleague who looked more like a hatchet man than a partner in her law office, and in general giving the impression of someone who was preparing a whopper of a case.

When it was her turn to plead, she laid out the same tired non-explanations that France 2 and Enderlin have been giving for the past six years. It always begins with Charles Enderlin is a respected, experienced journalist, he has been Jerusalem correspondent for X years, he is Franco-Israeli, he has written books and won prizes...and it goes on to say how respectable is France 2, how devoted to excellence in journalism... Then she starts trashing everyone on the other side. Karsenty, his witnesses, his sources, their sources, the Israeli army investigators, the Metula News Agency...they are all low class, unreliable, unrespectable, dubious, bumbling fools if not outright conspirators.

All these droopy snoops have been dogging Charles Enderlin for six years. Enough already. Staged scenes in the outtakes? Perhaps, she says, but none of them were in the news report. (Assuming of course as given that the al-Dura scene was not staged). Besides—and this was the best of her low moments—a journalist from l'Express told her that in certain situations a person will lie down and play dead in order to save his life.

She accused Karsenty of making such a big noise about the al-Dura affair in this incriminated article that it went all the way to the Wall Street Journal and other such international media. What a disgrace, for France to be dragged through the mud that way. And she concluded that her client was asking for 1 euro of symbolic damages, and let this story be put to rest forever.

What astonished me is that France 2 dared to take someone to court over the al-Dura affair and not come up with a single new argument. Everything that was said in court had been said before. It was and still is utterly beside the point.

If what we saw in court was really the trial, France 2 lost. And will certainly appeal the judgment. The only thing that could tip the balance in their favor would be orders from above.

[to be continued]

AL-DURA: THE TRIAL/ PART THREE
September 17, 2006

Erratum: the name of the pert and pertinent *procureur* is madame Alimi-Uzan, not Halimi-Selam. Richard Landes apologizes for the error. In mistakenly granting her the names of Sébastien Selam and Ilan Halimi, was he seeking justice for those two young Jewish men murdered by Muslims in France? The al-Dura blood libel certainly feeds the kind of hatred that inspired those crimes.

Disclosure: I make no pretense to objectivity in my reports on this trial. Philippe Karsenty is a friend and colleague; we have often discussed this case that was brought against him but aimed at all of us who share a commitment to destroying the al-Dura blood libel.

Philippe e-mailed me a transcript of the conversation with the *Figaro* journalist mentioned in Part Two. In my next report I will give a résumé of SDS's article (*Le Figaro*, 16-17 September 2006), which is comprehensive, coherent, well-written, and quite fair.

You can say that the journalist made the remark to me...here's exactly what was said:

Stéphane Durand-Soufflant: I was really surprised by the recommendations of the procureur.

PK: Why?

SDS: Because she was convinced [by the defense]. I wasn't. But after all, her name is Alimi-Uzan...

PK: Meaning?

SDS: Meaning she's Jewish!

PK: Enderlin is Jewish too!

N.B. I have no experience in court reporting and apologize in advance for approximations or errors. Accepted translations of legal terminology are often misleading because there is no exact correspondence between the French and American legal systems. *Procureur* is translated as "prosecutor" or "state's attorney." But I'm not sure that the function fits the translation.

The case is heard by a panel of three judges: the presiding judge, or *président*, and two *magistrats* who listen but do not participate in the debates. The case was heard in the *17e chambre correctionnel* or court of "summary jurisdiction." Except for one minor detail, too insignificant to develop here, the debate was conducted in language that any layman could understand, and the issues were framed in terms that we can grasp without any legal background. However, the acoustics in the courtroom are terrible. I may have missed important points. All that follows is from my notes, written in simultaneous translation. In the absence of a certified transcript, all "quotations" should be considered indirect.

THE TRIAL

[Dozens of cases are put on the docket, postponed, or dismissed before the Karsenty trial begins. Two lawsuits involving the president of the Front National, Jean-Marie Le Pen were scheduled; he is being sued for apology for crime against humanity. Hmmm...Le Pen is accused of apology for the last genocide of the Jews and Karsenty is defending the right to prevent the next genocide.]

I observe the France 2 lawyer, Maître Bénédicte Amblard, who is sitting about 2 feet in front of me. She is very busy shuffling stabilo-striped papers bedecked with fluoro postits. She rummages in her briefcase, takes out some CDs, puts them next to the thick file. Is she superprepared or throwing things together at the last minute? Her chignon falls apart.

I feel as if I too stand accused for all I have written on the al-Dura hoax. What if she has the proof!!! How do you feel when you are a lawyer for *France Télévisions*? Powerful.

Dr. Charles Gouz, his lawyer Aude Weill-Reynall, and Maître Amblard step forward to confirm their trial date. The judge asks if Charles Enderlin will attend. I cannot hear well but it seems like the reply is negative, and the judge shows his disapproval. After a short recess, the court reconvenes to hear Karsenty's case.

The judge gives a cogent presentation of the issues, showing that he has closely studied the documents. He calls Netzarim an *implantation [settlement]* not a "*colonie.*" I am impressed! The French love to call the disputed territories "colonies" and all that goes with it. Listing evidence that has been reviewed, he describes the Ména (Metula News Agency) video as "less interesting than Esther Schapira documentary, because it is focused uniquely on the hypothesis that the al-Dura incident was staged." The judge reads from the incriminated Media-Ratings article that accuses Enderlin-Chabot-France 2 of producing, broadcasting, and stubbornly maintaining a falsified news report [*English translation forthcoming*]; first, the passages cited for insulting language (*faux, masquerade, imposture*) then a longer excerpt that describes a falsified scene—the "wounded" man and the jeep. This is followed by projection of the original al-Dura news broadcast and two follow-up reports, and the Ména video.

The follow-up reports, broadcast in October and November 2000, are a revelation. Karsenty tells me his adversaries gave them as evidence! In fact those broadcasts are damning evidence against Enderlin, they show how he pushed and pressured to make the accusation against the Israeli soldiers stick. And right from the start he treated everyone who questioned that version of the incident as crooked and dishonest.

The judge gives a brief résumé of *Three Bullets and a Dead Child*, implicitly giving Esther Schapira credit for a reasonable investigation because it leaves questions open instead of claiming, like the Ména, to have the answers. I am firmly convinced that subsequent testimony made him reconsider.

Philippe Karsenty takes the stand. The judge's questions are pertinent, Philippe's answers are clear and compelling. Does he personally think the scene was staged or simply questionable? Philippe replies that he was initially convinced by the Schapira film, but realized after further investigation that the incident had to be staged. He gives an example: when it became clear from ballistics tests that the al-Duras could not have been hit by direct fire from the Israeli position, it was claimed they were hit by ricochets. But the father says he was hit 9 times, and the boy 3 times. Twelve ricochets? It's impossible.

Then comes the ten-gun question: why don't Israeli officials protest? Karsenty's answer is plausible: they think it would do no good to bring the image back to the forefront. Even if the truth could be established, it would turn against them.

Q: Denis Jeambar and Daniel Leconte, who viewed the 27-minute outtakes, said (Radio Communauté Juive) all the scenes were staged except the al-Dura scene. Jeambar cited a video of the father displaying his scars, a new element of proof shown by France 2 at a press conference.

A: I did not see the film because I was not allowed to attend the press conference. Leconte told me he was interested in the affair, and intended to investigate it. But Arte [French-German-Spanish cultural TV channel] warned him they would not work with his production company, Doc en Stock, anymore if he didn't drop the subject. Jeambar was under pressure from inside l'Express, notably Jacques Attali. Alexandre Adler told me that Charles (who is his brother-in-law) was tricked by his fixer. Many people have told me privately that they know the scene was staged, but they won't say it in public.

The judge's features tighten as if he is trying to hide his surprise...or distress. The hatchet man, Maître Guillaume Weill-Raynal, who has been coaching Maître Amblard since she came into court, whispers excitedly giving the impression that he has an ace of spades that will trump these revelations and make them explode in Karsenty's face.

The witnesses are called to the bar.

Francis Balle, professor of media, former member of the CSA (French equivalent of the FCC) describes how he had encouraged Karsenty to go ahead with his plan to launch Media-Ratings. When professor Balle viewed Karsenty's exposé of the al-Dura affair, he concluded that the images are dubious and their effect was drastic. He doesn't understand why France 2, an honorable network, has consistently refused to question its own material and open it to public scrutiny.

Karsenty's lawyer, Maître Dauzier asks the witness if France 2's refusal to show the 27-minute outtakes can be justified as protection of its source? Or does the public have a right to see them, to dispel doubt? Monsieur Balle replies that it has nothing to do with protecting a source; the footage should be shown so the truth can be told. Was Karsenty's language excessive? No, it is normal to use words with strong impact to attract attention on a controversial subject of public interest.

Judge Boyer asks two questions that clarify the debate: by presenting the outtakes to three journalists was France 2 not in fact "showing" them. And, further, how do we distinguish between valid controversies [as this one might be] and abusive "investigations" like the 9/11 conspiracy theories? The witness pursues the clarification by replying that there is a tendency in French society to blur the distinction between factual reports and commentary.

Witness: Luc Rosenzweig, 63 year-old retired journalist (*Libération, Le Monde*) whose last position was TV critic.

Rosenzweig says his attention was drawn to the al-Dura affair while he was attending a congress in Tel Aviv. He pitched the idea to Jeambar, then editor of *l'Express*, and began his investigation. [I have a draft of the article scheduled for publication on the 4th anniversary of the al-Dura incident. Jeambar wanted to double check. This led to their meeting with Arlette Chabot, the France 2 counter-offensive, and a wave of articles and interviews. But Jeambar never published Rosenzweig's article.]

Judge Boyer asks Rosenzweig if he started with the idea of finding out who killed the boy, or already posited that the scene was staged. Rosenzweig says he didn't have any hypothesis, he just found the report dubious. And when he finally saw the 27-minute footage? He saw that, contrary to repeated declarations by Abu Rahmeh and Enderlin, they did not have 27 minutes of al-Dura footage; it was 24 minutes of staged scenes. "My conviction is that the incident did not occur as it has been described."

Rosenwzeig tells what happened when he tried to do a proper journalistic investigation. Having gathered material from Shahaf and others on the Israeli side, he went after the other side of the story. He was told that the cameraman was receiving medical treatment in Paris; he left messages and has not had a reply to this day. He looked for a fixer who could take him to see Jamal—that didn't work either. He tried to see the doctors at Schifa hospital who reportedly received the corpse of a boy identified as Mohamed al-Dura [at noon or 1 PM, when the incident is reported to have begun at 3 PM]. He tried to go to Gaza but was refused entry. So, he concludes, I couldn't get the other side of the story. As a journalist I can't affirm that the scene was staged, but the probability that it was staged is much higher than the version presented by Enderlin.

Q: Did you see Enderlin?

A: Yes. He told me he couldn't show me the outtakes, they are locked in a safe in the France 2 legal department.

Q: What do you think of Enderlin's statement that the image "corresponds to the reality of the situation"?

A: That's not my conception of journalism.

Q: Have you written articles on the subject?

A: Yes. For example, I published an article on the Ména site. The title is "Charles Enderlin is a liar in all languages."

Did the witness see the additional proof provided by France 2? No, he was not allowed to attend the press conference. [This "invitation only" press spin conference was a low point in the al-Dura machinations. How could France 2 officials think they could get away with it, unless they think they can get away with anything? Sending Abu Rahmeh to film Jamal's wounds as proof that he was shot that way that day at Netzarim junction is like showing a man's teeth as proof that he ate twenty Dunkin' Donuts five years ago. But it worked. The hand-picked journalists who were invited to see the proof swallowed it whole and brought it up in articles and interviews in which they displayed abysmal ignorance of the entire affair. It is a story in itself.]

Witness: professor Richard Landes, medievalist Boston University

Professor Landes explains how he got interested in the al-Dura affair, showed the material to media professionals and, in the face of their indifference, put all the material on his website seconddraft.org so that people could judge for themselves. Charles Enderlin showed him the 27-minute footage in Jerusalem, in the presence of an Israeli photographer who laughed at the grotesque staged scenes. Enderlin commented, "They are always doing it." I said the al-Dura scene could be a fake too. Enderlin said they aren't smart enough to do that. I realized this [staged news] was an industry, I called it 'Pallywood.'"

Did Landes see the boy's death throes? What he saw was the few minutes of al-Dura footage that was cut: the boy moves, holds his hand over his eyes, looks at the camera. He is alive. Landes affirms that as a historian he would say there is a 95% probability the scene was staged.

Q: Did Charles Enderlin investigate further, after the fact? Did he interview family members?

A: I don't think he made any further effort to understand what had happened. He made a drawing for me [Landes holds out the paper]: it shows the Israeli position directly facing the al-Duras. In fact, that was a Palestinian position. Three years after the event he still doesn't know the lay of the land? Or did he think I was too stupid to check for myself? And he told me the bullets had been found. Oh? So where are they? In a bag, in the Palestinian general's desk drawer. You believe that? "I believe the Palestinians", he replied, "as much as I trust General Yom Tov Samia."

Witness: Gérard Huber, writer, psychoanalyst, author of *Contre-expertise d'une mise en scène* [excerpts available at World Net Daily].

Huber explains: I was Paris correspondent for la Ména when I undertook the investigation. I made every effort to contact France 2 to show them our findings and give them the opportunity to correct me if I was wrong. They refused. I read everything, viewed everything, spoke to everyone who would speak to me, and concluded that there is no logical version of the story. It is an enigma. The cameraman who filmed the scene retracted the testimony he gave to the PCHR, he declared under oath that the Israelis shot the al-Duras "deliberately, intentionally, in cold blood." I don't accuse Enderlin. No one is able to give a reasonable version of the incident. I suggested an impartial international inquiry. From time to time France 2 retracts elements of the story, but never makes the retractions public. I am in favor of a free, open debate.

Q: Your book is entitled *Contre-expertise d'une mise en scène* [re-examination of a staged scene]." Are you justified in concluding that it was staged?

A: Yes. My investigation supports that conclusion.

After each witness testifies, the judge asks Maître Amblard if she wants to cross-examine. She declines. And presents no witnesses for the accusation.

A ten-minute recess is allowed before the plaintiffs [*partie civile*] present their case. Though Arlette Chabot is included in the *partie civile*, there are almost no references to her role in covering the al-Dura affair and no defense of her good faith...as if the plaintiffs preferred to forget about her.

Maître Amblard comes forward, begins to speak, her voice is inaudible. Her small hands, too, are inaudible, gesturing like little mouse paws as she attempts to convince the court of the sincerity of her clients. Finally a microphone is brought over but she still manages to speak to the side of it. Fortunately for me, perhaps unfortunately for her clients, I have heard most of these arguments before. They are pathetically circular. Charles Enderlin is a distinguished prize-winning journalist, author of several books. He is an Israeli citizen, he served in the army. France 2 is a national television channel, reputable, reliable. On 30 September 2000 Talal Abu Rahmeh is caught in a crossfire, trapped. He takes refuge behind a panel truck, risks his life, films a scene that the other reporters could not film, they ran for cover, he filmed the death of a child, sent the images to Charles Enderlin, they were viewed by countless members of the press corps [at the Beth Agron Press Center in Jerusalem]. The images were validated. Talal Abu Rahmeh is a reliable cameraman, he has been working with France 2 since 1990.

In other words, the al-Dura scene cannot be a falsification because France 2, Enderlin, and Abu Rahmeh are above suspicion. Whereas, Philippe Karsenty and his so-called witnesses...

Karsenty makes terrible accusations. A *faux* is a criminal offense [yes, in the legal sense of "forgery" but Karsenty was not using legal language; in common speech, in this context, a *faux* is a falsification], there is no justification for this accusation. There is no proof of intention, no proof of motive. The day after the broadcast everyone agreed that the gunfire came from the Israeli position. Several days later other hypotheses were expressed; Charles Enderlin refuted them.

Karsenty's argument is based on the Ména's documents. Esther Schapira's film is also based on information from the Ména. Casting doubt on the death of the child is surrealist. It all comes from that Israeli government commission [implying that an Israeli government commission is by definition partial and invalid]. The Ména film is ridiculous. The Schapira film is a bit more modest. But full of false information. It is not true that the Israeli soldiers didn't have automatic weapons, they had M 16s and Kalashnikovs. She claims she interviews soldiers who were at the post that day, but they have Hebrew names, the soldiers were Druze.

To claim that Charles Enderlin was swindled by his cameraman is to hold him up for ridicule.Then Maître Amblard proceeds to hold the witnesses up for ridicule. Who are these so-called professors and journalists, what do they know about war reporting and death scenes? It's not true that France 2 didn't investigate. Direct witnesses were questioned, none of them contradicts Talal's version. They all say the same thing. Only the Ména disagrees. What of the so-called staged scenes in the outtakes? None of them appear in the al-Dura news report. And what proves they are really staged? We have a deposition from a journalist from l'Express: in this kind of situation with bullets flying people often lie down and play dead to save their lives, they may remain that way for hours until it is safe to get up.

Luc Rosenzweig admits himself, it has been several years since he wrote about the Middle East. Besides, he works for la Ména. Professor Landes, hmph, what does he know about these matters? Gérard Huber? Aha!!! He is not simply psychoanalyst and author, he is the Paris correspondent of the Ména!!!! [Apparently she didn't listen to his testimony: he was their Paris correspondent, and said so in his testimony. He resigned several years ago.]

Item: The Israeli commission that investigated the al-Dura affair was disavowed by the judgment of a Tel Aviv court, not known for its pro-Palestinian positions. The commission was judged partial, unscientific, incompetent, unqualified. Harrumph!

Item: Chief investigator Nahum Shahaf claims to possess a dramatic photo that changes the version of Rabin's assassination. Harumph!

Item: The Israeli daily *Haaretz* wrote, "It is hard to find words to describe the stupidity of this investigation [of the al-Dura affair]. Harumph!

Item: the defamation was inspired by personal animosity. She reads a message from Karsenty to X, promising to bring down Enderlin.

Item: there is no legitimate aim. What could be legitimate in this relentless attack pursued for six years! For what? To destabilize Enderlin. Why?

Item: this campaign spread beyond our boarders, beyond the limits of sites and blogs—she cites the WSJ article—look at what they say about France… and it is all based on one source, one disqualified investigation, the Ména.

Item: the vocabulary—falsification, hoax, masquerade—is insulting, and goes way beyond what is permissible.

My client is asking for 1euro of symbolic damages; we want to put an end to this shameful campaign that has been going on for years, spreading untruths.

[So, that's it, they don't have a shred of proof, not a hairpin of an argument. Questioning the veracity of a patently dubious report is an insult to the honor of France 2 and Charles Enderlin because they are honorable and those who question them are dishonest, confused, shabby, worthless hecklers who don't know when to stop. Guillaume Weill-Raynal, her volunteer coach, turns around and glares at the people in the courtroom as if they are all right wing Zionists. Elisabeth Schemla (journalist and director of the recently bankrupt site proche-orient.info) sat in the bleachers, listening with eagle ears, whispering, sending signals. At one point a note was passed from behind (I think from E.S.) to Maître Amblard via me and a friendly colleague.

Drats, are we real journalists? Why didn't we keep it? Maybe it was meaningless scribble, or nasty gossip, nothing that could help their case, they had no case, they thought they didn't need to have a case, the legal work was as shabby as the al-Dura broadcast itself. We, the collective accused, work our heads off, work our fingers to the bone, double check, cross check, search our conscience and they, the perpetrators of the blood libel, don't even bother to build plausible lies. They believe they live in a world where their word is good no matter how bad it really is.

That's what we are dealing with: slipshod blood libel.]

The *procureur* stands and I can finally see her, or at least her head, in profile. Her long red hair is piled in a youthful mass. Her cheeks are round and her lips are full and pinkly lipsticked. She speaks for a society that doesn't seem to know it needs her firm voice of integrity, she speaks to our Jewish people who have not turned out en masse to witness the trial of 21st century blood libel, she speaks to Israel that does not know how to reply to these pernicious accusations, she speaks to the press that did not bother to come to hear a magisterial lesson on their responsibility. She speaks, bless her heart, of "verifiable facts." Hear ye hear ye French journalists, madame la Procureur du 17e correctionnel reminds you that you are supposed to be dealing with verifiable facts.

All the more so, according to the *procureur*, in the tense climate that prevailed when this report was broadcast and given the grave consequences that followed on publication of this image. The media have a responsibility to the public. We are asked to judge the statements made by the accused to denounce a situation and, on the other hand, the image and commentary broadcast by the plaintiff.

Is this a case of defamation? Yes, the article does cast a shadow on the honor of the person. But the accused is asked to offer proof of the truth of his statements and we have here an order of proof that is convincing if not total. Staged scenes are effectively included in the footage provided by the cameraman. The alleged scene of the child's death throes does not appear in the raw footage as alleged. If that scene doesn't exist, this is pertinent to the debate. As is the debate on the ballistics, the angle of the Israeli position, the type of weapons used, the possibility of seeing the man and boy from the Israeli position. All of this should be taken into consideration.

There is a war of images. Al-Dura was a symbol. I saw a serious documentary on television that showed this kind of staging. The fact that these are scenes of war does not excuse the absence of verification. It was not done. Charles Enderlin was not at Netzarim Junction when the incident occurred. The plaintiffs initiated this procedure, they should have brought witnesses, they should have presented proof to sustain their affirmations, the outtakes should have been shown here during this trial.

The *procureur* concludes in answering, one after the other, the elements of decision that should guide the court.

Was the information contained in the incriminated article justified? Yes. The public has a right to be informed about this controversy.

Was the article inspired by personal animosity? No. The plaintiff has not given proof of personal animosity. Monsieur Karsenty directed his criticism at Charles Enderlin in his role as journalist.

Was the tone of the article acceptable? Yes. Freedom of tone in such a controversial subject is authorized.

Was the accusation based on a serious investigation? Yes. It cannot be dismissed out of hand, as France 2 has done. The accused made a serious effort to test hypotheses, verify information, engage in honest debate with France 2.

The plaintiff's arguments are weak. Why were these journalists excluded from the press conference?

The procureur concludes in recommending that Karsenty be acquitted.

Maître Dauzier makes his closing arguments. Philippe Karsenty reads a statement. [elements to follow] The session is adjourned. The verdict will be announced on October 19.

My verdict is announced here: on the face of things, Karsenty won this case hands down. The judge is free to follow or ignore the *procureur's* recommendations; I think he will follow them, though he may not have the same level of lucidity and conviction. He too recognizes that France 2 failed to argue its case. Honest observers may disagree on the authenticity or falsification of the al-Dura scene but no honest observer could fail to recognize that France 2 did not verify, has no proof, should have opened the question to public debate and made the outtakes freely available years ago. If there is any acrimony, it is on the side of France 2. I think the court does not appreciate being exploited by France 2 to silence opposition and avoid the issue. I think the court has enough genuine independence to implicitly condemn France 2 by acquitting Philippe Karsenty. Will France 2 appeal? Will France 2 drop the other two cases? I don't know.

AL-DURA ICON ON TRIAL IN FRANCE
September 25, 2006

Six years after the Mohamed al-Dura death scene kicked off the "Al Aqsa Intifada" the Palestinian icon was at issue in a French court. The state-owned France 2 television network sued Media-Ratings director Philippe Karsenty for defamation, slander, and slurs on their good reputation in an article published online in the fall of 2004, accusing France 2 and Jerusalem correspondent Charles Enderlin of broadcasting a fake, a hoax, a sham, and a swindle. Karsenty, along with many analysts, claims the Palestinian boy's death scene was staged.

The case was heard on September 14th before Judge Joel Boyer of the 17th Chamber of the Tribunal de Grande Instance. Contrary to what might have been expected, the court lent a sympathetic ear to the defendant's arguments and seemed to be offended by the cavalier attitude of the plaintiff. The verdict will be announced on October 19. Two similar cases against other defendants are pending.

September 30, 2000, Netzarim Junction in the Gaza Strip: viewers were stunned by the scene that became the emblem of Israeli (= Jewish) cruelty and Palestinian martyrdom: Jamal al-Dura and his twelve year-old son Mohamed crouched with their backs to a wall, their faces contorted in fear.

Charles Enderlin, who was not present when the incident occurred, commented in a dramatic voiceover: the man and the boy are "targets of gunfire coming from the Israeli position..." And, seconds later: "Mohamed is dead, his father is critically wounded." Cameraman Talal Abu Rahmeh, who won dozens of prizes for the scoop, swore before the Palestinian Center for Human Rights that Israeli soldiers wounded the man and killed the boy "deliberately, in cold blood."

The image of the "intifada" poster boy, Mohamed al-Dura, has inspired violence against Jews all over the world and served as an excuse for barbarous acts such as the lynching of two Israeli reservists in Ramallah and the beheading of Daniel Pearl. Measured against a recent NIE report that pinpoints American presence in Iraq as a focal point for recruiting terrorists, the martyrdom of the Palestinian child has been a far more effective recruitment tool. It was used in a pre-9/11 Al Qaeda recruitment video.

The al-Dura scene, which lasts about 55 seconds, is in fact devoid of action and drama. The emotional impact comes from Enderlin's commentary and the human interest story that was spun around it and uncritically swallowed. Charles Enderlin and France 2 officials, with French media complicity, have kept the lid on the controversy, dismissing serious investigators as "right wing Zionist extremists" concocting wild conspiracy theory.

France 2 claimed to have 27-minutes of raw footage of the incident but refused all requests to show the "foolproof" evidence...until the fall of 2004, when news director Arlette Chabot showed it to three reputable French journalists. They discovered the real context of the al-Dura incident— 24 minutes of staged battle scenes filmed by Palestinian stringers, including Talal Abu Rahmeh.

The demonstration of proof backfired and the case came back into the news, reaching high profile English-language media including *National Post*. France 2 retaliated with a threat to sue anyone who accused them of falsification; only three people have been sued to date. The incriminated Media-Ratings article, calling for the immediate dismissal of Charles Enderlin and news director Arlette Chabot, is backed up with a summary of anomalies and discrepancies that have led investigators to doubt the authenticity of the death scene.

The trial lasted four and a half hours. Judge Boyer began with a thoughtful summary of the issues at stake. The original al-Dura news report was projected, followed by two subsequent newscasts in which Charles Enderlin dismissed an Israeli army investigation that concluded the victims could not have been hit by Israeli gunfire. The "staged scene" hypothesis was presented in a Metula News Agency film and the "less radical" conclusions of a German documentary were succinctly described.

Karsenty's lawyer, Maître Dauzier, presented a coherent argument for his client's good faith in challenging the al-Dura story. The defendant took the stand, followed by four witnesses—Francis Balle, Luc Rosenzweig, Richard Landes, and Gérard Huber. Each in turn described the step by step process by which they had finally concluded that the al-Dura incident was staged. The plaintiff's lawyer, Maître Bénédicte Amblard, declined to question the witnesses.

Serious analysts who have studied the al-Dura affair were intrigued to learn that France 2 had decided to take critics to court. Enderlin and his hierarchy had been holding the lid on this story for six years; if they had conclusive evidence they would have produced it long ago. How could they take the risk of standing before a judge, empty-handed? Were they assured of protection from the highest government spheres? Did they think the court would automatically take their side, despite the lack of evidence? Are they convinced of their good faith, against all evidence?

The plaintiff's case was incoherent, based on circular logic: they could do no wrong because they can do no wrong; Enderlin, Abu Rahmeh, and France 2 are above suspicion; the defendants and his witnesses are beneath contempt. But the bullying techniques that have been used to silence criticism did not look so brilliant in court.

The *procureur* (roughly equivalent to the state's attorney), Sandrine Alimi-Uzan, argued for the defendant's right to express his opinion in strong language that does in fact defame the plaintiff, but is not legally punishable because it is based on an honest, serious investigation of the disputed news report, and is not animated by personal animosity. She criticized the plaintiff for dismissing the competence of the defendant's witnesses while failing to present witnesses or evidence to uphold the complaint. The *procureur* eloquently stated the basic principles of press freedom: the responsibility of the press to present verifiable information—all the more so in this case where the impact of the image was lethal—and the right of the public to challenge the media and obtain honest answers. Arguing that France 2 should have presented the 27 minutes of raw footage in court, she recommended acquittal.

Most observers who covered the trial concur that France 2 lost in court. The verdict will be announced on October 19th.

— *National Post, Canada*

AL DURA: THE VERDICT
October 19, 2006

Charles Enderlin has irretrievably lost his honor today, and it looks like France 2 and the rest of the French media have thrown theirs in the same murky al-Dura pool.

Judge Joël Boyer who personified the search for the truth as he presided over the hearing one month ago pronounced the verdict in a weak, anonymous, impersonal voice. (If I were writing as a novelist I would say he was ashamed of the verdict he had to announce. As a reporter I cannot so presume). Philippe Karsenty is convicted of defamation and ordered to pay a fine of 1000 euros. In addition, he must pay damages of 1 euro to each of the plaintiffs, Charles Enderlin and France 2, plus 3000 euros of legal expenses. The financial penalty, it would seem, is deliberately light. The intention of France 2 was to save its honor. I repeat, they threw it away for a hill of beans. Karsenty is appealing the verdict. That case will most likely be heard a year from now. It involves further heavy expenses for the defendant.

But there is a higher court, beyond the series of appeals courts through which Philippe Karsenty may drag his burden of truth, beyond the European Human Rights Court, which stands outside the huis clos that is France, and might judge in a more reliable light. There is a higher court that is convened in the mind of every courageous human being who is able to examine the evidence, reach a judgment, and defend it against the pressure of powers that be and powers that should not be.

Luc Rosenzweig, one of the four witnesses who testified in Karsenty's favor, is a grizzly, endearing retired journalist and active author. He was one of the three journalists who viewed the 27-minutes of outtakes in November 2004 and saw that France 2 had been bluffing for four years; there were no other al-Dura images to be seen. Fifty-five seconds, that's the whole story. Rosenzweig wrote an article exposing the hoax. It was supposed to be published in L'Express. L'Express opted out. Lost interest in the al-Dura affair, didn't cover the trial, couldn't care less...until, bingo, France 2 wins a lawsuit in a French court and the story is on the wires before the accused can go home and take off his tie. Well my friends, that's a laugh! The French media are in a tizzy, trumpeting the triumph of Charles Enderlin. Is there no danger that their readers might wonder why this juicy story was kept in the larder all these years?

Metula News Agency published a grizzly, endearing article in which Luc Rosenzweig, who has been in the upper spheres of French journalism, mapped out the Enderlin-France 2 strategy. He explained that they prudently bypassed some very thorough analyses published in prestigious outlets such as *Commentary*, the *Wall Street Journal*, the *Reader's Digest*, etc., and aimed their venom at what they thought to be three easy targets. Confident of winning in a French court, Enderlin would then extract the judgment for libel, graft it onto the original trunk—the al-Dura news report—and claim that the court had validated the authenticity of the news report. Rosenzweig shouted loud and clear: Enderlin is a liar, he lies in French, in English, in Hebrew. And two-gun Luc stood there, metaphorically, and dared Enderlin to stand up and fight like a man.

Reuters didn't send anyone to cover the hearing but they sent two journalists to pluck the verdict and deliver it fresh and crunchy over the wires. A Reuters stringer was present at Netzarim Junction on the day the al-Dura story was produced. Many of us have seen his outtakes. They are pure Pallywood. Did he think no one would notice, or was he deliberately or unwittingly providing evidence for that highest of courts?

I was sitting next to one of the Reuters guys in the press box. He was so opaque, it took me a while to realize he was being deliberately hostile. OK, so maybe I joke too much. But I told him a bit about Pajamas Media, and how our very own Little Green Footballs had exposed their very own fauxtography.

The verdict in the case of France 2 versus Philippe Karsenty was announced just seconds after the session was convened. We—those of us who stood with the defendant—hardly knew what hit us. The words were so alien, after what we had thought was a highly civilized search for the truth, a fair trial. We filed out of the courtroom, gathered in the vast marble hall, talked, filmed, interviewed each other. I found myself again with a Reuters reporter. He was so opaque, I can't tell if he was the same one who had been sitting next to me, or another who looked just like him. He was interviewing Maître Rosine Goldberg, a lawyer who had attended the Karsenty trial but was not directly involved. She had many interesting observations about legal aspects of the case. But when the Reuters guy started asking about the difference between a mistaken news report and a staged report, the bright lawyer obviously didn't have the goods. I tried to offer some pertinent details. His opacity opacified.

The Daniel Pearl foundation is holding its annual memorial concert in Paris next month. This empty victory in a hollow court (oops, careful, I think you are not supposed to criticize judicial verdicts in France) will be another pang in the heart of his father Judea Pearl. Judea contacted me after reading my *New York Sun* article on the al-Dura affair. He learned, from that article, that images of al-Dura were interspliced with footage of the beheading of his son. He had never watched that video. I have never seen it either. Someone told me about the use of al-Dura in the beheading of the glowing-with-life Wall Street Journal reporter.

The hatred fueled by the al-Dura death scene did not stop with Israelis, did not stop with the Jews. French police are now using the term "intifada" to describe the situation in the banlieue. Four major incidents have occurred in the past month. Paramilitary actions against the police. Carefully prepared ambushes, hundreds against two or three, murderous violence. You may have read about youths attacking with stones. They are rocks, not stones. The punk jihadis go for the head. They smash skulls. Leave policemen permanently damaged. Over a thousand have been injured this year. Or is it in the past few months? I'll check my figures tomorrow.

I don't draw a direct line from the al-Dura blood libel to these skirmishes that will, according to police sources, soon lead to another major outbreak of organized violence. The line is jagged. And the contradictions are closing in.

The police fired into the air during the last incident. One of the youthful jihadis fired into the air too. Will policemen fire into the crowd to save their lives? Or let themselves be torn to pieces and smashed to pulp? If they defend themselves, if they wound or kill one of their assailants, the banlieue will declare all-out war.

And that puny victory in the 17e Correctionnel will be of no use when the French police find themselves in the same position as Israeli police and soldiers in October 2000. The media that are gloating over Karsenty's defeat poured hellfire and damnation on Israel trying to defend itself in those years.

Don't they understand? It was not a trial to determine the authenticity of the al-Dura report. A French court won't raise that question, won't deliberate on that evidence, won't even ask for the 27 minutes of outtakes. Where does it get you when you keep winning in a rigged game?

The video report of today's round trip to the Palais de Justice is on its way. A summary of the judgment will be posted as soon as Maître Dauzier, Karsenty's lawyer, gives me a copy. He explained today that he is not allowed to disclose those details until the document has been signed by the presiding judge...perhaps a week from now. Apparently someone else's lawyer had no such scruples. The pro-Enderlin press is gleefully disclosing tonight.

Chapter 4

AL DURA: SECOND TRIAL
October 24, 2006

Different courtroom but same 17e Chambre (don't ask why the 17e meets in the 16e on Tuesdays); different defendant—this time it's Pierre Lurçat defended by Maître David Dassa-Le Deist; different judge; different *Procureur*—this one couldn't care less; same plaintiff defended by the same Maître Amblard who gave the same France 2 is above suspicion arguments. Okay, so this time I'm not naïve, the show was less inspiring, and I suppose it's a foregone conclusion. If Maître Amblard is not embarrassed to reiterate, from trial to trial, flimsy arguments that couldn't hold water in a third grade debating society, I guess she knows her way around the Palais de Justice. There is no way that the accused could prove that the defamation was pronounced without personal animosity, in good faith, after a diligent investigation. But we are tireless, and we will study this case in the strong light of our commitment to freedom of speech. Stay tuned.

SUE ME TOO CHARLIE MON VIEUX
October 27, 2006

During this period of infamous "al-Dura" trials, which I have been covering closely for Pajamas Media, I spend a lot of time with colleagues who, like me, have been striving to erase the vicious al-Dura blood libel relayed by France 2 in September 2000 and still going strong. This affair is a bit like last summer's Hizbullah war: no one wins, no one loses, and the verdict pronounced in the court of public opinion is just one more skirmish in an endless war.

I want to write the truth, the whole truth, nothing but the truth about the al-Dura affair. A text that will take life, live and breathe, go forth in the world, take action, obtain results. A supertext that will soar over the heads of Gotham, Sodom & Gomorra, Paris, and El Buredj, swoop down on the villains, knock their heads together, and restore the harmony of the universe.

Charles Enderlin and France 2 are on a winning streak in the French courts. Victorious against Philippe Karsenty, Maître Amblard used the same arguments against Pierre Lurçat, and will most likely attack Dr. Gouz with carbon copy righteous indignation. She swore that her clients respect freedom of the press, including freedom to criticize journalists, but they cannot accept harsh insulting language. Somehow in the logic of the court you have to find a way to accuse Charles Enderlin and France 2 of lying, Jamal al Dura of play-acting, Talal Abu Rahmeh of filming a staged scene, and all of them of viciously maligning Israel...without using harsh language.

If insults are the problem, why has Charles Enderlin initiated a new round of lawsuit threats, aiming at high profile authors who report on his imbroglio in polite, reserved, journalistically acceptable terms?

Misled by his own sense of self-importance, Enderlin stubbornly defends an unsubstantiated "news report" that collapses after ten seconds of unbiased examination, a worthless news report that has one and only one function—blood libel.

It is fabricated as blood libel, it functions like blood libel, it is maintained on life support only because it is blood libel. Why do normally intelligent people think this slapdash production is a credible news report? Because it is blood libel, blinding blood libel. Why do France 2 and French media and French society defend Charles Enderlin to the point of losing their own honor? In defending Enderlin, a simple messenger boy in this affair, they defend the blood libel he conveyed and, inadvertently, flatter his inflated self-image. Enderlin gets a free ride on a blood libel that could eventually swallow him up in its maw but in the interim enjoys the privilege of pushing himself in your face every time you try to shed light on the blood libel. He gets interviewed by *Télérama* (but doesn't seem to have pull with big international media); he or his allies feed information to hapless journalists like Michel Zlotowski, who used to write for the JPost. His mediocre films are shown on French TV, his boring books are published all the way to the USA, his amateurish interpretation of the Mideast conflict is praised by President Chirac. His journalistic qualities can be judged by the way he digs in his heels and insists that the Mohamed al-Dura blood libel is a legitimate news report.

The 55-second al-Dura death scene filmed on September 30 2000 by T. A. Rahmeh, produced by France 2, and broadcast worldwide, is not a news report. It does not respect the criteria of news reporting, it does not resemble a legitimate news report, it does not function as a news report, it cannot be defended as a news report. It has no context, no depth, no duration beyond itself, and no connection with any other point in space or time. It is cut from whole cloth and pasted onto the real setting of Netzarim Junction, but has no relation to the myriad events that actually took place there. It doesn't even fit in with the Pallywood fake battle scenes filmed at the Junction that day.

I defy anyone to give a coherent description of what happened to Jamal and Mohamed al-Dura on the afternoon of September 30 2000. It can't be done.

Jamal himself, Talal the prize-winning cameraman, France 2 officials, journalists of all stripes and nationalities tell, retell, repeat, and reiterate a story concocted like the video, a story that respects none of the rules of news reporting or story-telling, that works only as blood libel. When a detail gets in the way, it is smudged. But it can't be eliminated without undoing the blood libel. Here's an example: Israeli soldiers shot directly at the man and the boy—sitting ducks—for 45 minutes, with the sole intention of hitting them and, finally, at the term of those 45 minutes managed to kill the boy and critically wound his father.

Try to make that detail stand alone. Does anyone in his right mind believe an Israeli soldier would need 45 minutes to hit a stationary target clearly visible in his gun sights? The answer is no. The story should choke on that detail, but it gets smudged: sophisticated journalists find urbane explanations for a "minor" anomaly; Talal sends his hierarchy a self-serving disclaimer some years after the fact; your average gullible news consumer swallows and spins...

The problem is, none of the details in the al-Dura blood libel stand up to examination. They can all be spun, dismissed, hid behind someone's back, shrugged off, swallowed, whatever. And yet the ensemble remains intact because it is true as blood libel and only as blood libel. The details were faked to make it look like a news report. Debunking them is a trap too. It gives credibility to the illusion that the scene is somehow, in some way, vaguely if imperfectly, a news report.

Rational journalists and black-robed judges might feel comfortable with the idea that Al-Dura was killed by Palestinian gunfire in a shootout with Israeli soldiers. But how do they explain his status as icon of the al Aqsa intifada? A Palestinian child killed by Palestinians can't be an icon. Kids like Mohamed are getting killed—by Palestinians—in great numbers right now in Gaza. Have any of them turned up as icons?

The image of Mohamed al-Dura is worthless unless it is blood libel. It must show that bloodthirsty Jews deliberately kill our children. If anyone really believed the soothingly well-balanced compromise interpretations of those seemingly rational analysts, the image would be deflated to near invisibility.

Ah, but the reasonable analysts will say al-Dura is only an icon in the Arab-Muslim world...implying that nothing we could do here in our civilized neighborhood would discourage them from misusing it. Thanks a lot! First of all, they got it from France 2. And, second, it is working beautifully here too, pumping out more Jew hatred than Saudi Arabia pumps oil, facilitating mini blood libels—massacres in Jenin, on a Gaza beach, in Qana— that keep the pot boiling and win wars by losing them.

Graphically, the al-Dura scene does not look like a news report. The shooting angle, the framing, the postures, the sequences, the zoom all ring false. It's not a news report that became an icon, it's an icon misrepresented as news. If it weren't blood libel, trained and untrained eyes would see that it doesn't look like a news report. It is blood libel, blinding blood libel, so blinding that freeze frames that <u>prove</u> the report is faked are used to illustrate articles reporting that Charles Enderlin is vindicated, the famous France 2 Jerusalem correspondent is an honorable man, Charles Enderlin trusted his trustworthy cameraman, and extremists who try to sully their good reputation are beneath contempt. Neither the journalists nor their photo editors bother to find out where the freeze frame stands in the sequence and why it contradicts Jamal's testimony.

The al-Dura scene is not a news report. There is a serious disconnect between the images, the voiceover commentary, and the enveloping narrative peddled along with them. This is glaring evidence of falsification and yet the eyes of reasonable people glaze over when you point it out. If I showed you the image of a shaggy dog sitting in a broken down jeep and said, "Airbus is proud of its jumbo carrier, the A 380... Singapore Airlines has ordered a dozen of these luxurious cruise ships on wings..." the disconnect would arouse your suspicion. The al-Dura disconnect is no less obvious. But blood libel mobilizes base emotions that refuse rational control. Though every word said or written to flesh out the al-Dura myth actually tears it apart, the enveloping narrative was used uncritically as fodder for a slew of articles worldwide. People aren't bothered by the clumsy storytelling. It works because it's blood libel, hysterical incoherent accusations that awaken ugly instincts in the pit of some stomachs and self-defeating guilt feelings in the hearts of others.

The al-Dura story is a sham news report but it's a real blood libel relayed by high tech 21st century media...

It will be dismantled somehow, some day, somewhere out of the reach of the French *huis clos*.

And all the lawsuits of Charles Enderlin will never put it together again.

— *Makor Rishon*
— *Augean Stables*

AL DURA AFFAIR: FRANCE 2 WINS BY A DECISION

January 18, 2007

The decision in the last of a series of three "al Dura trials" was so arbitrary, so discriminatory, so murderous of free speech that I am almost too disgusted to report it. Dr. Charles Gouz, editor of a modest home-made website, désinfos.com, was convicted of defaming Charles Enderlin and France 2. And that wraps it up! With a healthy 2 out of 3 wins, the state-owned TV channel and its Jerusalem correspondent can claim victory and dress in an illusion of justice. The first and most substantial case, against Philippe Karsenty of Media Ratings, was won against all evidence and used as proof of the authenticity of the al Dura "news report." The second, against Pierre Lurçat, was lost on a technicality. And, in the opinion of Karsenty, Dr. Gouz had to lose because France 2 must win against his appeal in September.

If the Gouz case actually establishes any legal precedent, it would mean that no one can publish a blog in France, no one can post a compilation of articles on a web site, no one can write freely about anything at any time. Dr. Gouz, like many others and particularly many Jewish people all over the world, was horrified by the outburst of anti-Zionist Jew hatred sparked in September 2000 by the "al Aqsa intifada." He created a website and posted—without commentary—articles of interest to counter the "disinformation" peddled by mainstream media.

In 2002, twenty big and small associations organized a demonstration outside the France 2 building to protest the station's refusal to broadcast the Esther Schapira film-investigation of the al Dura affair. The film was projected on a big outdoor screen, and the associations awarded France 2 the prize for disinformation. This would seem like a perfectly normal action by free citizens in a democratic country. Dr. Gouz did not join the call to demonstrate. He simply posted a Metula News Agency release advising <u>against</u> participation in the protest and recommending other methods to achieve full disclosure of the facts surrounding the production and broadcast of the al Dura report and obtain a retraction of the false accusation against Israeli soldiers. (Pierre Lurçat was accused of publishing an appeal to participate in that same demonstration).

Both the appeal to demonstrate and the call to refrain from demonstrating are, in the court's opinion, defamatory to the extent that they incorporate harsh criticism of the al Dura news report. Charles Enderlin is using those victories to silence critics, prove the report was legitimate and, stealthily, sustain the original accusation: The man and the boy were "targets of gunfire from the Israeli position."

Technically the defendant's lawyer should have been given the judgment in full immediately after the verdict was pronounced. But it wasn't ready. Maître Aude Wiell-Raynal managed to get a few passages that were passed around among the rare journalists and sympathizers gathered in the cold marble hall outside the courtroom. From what we could understand, Dr. Gouz was guilty, half guilty, two-thirds guilty...acquitted on one sentence and part of another, convicted on another sentence...such a garble it's almost shameful to repeat. Try to remember that Dr. Gouz, a GP who looks like exactly the person you would want at your bedside in times of illness, did not criticize the al Dura report, did not accuse Enderlin or France 2 of lying, cheating, or stealing. He did not and does not to this day claim that the al Dura report was staged. However, in the eyes of the court, Dr. Gouz is inseparable from the Metula News Agency release he posted.

The court picked through the release, found that Dr. Gouz-Metula-News-Agency could, without slandering, say that Charles Enderlin had committed a serious professional error but could not say, without sufficient proof, that the bungled newscast was "disinformation," but could go on to say that the said news report functioned as an incitement to ethnic hatred...

For this mixture of alleged slander, insufficient proof, lack of diligent investigation allegedly committed, I cannot say often enough, by Metula News Agency, the good doctor who copied and pasted it was slapped with a suspended fine of 1,000 euros. If, in the space of five years, he does not commit further slander, the fine will be dropped. That's the criminal penalty. In addition he is sentenced to pay 1 euro symbolic civil damages to each of the plaintiffs.

Nothing that was said by the witnesses who testified forcefully in Dr. Gouz's favor, nothing in the eloquent plea for acquittal delivered by *la procureur* Sandrine Alimi-Uzan, nothing in the dazzling defense of Maître Weill-Raynal who deftly attacked every weakness in the plaintiff's case, nothing of the resounding defense of press freedom and concomitant demand for journalistic responsibility of all of the aforementioned could weigh even 1 gram against the thrice-repeated plea of France 2 lawyer, Maître Bénédicte Amblard: Charles Enderlin has been France 2 Jerusalem correspondent for twenty years; he is an honorable man, a respected journalist and author of several authoritative works on the Middle East conflict. Talal Abu Rahmeh is an honorable cameraman; he has worked with Charles Enderlin for over ten years. Metula News Agency has orchestrated a virulent campaign to slander Charles Enderlin and France 2. France 2 is an honorable television channel. President Chirac himself has expressed in writing his admiration for Charles Enderlin. And so forth and so on.

Maître Amblard pleaded with the court to judge in favor of her clients and stamp out, once and for all, this vicious campaign that has been going on for six years, instigated and orchestrated by Metula News Agency. (PS: the agency in question has been trying to get France 2 to sue it...to no avail.)

The court heard her plea, ruled in her favor and, I would suppose, heaved a sigh of relief. Now that's done with! No one will ever again dare to question the al Dura report in France. And we won't have to hear any more of these cases. Phew!

Did Charles Enderlin, basking in the warmth of the decisions rendered in the Palais de Justice, glimpse the light dawning on the shores of Herzliya? Could it be that the tide is turning? Watch these Infolive TV interviews with Israeli officials and judge for yourself. One of the most notable accomplishments of the "Media as a Theater of War Conference" (see below) was to bring home the full significance of the al Dura blood libel and spark awareness of the need for Israel to stand up and talk back to this false accusation that has opened the floodgates of slander, libel and defamation against the state of Israel and those who defend it everywhere and anywhere.

For six years Charles Enderlin has been posing as the innocent victim of a vicious campaign to discredit his faultless reporting, simply because it—in his opinion, deservedly—makes Israel look bad. If France 2 had acted in good faith and released the al Dura outtakes within a month of the dubious news report, the facts would have been exposed to public scrutiny, the unsubstantiated report would have been withdrawn, and no one would have had to relentlessly pursue the truth.

The temporary relief offered by using the Parisian court to squelch the affair and punish honest citizens who courageously defend press freedom may well be short-lived. The refusal to release the outtakes implicitly proves that the seasoned France 2 journalist did not make the serious investigation that the court demanded of the three mangled defendants. As the affair al Dura enters a new phase in an international arena, this easy victory may turn out to be a serious tactical error.

One cannot do justice to the Conference organized by Professors Richard Landes and Uzi Arad at the IPS (Institute for Policy and Strategy) in Herzliya: The Media as a Theater of War, the Blogosphere, and the Global Battle for Civil Society, December 17-18 2006. The program and background information can be consulted on the Herzliya Conference site. Audio, video, and text of the proceedings will eventually be available. There is no way to dash off a concise comprehensive account of the rich hours we shared in the halls of the beautiful Daniel Shizen Hotel, looking out on white sands and blue seas but bravely concentrating on the work at hand. A mood of exhilaration was sustained from the luscious breakfast banquet, through hours of informative, inspiring formal sessions, and late into the night of rich conversation.

It was quite exceptional as Conferences go. All the speakers respected the draconian 15-minute limit. There was no ego tripping, no boring overwritten texts read in a monotone. Speakers spoke, but they also listened. The attitude was mutually respectful and democratic. No one pulled rank. There were no guest appearances. Big names sat for hours and listened to the other panels. The audience was attentive, the questions challenging. Differences of opinion were aired politely. Richard was visibly and deservedly pleased by the dynamics he had set in motion and the potential it was generating, so I asked him whether he had any disappointments. "The mainstream media. We invited them all, they didn't show up. Can't they listen to criticism?"

Pajamas Media was present and accounted for. East met West and North met South as the blogosphere came to life in three dimensions. The role of the new media was explored with some well-deserved pride in the stunning exposure of fauxtography and staged news in this summer's Lebanon war. The Conference functioned as a two-day think tank convened to formulate a paradigm shift in Israel's public diplomacy. Greater understanding of the sources of virulent anti-Zionism dictates a less apologetic, more assertive presence on the international scene.

The al Dura affair is at the heart of that paradigm shift. Philippe Karsenty, scolded and shamed in the musty chambers of the 17e Correctionnel in the Palais de Justice, was received with a standing ovation at the Herzliya Conference. Convicted in France of defaming France 2 and Charles Enderlin, Karsenty was honored in Israel. Ranaan Gissin, former advisor to PM Ariel Sharon, stood up and apologized for failing to act against the al Dura accusation. Daniel Seaman, chief of the Government Press Office, declared that the al Dura report was staged, Enderlin was dishonest, his cameraman was working for terrorist factions.

The verdict against Doctor Gouz was announced at 1:45 PM on the 18th of January 2007. On that same day, France rendered a belated tribute to the "Righteous Gentiles," French people who braved mortal danger to save Jews from certain death in the Shoah. President Chirac wiped a tear from his cheek as his voice, choked with emotion, echoed in the vaulted hall of the Pantheon. Grant him the sincerity of that tear.

And then ask how he can actively sustain the al Dura blood libel?

TRIALS: THE APPEAL

9/18/07 Al Dura Affair / Brief recap on the eve of the hearing

Philippe Karsenty, director of Media-Ratings, has appealed his November 2006 libel conviction in the case brought against him by state-owned France 2 Television and its Jerusalem correspondent Charles Enderlin, in what has become known as the al Dura affair. The case will be heard tomorrow in the Appeals Court at the Palais de Justice. A major turning point in this case is the Israel Defense Force's imperative demand for handover of the 27 minutes of raw footage filmed by France 2 stringer Talal Abu Rahmeh and purportedly showing additional images of the alleged victims of Israeli gunfire, identified as Jamal al Dura and his son Mohamed.

Abu Rahmeh affirmed, in sworn testimony, that Israeli soldiers fired deliberately and continuously at the man and the boy for 45 minutes, until the boy was dead and the man critically wounded. He claimed to have filmed 27 minutes of the 45-minute incident. France 2 journalist Charles Enderlin insists that the 55-second segment broadcast by his network and distributed free of charge to international media, is an excerpt from more ample coverage of the incident contained in that 27-minute video. France 2 has refused countless requests, including several from the Israeli army, to release the 27 minutes of raw footage. Charles Enderlin and his hierarchy continue to insist that the withheld footage substantiates claims that the boy and the man were shot ... by Israeli soldiers...or by gunfire from an undetermined source.

To my knowledge, four people have viewed the 27-minute video:

Richard Landes (professor of history at Boston University, director of seconddraft.org and Augean Stables), Luc Rosenzweig (retired, reputable, first class French journalist), Denis Jeambar (former reputable editorial director of the news weekly l'Express, currently director of Editions du Seuil), and Daniel Leconte (reputable journalist and director of Doc en Stock, producer of documentaries for French TV).

All four witnesses have testified, formally or informally, to the absence of images of Jamal and Mohamed al Dura in the 27-minute outtakes. They have all, in differing degrees, noted extensive footage of staged battle scenes in the 27-minute segment. None of the four have claimed that the 27-minute segment includes any image that could substantiate the voice-off narrative of the "death scene" as broadcast by France 2 on September 30, 2000.

Landes and Rosenzweig maintain that the 55-second video is a staged scene. Jeambar and Leconte maintain that the boy was killed and the father injured in a crossfire.

There is no evidence of a crossfire in the 55-second "death scene" video. There is no other image of Jamal and Mohamed al Dura in the 27-minute outtakes. This is why I dismiss the "crossfire" explanation as a deus ex machina.

To my knowledge, the only mention of the upcoming hearing in French media is a Radio J interview of Philippe Karsenty by Michel Zerbib, the only French journalist to have given serious attention to the al Dura affair over the past few years. Mainstream media that reported on Karsenty's conviction, misinterpreted as proof that the al Dura "death scene" was not staged, have not mentioned the IDF demand for handover of the outtakes despite the fact that it expresses serious doubts about the credibility of a major news report.

Asked if the change in government might influence the outcome of his trial, Karsenty replied that there are two possible avenues of success: the court could rule in his favor and/or President Sarkozy could instruct Patrick de Carolis, director of France Télévisions, to turn over the outtakes as requested. Recalling that a letter of praise for Charles Enderlin from then president Jacques Chirac weighed heavily in the case against Karsenty, we will be curious to observe the attitude of the Court during tomorrow's hearing. A brief report will be posted tomorrow evening, followed shortly by a full report.

STUNNING TURN OF EVENTS IN THE AL DURA AFFAIR
The Court requests hand over of the raw footage
September 19, 2007

Maître Bénédicte Amblard, representing Charles Enderlin / France 2 in their libel suit against Philippe Karsenty (Media Ratings) dropped her pencil and lost her composure when presiding judge Laurence Trébucq, overriding the opinion of the Avocat Général, firmly demanded handover of the 27-minute unedited film shot by Talal Abu Rahmeh at Netzarim Junctin in the Gaza Strip on September 30, 2000. The Maginot Line of France 2 collapsed then and there. From here on in, anything is possible.

Karsenty is appealing his October 2006 conviction for defamation in a case brought by state-owned TV channel France 2 and the station's Mideast correspondent, Charles Enderlin. In the incriminated Media-Ratings press release, Karsenty had called for the immediate revocation of Enderlin and then news director Arlette Chabot for their respective roles in broadcasting and upholding a hoax—the famous news report of the "death" of 12 year-old Mohamed al Dura, "target of gunfire from the Israeli position."

While the court of first resort had granted Karsenty's right to question the authenticity of the news report, it followed the plaintiff's arguments and found him guilty of bad faith and publication of unsubstantiated accusations based on a single source (Metula News Agency). Karsenty appealed.

Things looked grim for Karsenty as the hearing began. There was a technical problem with the large screen he had been authorized to bring into the courtroom (which is normally equipped with a tiny outmoded TV). And the judge sternly rejected his proposed projection of a didactic montage of the disputed al Dura images. After a brief recess during which the technical problem was solved, the hearing began with a brief interrogation on Karsenty's professional and financial situation, followed by a rather awkward résumé—by the second judge, designated as the "advisor"— of the initial case and conviction

Karsenty's counsel, Maître Marc Lévy, interjects a request for an expertise on the 27-minutes of unedited footage, which had been viewed by three journalists—Jeambar, Leconte, and Rosenzweig—who testified that they consisted of 24 minutes of staged scenes, with no images of the al Dura boy and his father and no trace of the boy's "death throes" that Enderlin claimed had been edited out because it was "unbearable."

Readers should know that "discovery," as understood in the U.S., does not exist in the French system This is how France 2 could accuse Karsenty of making unfounded accusations without facing the obligation to produce the raw footage that might substantiate them.

The judge immediately grasps the importance of the raw footage and asks "Do we have the film?" Maître Amblard replies, supremely self-confident: "Of course not." She seems to assume that the Court will bow to the higher authority of France 2. Maître Lévy argues with subdued indignation that it is unacceptable to refuse to produce the outtakes, which are composed for 90% of staged scenes and 10% of "al Dura."

The Avocat Général concludes, on the basis of jurisprudence, that the Appelate court does not need to examine the raw footage because the court of first resort had ruled on the case without seeing it. Maître Amblard seizes this favorable wind to embark on a typical Enderlin argument—just because 90% of the film is composed of staged scenes, it doesn't mean that the remaining 10% is also staged. How could it be? It is the death of a child!

The judge calls a brief recess to deliberate on the request; the judges decide to examine further evidence and leave the request for expertise in abeyance. A setback for France 2, an opportunity for Karsenty.

The first exhibit is set in motion—the infamous news report of the death of the Palestinian child. The judge rejects Karsenty's request to be allowed to interrupt the projection and explain, frame by frame, why the images do not correspond with the voiceover commentary. Things get prickly. Karsenty's counsel fades into the background, the judge insists that she and her associates can see for themselves without Karsenty's comments, he overrides the judge, the mood is tense but slightly comical.

Will she cut the projection and throw him out of court? Is he upsetting his apple cart? For anyone who has worked on the al Dura affair, it's agonizing to hear Karsenty go through the tedious details while the judge, like any innocent observer, makes the same objections we've heard a thousand times. The shooting angle, the Israeli position, no blood, the wall intact after 45 minutes of alleged gunfire, the Reuters cameraman right next to them... The judge objects, obstructs, interrupts, but keeps watching, keeps listening, follows intelligently, assimilates large doses of information as Karsenty projects news reports from the days following the incident. Charles Enderlin and Talal Abu Rahmeh stick to their story, embellish it with details that have withstood examination for seven years but may soon be turned against them.

The projection continues with a news broadcast in which Enderlin, in all his glory as "objective reporter," trashes the army investigation led by General Yom-Tov Samia... and ends by quoting from Haaretz: "The Israeli army shot itself in the foot."

The Judge turns to Maître Amblard: "Are there any staged scenes in any of these news reports we've just viewed?"

Maître Amblard falters. She tries to refocus attention on the al-Dura report. But the judge insists. "Are there any staged scenes in the 27 minutes of raw footage that might have appeared in the news reports we've just watched?"

Maitre Amblard fumbles. Backs up a step as if she had been pushed. And whispers a most unconvincing "No."

The court recesses. (Even though an informed source has already whispered the result in my ear, I am gripped with suspense.) The judges return and report their decision on the question in suspense. The expertise. The raw footage. They want it. They will not go forward until they have seen it. Maître Amblard drops her pencil. She is sincerely stunned.

Finally she mutters, "If the court orders my client to produce the footage...of course...but I don't know where it is."

Maître Lévy leaps forward and places a letter in the judge's hands. It's Charles Enderlin's response to the Israeli army request for handover of the raw footage. Enderlin explains that it is in Paris, in the hands of the France 2 legal service.

One more brief recess as Maître Amblard attempts—in vain— to reach a France 2 official who can confirm the availability of the material.

If the footage is not turned over voluntarily by the 3rd of October, the court will issue a formal request. The next hearing is scheduled for November 14th, to view the said footage. A relay hearing is scheduled for January 16, and the case will be heard in full on the 27th of February.

Philippe Karsenty has scored a significant victory. The al Dura report has been questioned ever since it was first broadcast seven years ago.

The 27-minutes of raw footage have served as a protective shield for Charles Enderlin and France 2—the "proof" that was never presented. Even after reputable journalists had viewed the footage and testified to its nature, it retained its magical quality and was used to discredit anyone who questioned the veracity of the al Dura report.

Today, a French Appelate Court destroyed that magic. The raw footage is forced to enter the sphere of reality, where it will be judged by rational standards.

The outcome remains uncertain.

Will France 2 discover a way to slip out of this injunction? Will the court temper its demand? Will the footage be produced, viewed, and dismissed as irrelevant?

Will President Sarkozy exert his authority and imperatively request state-owned France 2 to come forward, produce the evidence and, eventually, dismiss collaborators who have participated in this hoax...as requested in the incriminated Media Ratings release?

And, finally, when will the French media tear off their false faces and admit what they know about the al Dura affair?

Despite an AP release and extensive international coverage over the past few weeks, no mainstream media reporters attended today's hearing. They missed an early warning that the rules of the game may well be changing.

IT'S OFFICIAL—AL DURA WAS STAGED
October 2, 2007

Ainit the truth! You work on a story for years, and the day you oversleep your mailbox spills over with breaking news. "Al Dura death was staged. It's official." Everybody and his brother gleefully informed me of the breaking news: Haaretz, Ynet news, atlas shrugs, MSNBC, Guysen Israel News, and Sharansky in the Wall Street Journal.

Dany Seaman, director of Israel's Government Press Office—responding to a letter from chairwoman Nitzana Sarshan-Leitner, informing him that Shurat HaDin intends to sue France 2 Jerusalem correspondent Charles Enderlin—declared officially that the France 2 al Dura report was staged. Shurat HaDin wants the GPO to cancel France 2 credentials unless and until the state-owned French TV channel turns over the raw footage as formally requested by Israeli army officials.

Stopping short of this measure, in accordance with the recommendations of Attorney General Menachem Mazuz, Seaman officially declared that the al Dura report was a hoax that had caused untold harm. The Prime Minister's office—no surprise—has officially declared that it has made no official declaration on this issue.

As it happens, I got the scoop when I visited Dany in July. Here's what I wrote [Facts & figures in Jerusalem July 2 2007]

"The next day, a pleasant walk through Independence Park leads me to the Beit Agron Government Press Office and one of my favorite straight talkers, GPO chief Danny Seaman. My man hangs in there, warding off varied and sundry militants and freeloaders trying to wrangle press credentials, and resisting pressure from a Foreign Office that thinks giving-in is a way of making friends and influencing people. We go over the latest developments in Gaza, he deplores the wasted opportunity. 'Israel should give Hamas an ultimatum, release Gilad Shalit in 5 days or we'll cut off the electricity, shut down the water supply...' The Foreign Press Association is already negotiating with Hamas —'safe' passage into Gaza in exchange for 'fair' coverage. And how about this zero-approved Israeli government? The left wing media and establishment won't let Netanyahu win. It doesn't even matter anymore. We need Giuliani in the US, Sarkozy in France, Merkel in Germany... They're starving in Gaza? So why don't they smuggle in food instead of weapons? Gaza will be the first successful Muslim Brotherhood country; all the surrounding Arab nations will be endangered if it succeeds.

"I leave with these and other words of wisdom, and a temporary GPO press card, renewable at each visit to Israel."

And here's what I didn't write:

Dany told me that Shurat HaDin is going to sue Enderlin for the al Dura hoax and the terrible damages it has entailed. Dany asked me not to publish information about the lawsuit until it was officially announced. Charles Enderlin, the France 2 Jerusalem correspondent who has been peddling and defending the al Dura hoax beyond belief, is known by his detractors in France as "Scoopy." I kept my word, didn't scoop the story, went about my business, and here it is, full blown and sweetly perfumed. Everyone who has worked on the al Dura affair knows there is no magic bullet. It is an intricate puzzle, and it will be put together by painstaking efforts from many directions. But recent developments, stimulated by Karsenty's appeal of his 2006 conviction for defamation of Enderlin and France 2, are more than promising.

So, the first thing you want from me is a résumé of reactions in the French press. That's easy. I heard an extensive account of the affair this morning on Judaïques FM. What else is new?

A quick review of today's reports of Seaman's official declaration demonstrates the chilling success of the al Dura hoax: many journalists describe events at Netzarim Junction on September 30, 2000 as if they were an authentic context for a questionable incident. If and when the 27-minutes of raw footage is projected in the French appellate court (the court order will be issued tomorrow, PJ Media will be there), the whole truth will begin to emerge. September 30, 2000 was almost entirely staged!

Jamal al Dura and the boy identified as his son Mohamed were not caught in the middle of a relentless firefight between Israeli soldiers and Palestinian gunmen and/or policemen; they were performing the lead roles in a day-long production organized to trigger the "al Aqsa Intifada." The al Dura "death" scene is one of countless scenes staged that day. Raw footage shot by a Palestinian cameraman working for Reuters, turned over to Israeli physicist Nahum Shahaf, is available for viewing on the seconddraft site created by historian Richard Landes. Landes, who has also viewed the 27-minutes of footage shot by Talal Abu Rahma, testifies that it is composed of approximately 24 minutes of the same type of staged scenes found in the Reuters tape.It appears that there was one brief firefight between Israelis and Palestinians at the junction that day. The al Dura scene was not filmed during that episode.

As I explained in a Commentary article published in September 2005, distracted commentators maintain the authenticity of the al Dura "death" scene based on what they think they see in the scene itself, and what they have been led to imagine as its realistic context in a zone of fierce combat. They do not even examine, let alone question the narrative by which the al Dura story has been inserted into current events.

Countless journalists are describing the 27-minutes of raw footage as if it were—as Charles Enderlin has consistently claimed, as his cameraman declared under oath—27 minutes of the 45 minute ordeal of a man and a boy pinned down by Israeli gunfire. I saw raw footage of Esther Schapira's interview with Talal Abu Rahma; the cameraman explains why the 55-second excerpt (from the 27-minute film of the 45-minute incident) looks as if it were filmed in real time. The dramatic gestures that engraved the al Duras on the world's psyche—the crouching, the waving, the shouting in horror, etc.— says Abu Rahma, were repeated off and on throughout the 45-minute incident. Filmed intermittently, then mounted, they give the effect—he claimed—of a single incident in a 55-second time frame.

My eye!

Charles Enderlin is defending his news report and his cameraman all the way down to the finish line. Far from cringing in horror at the thought of what the world will discover when the raw footage is projected, he is waving the V for victory:

"We plan to show the film in court in France, and I am certain it will end the repeated mudslinging." (quoted in Ynetnews.com)

Has he already forgotten that last year's three defamation trials were supposed to put the affair to sleep forever?

Your correspondent will be on the lookout for reactions in France ...expect a long list of no-comments...

ISRAEL'S GPO SAYS AL DURA REPORT IS A HOAX

10/2/07 Daniel Seaman, chairman of Israel's Government Press Office, has officially declared that the al Dura news report—filmed on September 30, 2000 at Netzarim Junction in the Gaza Strip by a Palestinian cameraman employed by state-owned French channel France 2— was staged. The news broke in the Israeli media this morning, is spreading in the United States, but has not pierced the firewall of mainstream media in France.

In the voiceover, France 2 Jerusalem bureau chief Charles Enderlin dramatically described the "death" of the 12 year-old Palestinian boy, Mohamed al Dura, "target of gunfire from the Israeli position." The 55-second video was immediately broadcast worldwide and assimilated by unsuspecting viewers. It functioned as blood libel, justifying atrocities against Israelis and Jews.

For seven years investigators and analysts have labored relentlessly to counter that unfounded accusation. For seven years Charles Enderlin and France 2, protected by the Chirac government and upheld by mainstream media, have stifled criticism and discredited these investigators.

The Israeli government, pursuing a "let sleeping dogs lie" policy, discouraged efforts to expose the hoax. Jewish organizations shied away from the controversy.

The al Dura affair is a smudge on the face of coverage of the "Middle East conflict"; every attempt to wipe it away spreads and deepens the stain. In 2005, France 2 and Enderlin, apparently confident that they could wipe away the smudge, brought defamation lawsuits against three French-based websites that had posted material questioning the authenticity of the al Dura video.

The cases were heard in the autumn and winter of 2006-7. France 2 lost one on a technicality, and won the other two. Suddenly mainstream media in France discovered the affair...long enough to report that the al Dura scene was not staged! But one of the defendants, Philippe Karsenty, director of the Media-Ratings watchdog site, appealed his conviction and has achieved a major victory—the Appellate Court asked France 2 to produce the 27-minutes of raw footage from which the 55-second "news" video was excerpted. If France 2 has not spontaneously turned over the document, the Court will issue an order to that effect on October 3rd. The raw footage will be projected at a hearing scheduled for November 14th, and the case will be heard in full on February 27th 2008.

The Palestinian cameraman, Tala Abu Rahma testified under oath that Mohamed al Dura and his father Jamal were pinned down by uninterrupted gunfire from the Israeli position for 45 minutes. He claims he filmed the incident off and on from beginning to end for a total of 27 minutes, from which Charles Enderlin excerpted 55-seconds for the news report. Enderlin, backed by his hierarchy, insists that the raw footage confirms the authenticity of the news report...but has refused to make it available for public scrutiny. Four reliable witnesses who have viewed the footage testify that it is composed of staged scenes, faked injuries, falsified ambulance evacuations. There are no images of the al Duras.

If the raw footage is projected in the courtroom, the battle will be half won, no matter how the Court rules on Karsenty's appeal. If a dozen world class journalists attend the November 14th hearing, the al Dura affair will be brought out of the dark alley and into the agora of democratic societies where it should finally be judged.

— *Commentary / Contentions*

MORE ON AL DURA
October 3, 2007

In a brief hearing today, Appellate Court judge Laurence Trébucq read out the court order enjoining France 2 to hand over, no later than October 31, the raw footage filmed by cameraman Talal Abu Rahma on September 30th and October 1st 2000. Maître Bénédicte Amblard, representing France 2, confirmed her client's intention to comply. This confirms the request announced on the September 19th hearing of Philippe Karsenty's appeal of his October 2006 conviction for defamation against France 2 and Charles Enderlin in the "al Dura affair." (The videos will be projected on a modern screen furnished by the defendant for lack of adequate material in the antiquated Palais de Justice.) In the absence of mention of a *huis clos* it is assumed that the November 14th hearing will be open to the public. An overflow crowd is expected.

This court order, which would seem perfectly reasonable to someone acquainted with the United States legal system, is apparently unprecedented in France. In fact, in the October 2006 defamation suit had been brought in an American court, the defendant's lawyer would certainly have asked to examine the outtakes. "Discovery" as we know it does not exist in French law. The burden of proof in a defamation case rests on the defendant. The court of first resort had ruled that Karsenty's public accusation of France 2 and Jerusalem correspondent Charles Enderlin, on his watchdog site Media-Ratings, was not based on a serious investigation of the facts. Further, the court discredited Karsenty's arguments, "drawn from a single source—Metula News Agency." The irony of this judgment is that Charles Enderlin relied on a single source—Palestinian cameraman Talal Abu Rahma— for the report of Mohamed al Dura's "death," and failed to investigate the report after he received the raw footage, which contradicts the sworn testimony of the cameraman.

As for the single source, all investigators and analysts working over the past seven years to unearth the truth about the al Dura affair have drawn on documentation collected and developed by Israeli physicist Nahum Shahaf. The mass of documentation, analysis, and reasoned argumentation subsequently accumulated would fill several books in several languages. On the other hand, France 2 and Charles Enderlin are still presenting the same flimsy arguments used ever since the report was aired, immediately provoking serious inquiry from many quarters. It should be noted that CNN rejected the al Dura report proposed by Abu Rahma on September 30th.

Skeptical readers suggest that even if the truth about the al Dura report were to be fully and convincingly exposed it would not change the underlying story or the attitudes it has fostered. Beyond the realistic assessment of the enormous difficulties facing those who would try to expose one gigantic media lie stands our hope in the capacity of democratic societies to demand a minimum of integrity from the journalists who claim to inform us. Recent developments in the al Dura affair should encourage us to persevere.

French mainstream media do not even want to admit they know about this turn of events in the al Dura affair. But Charles Enderlin whistles in the dark on his France 2 blog. "Finally," he exclaims, "the raw footage will be projected..." promising that his critics will finally be silenced.

We shall see...

— *Commentary/Contentions*

THE "DEATH" OF MOHAMED AL DURA COMES BACK TO LIFE

October 9, 2007

The "death of Mohamed al Dura" myth is back in the news, and this time Charles Enderlin & France 2, respectively producer and broadcaster of the questionable "news report," are on the defensive. In a surprise reversal of previous procedure, Appellate Court judge Laurent Trébucq has ordered France 2 to turn over the raw footage filmed by France 2 stringer Talal Abu Rahma at Netzarim Junction in the Gaza Strip on September 30, 2000. Analysts familiar with the affair know that projection of the 27-minute video will prove that the sole witnesses to the purported incident—Abu Rahma and Jamal al Dura—are not telling the truth. How will the inflated reputation of Charles Enderlin resist this laser scalpel?

Philippe Karsenty's lawyer, Marc Levy, interjected the request for examination of the raw footage at the September 19th hearing of his appeal of an October 2006 defamation (libel, slander) conviction. On October 3rd the judge read out the court order to produce footage on or before October 31st, to be viewed in the courtroom on November 14th. The case in full will be heard on February 27th 2008.

The court order is all the more notable in that the authenticity of the al Dura report was not, strictly speaking, at issue in the original lawsuit. The court of first resort convicted Media-Ratings director Karsenty of slander on the grounds that the release he published, accusing Enderlin, France 2 and news director Arlette Chabot of producing, broadcasting, and defending a fake, was couched in unduly harsh language and based essentially on a dubious Metula News Agency investigation. Further, the court sustained the plaintiff's argument that the absence of protest by the Israeli government indicated that Karsenty's accusations were unfounded.

Setting aside the peculiarities of the French judicial system, let us focus on the raw footage that will be exposed to its eagle eye. Testifying under oath a few short days after the alleged al Dura killing, Abu Rahma swore that Israeli soldiers fired at the man and boy relentlessly for a total of 45 minutes during which he filmed, intermittently, for a total of 27 minutes. The 55-second "news report" broadcast by all the world's networks within hours of the alleged incident is excerpted from those 27 minutes of raw footage. Jamal al Dura, identified as Mohamed's father, corroborates—to this day—Abu Rahma's version of the ordeal.

Jamal, Talal, and Charles all insist that the Israeli position was squarely opposite the innocent civilians they heartlessly targeted. This curious "error" suggests that they behaved as if the simple truth of the layout of the junction would never be revealed. (A Palestinian position known as the pita stood directly opposite them. The Israeli position was at a 30° angle and a distance of 110 meters). Or did they believe that the simple truth, no matter how simple, how true, how convincingly revealed, would never operate?

The same would hold true for the outtakes. If the cameraman is to be believed, they are composed entirely of images of Jamal and Mohamed al Dura pinned down by Israeli gunfire. Enderlin has nurtured this belief for seven years. Hiding behind the misconstrued right of a journalist to protect his sources, he withheld the outtakes from public scrutiny with a self-confident smirk, showing them occasionally to select accomplices who dutifully declared that the raw footage contributes nothing to the al Dura controversy.

The raw footage should conform to the cameraman's description—27 minutes scooped out of a 45-minute incident. Screening might lead to more haggling about shooting angles, visible or invisible wounds and blood...another round of fencing between defenders and detractors would try the exhausted patience of "reasonable" commentators.

In fact, the raw footage has nothing to do with the al Dura scene. It is composed essentially of crudely staged Intifada games played by amateur Palestinian actors safely out of range of gunfire from the lone Israeli position. Similar scenes were filmed by a Reuters stringer that same day at Netzarim Junction; his footage, obtained by Israeli physicist Nahum Shahaf, can be viewed at seconddraft.org. Professor Richard Landes, director of that site, is one of the privileged few to have seen Abu Rahma's 27-minute outtakes. Enderlin unwittingly showed the video to the medieval historian, never imagining that he was dealing with a practiced eye. Later, under instructions from her superiors, Arlette Chabot showed the outtakes to three seasoned journalists—Denis Jeambar, Daniel Leconte, and Luc Rosenzweig. Jeambar and Leconte—unlike Rosenzweig who calls the al Dura report the biggest media hoax of our times—preferred to reserve judgment about the al Dura scene, but they did publicly declare that the footage was composed of at least 90% of obvious falsifications.

Where does that leave the al-Dura scene? Is it not, actually and exclusively, what it became: the poster boy of the "Al Aqsa Intifada"? A giant 3-dimensional postage stamp pasted on a poisoned letter to the world: Israel kills Palestinian children.

Whatever it is, it is not a news report. It is not 55 dramatic seconds excerpted from 27 rough minutes of a 45-minute horrifying ordeal. It is 55 seconds in and of itself. What does not happen then and there before the viewer's eyes did not, journalistically, happen. It does not corroborate Abu Rahma's statements, it contradicts them absolutely.

Charles Enderlin, writing on his France 2 blog, says he is delighted that the court has decided to look at the footage. It will finally bring an end to the "mudslinging," he says, conveniently forgetting that he has systematically and repeatedly refused to hand it over to the Israeli army. In reply to the September 10th request from Dover Tsahal deputy commander Col. Shlomi Am-Shalom, Enderlin said he doesn't have the footage, it is in the France 2 legal bureau. Shortly thereafter he made an open invitation to a Maariv journalist to view the outtakes in his Jerusalem office, while back in the Appellate Court Maître Amblard, of the said legal bureau, stammered that she didn't know where the tape was.

Enderlin, the wily Mideast "expert," failed to see the irony of blogging—under a France 2 logo—about a surprising development in the Appellate case that has gone unreported in French mainstream media. What's more, victory in last year's libel suits was supposed to put an end to the "mudslinging." What happened?

Attempts to expose the al Dura hoax began immediately after it was aired. Over the years, lawsuits, articles, books, videos, websites, documentary films, workshops, demonstrations, press conferences, lectures, and colloquia inched forward in a dark tunnel. But it was still too much for Charles Enderlin and France 2. They instigated libel suits in a French court, apparently serene in the conviction that no one would ask for evidence to prove—or disprove—the authenticity of the video.

September 2006: Philippe Karsenty presented voluminous evidence, articulate witnesses, and ample documentation; France 2 offered platitudes clinched by a non-committal letter from then president Jacques Chirac expressing vague appreciation for the general qualities of journalist Charles Enderlin, who never appeared in court. France 2 / Charles Enderlin—who had based the child-killer accusation against Israel on the testimony of one cameraman—were vindicated and Philippe Karsenty, who drew his conclusions from a large body of evidence collected by multiple investigators and analysts, was convicted of bad faith and insufficient diligence. French media that had chosen to ignore the controversy and the trials awoke and declared with fanfare: The Icon of the Intifada was not Staged! (complete coverage of the trials available at pajamasmedia.com)

That legal action now looks like a tactical error: Chirac is no longer president, anti-Zionism is not the cornerstone of his successor's foreign policy, and Philippe Karsenty is more diligent than Charles Enderlin /France 2 could have imagined. He appealed his conviction, came to the antiquated ill-equipped Appellate courtroom with his own large screen and a new lawyer who stopped the show with a demand for examination of the unedited raw footage. The Avocat Général (roughly the public advocate) dismissed the request on the grounds that the raw footage had not been at issue in the court of first resort. (The "procureur," his counterpart in that trial, made an eloquent plea for the right of citizens to question the media and seek verification in the case of dubious reporting. The judges ignored her recommendation for acquittal.)

September 2007: The Appellate Court judge, Laurent Trébucq, set the issue aside and began to hear the opening arguments. Maître Bénédicte Amblard, representing France 2 / Charles Enderlin, followed the same script she'd used in all three trials last year: Enderlin is a respectable respected journalist; a small clique of vindictive pseudo-analysts spawned by the disreputable "Franco-Israeli" Metula News Agency has been persecuting monsieur Enderlin; the court should confirm the conviction and put an end to this disgraceful spectacle.

Then Karsenty projects the infamous al Dura news report. We hear Enderlin intone in his 0.4-carat gold-plated voice: "3 PM... Netzarim...dramatic turn of events ...Jamal and his son Mohamed are targets of gunfire coming from the Israeli positions..." Karsenty interrupts the projection every few seconds to point out anomalies, inconsistencies, shooting angles... The judge balks. She wants to see for herself. Karsenty insists. The judge chides him. He persists. The judge complains one last time, then slowly lets Karsenty guide her through the tangle of details that confuse and enlighten whoever would listen and watch with a fresh eye.

The small audience was stunned and Maître Amblard was dumbfounded by the judge's decision to adjourn the hearing and request handover of the raw footage. In the courtroom on October 3rd for a reading of the court order, Maître Amblard had regained her composure, prettified her coiffure, and located the video. She replied in the affirmative when asked if her client will comply with the order before the 31st of October. Several influential foreign journalists are planning to attend the November 14th screening. Will the French media dare to take a peek at the handiwork of multi-prize-winning Talal Abu Rahma?

In another breakthrough, Nitsana Darshan-Leitner chairwoman of Shurat HaDin, who is preparing a lawsuit against France 2 /Charles Enderlin for their responsibility in inciting hatred with the falsified news report, asked the Government Press Office (nine months ago) to withdraw press credentials from France 2 and Jerusalem bureau chief Enderlin.

GPO Director Dany Seaman, who has consistently declared that the al Dura story is a fake concocted by Palestinian stringer Talal Abu Rahma, peddled by Enderlin, and maintained with the hechser of state-owned France 2 with the express intention of maligning the State of Israel and its army, didn't pull France 2 /Enderlin's credential (Mazouz advised against it) but he confirmed, in a September 23 letter to Shurat HaDin, that the al Dura "news report" is a fake. Seaman's "official" position was transferred to his statement, which became breaking news: it's official, the "death of Mohamed al Dura" is a fake. As usual, the PM's office lost no time in dissociating itself from Seaman's statement and most likely the Foreign Ministry was biting its nails over his undiplomatic rectitude.

This renewed interest for the al Dura affair has provoked defensive criticism from some quarters. Jamal al Dura, interviewed by Ali Waked, repeats his certainties— the Israelis are always trying to deny responsibility but the bullets are proof [what bullets?] they come from Israeli weapons, the Israelis fired from their position directly facing him and his son... Former IDF spokesman Nachman Shai, quoted in an article by Matthew Kalman (Oct 4 SFGate.com) said Enderlin showed him the tape: "From what I saw, we don't learn anything more. There is no new evidence there..." No new evidence? Isn't that the point? Anyone acquainted with the written documentation would know that the tape is conclusive evidence that the reporter, Abu Rahma, is lying. Do truthful journalists and lying journalists have equal value when it comes to reporting what happens? And what doesn't!

Kalman's thorough, informative article begins with this string of errors: "Mohammed al-Dura's gut-wrenching death is running again on television screens across the world, seven years after the 12-year-old boy died in his father's arms in a hail of bullets." The "gut-wrenching death," which is nowhere to be seen in the 55-second video, becomes a foregone conclusion in an article that purports to examine the controversy. "...running again on television screens across the world"? Dozens of articles, blogs, and private messages on the subject are currently circulating; no one has mentioned TV reruns of the controversial scene. Certainly not in France! "...the 12 year-old boy died in his father's arms in a hail of bullets." He is never once seen in his father's arms. The hail of bullets consists of a few shots hitting the wall, widely missing the man and the boy.

Kalman claims "Israeli officials ... have spent the subsequent years trying to prove that [the boy] died from Palestinian bullets." Not so.

Israel officials have been avoiding the issue to such an extent that their indifference was cited in the October 2006 judgment as a reason for discrediting Karsenty's denunciation of the "fake." While clearly trying to give expression to two sides of the issue, Kalman seems to be handicapped by the lack of accurate background information.

Gideon Levy couldn't care less about background information. He bares his chest and hammers away at the al Dura debunkers, shameful apologists for unfettered Israeli child-killing. His apoplectic diatribe rattles and sputters. Who cares if the al Dura report was staged or scooped? What does it matter, why worry about one fake when there are, dixit B'tselem, 850 real child murders to atone for!

The mile-long talkback demonstrates the method and effects of the al Dura scene. "Israel kills Palestinian children" is not the same as "Palestinian children are killed in the conflict with Israel." The al Dura death scene serves precisely to justify the accusation that Israel—or Zionists or Jews— kill Palestinian children. Levy argues that one al Dura balances out hundreds of real child-killings that do not "exist" because they were not filmed. In fact, al Dura was faked to make the phenomenon of deliberate Israeli child murder exist <u>before</u> those other children died. Levy and his supportive readers claim, falsely, that Israelis are trying to prove they didn't kill al Dura; they say Israel should stop harping on this one case and face up to its overall guilt.

Why don't they stop harping on it? Why can't they say OK, that one was faked, the others are true? They can't let go of al Dura because it gives them the right to say Israelis are heartless murderers of Palestinian children. Enderlin can't let go of the patently false story parroted by Talal & Jamal because the al Dura report falls flat without evil Israeli intentions. Talal and Jamal can't let go of their ridiculous assertions—the 45 minutes of head-on fire deliberately aimed at them— because it proves Israelis are heartless bloodthirsty savage child-killers.

Why else would they kill Palestinian children? That's not how you win a war. The children are, according to Levy and his allies, totally innocent. Uninvolved bystanders or, even worse, sought out and gunned down inside their homes. So Israelis kill Palestinian children for the cruel pleasure of it, the way they killed al Dura; even though the al Dura scene is false we have to defend it because it shows the true nature of Israelis.

Gideon Levy and Charles Enderlin, Israelis who accuse Israel of systematic child murder, need the al Dura blood libel to dress their inflated egos. Cheating along with the jihadis, covering up their lies, swallowing their crude falsifications, espousing their jagged reasoning... it's no big deal. Spokesman for the universal conscience of humanity is more flattering.

It looks like they hitched their star to a losing martyr.

— *Makor Rishon*

AL DURA RAW FOOTAGE: A MINUTE OF TRUTH
November 11, 2007

The hour of reckoning in the case of France 2 and Jerusalem bureau chief Charles Enderlin versus Phlippe Karsenty is fast approaching. On November 14th the raw footage of Palestinian cameraman Talal Abu Rahma's film of the al Dura incident will be screened at a special hearing of the Appellate Court. Mohamed al Dura is the 12 year-old Palestinian boy allegedly shot dead by Israeli soldiers at Netzarim Junction in the Gaza Strip on September 30, 2000. The cameraman and the boy's father are the sole living witnesses who attest to the veracity of the news report which was broadcast worldwide with a commentary by Enderlin.

In order to understand what the raw footage might reveal we have to look behind the visual evidence and retrieve official and unofficial testimony from the witnesses. The man and boy, they say, were pinned down by uninterrupted Israeli gunfire for 45 minutes; the boy (elsewhere described as killed instantly) bled to death as heavy gunfire continued for another 20 minutes; the ambulance driver sent to evacuate him was shot. The cameraman said he captured a total of 27 minutes of the dramatic incident, filming intermittently so as not to exhaust his battery (before the end of the incident?).

This should leave no doubt about the general nature of the footage that will be viewed in court. The images may not show the source of the gunfire aimed at the victims, they may not explain dozens of anomalies, but they will be focused on Jamal and Mohamed al Dura, caught off and on in the course of the terrible 45-minute incident.

In fact, there are no images of Jamal and Mohamed al Dura in the raw footage, except for a few seconds in which the boy changes position voluntarily after he was allegedly shot dead.

A handful of people have been allowed to see the raw footage over the past seven years. Richard Landes and Luc Rosenzweig say the raw footage confirms their conviction that the al Dura scene was staged. Journalists Denis Jeambar and Daniel Leconte, who viewed the footage at the same time as Rosenzweig, remarked that 90% of what they saw was faked but could not find proof that the al Dura scene was also staged. Still others assert that the raw footage "changes nothing."

But the raw footage contradicts Talal Abu Rahma's assertions. He said he witnessed and filmed the incident, intermittently, over a period of 45-minutes. And all that remains, concretely, is less than one minute? By what stretch of the imagination, by what frivolous notion of journalism could such a baseless report be accredited?

This is the simple irrefutable truth: There is no material evidence to substantiate the al Dura incident beyond the 55-second scene etched into the public mind. But no one—least of all those who dismiss debunkers of the al Dura myth—can describe the "tragic" circumstances of the man and boy "caught in the crossfire..." without referring to details drawn from a nonexistent source beyond those 55 seconds and outside the realm of verifiable reality.

To date, Charles Enderlin and France 2 have maintained the illusion that the 27-minutes of raw footage corroborate the al Dura story. Will they bring to the courtroom images that no one has ever seen, that would demolish everything claimed herein? They would like us to think so.

— *Commentary Contentions*

AL DURA RAW FOOTAGE: 27 MINUTES OF WHAT?

[At the request of one of those involved in the al Dura litigation I did research on the question of the duration of the raw footage. This issue is treated in many of my articles on the affair, but it is enlightening to look at some of the raw material. We see from these excerpts that the al Dura broadcast was never handled with even a minimum respect for the facts. The initial reference to 27 minutes of raw footage of the al Dura incident was reduced to 55 seconds without setting off any alarms. The 27 minutes that allegedly contained abundant evidence turns out to be 26 minutes of staged scenes, but that doesn't upset the France 2 /Enderlin applecart. The death throes ["agonie"] too horrible to broadcast turn out to be a questionable sequence in which the youth,

declared dead, is obviously alive, but that doesn't mean Enderlin, Abu Rahma, and Jamal al Dura are unreliable. Journalists know as well as I do that "agonie" means death throes, not an ordeal, not suffering, but they don't wince when Enderlin explains that the death throes ["agonie"] are the whole ordeal that lasted 45 minutes, was filmed for 27 minutes, but left only 55 seconds of footage. The excerpts that follow are a sort of cross-examination of the plaintiffs in the al Dura lawsuits... a cross examination that never happened in the French court.]

11/13/07 On the eve of the Appellate Court hearing scheduled for the precise purpose of screening the unedited raw footage surrounding the al Dura news report, we learn that France 2 is presenting 18 minutes of said footage. We expected 27 minutes. What does this mean?

Would they dare to withhold 9 minutes and claim that the proof of the veracity of the disputed news report lie in those precious minutes that will not be surrendered under any conditions short of war?

What does it matter—eighteen or twenty-seven minutes?

4/04/03 Amnon Lord, Makor Rishon,

[Yom Tov] Samia questioned the attitude of France 2 that, despite the importance of the incident, refuses to show all the footage of this shootout, centered on the child Mohammed Al-Dura.

According to the cameraman Talal Abut-Rahma, there remain 6 minutes of footage that do not directly follow the account of the shootout. Both Yom Tov Samia and Nahum Shahaf, who led the investigation, ensure that France 2 still has at least 27 minutes of raw footage of the incident. They think there is in fact much more, but France 2 refuses to release them.

"Charles Enderlin (France 2 journalist) lies on two accounts," Samia accuses. "First, when he says he is ready to release the raw footage on request; second, when he says he handed them over to whoever asked for them."

Luc Rosenzweig *(article commissioned & killed by Denis Jeambar, editor in chief of l'Express)*

It is strange that the cameraman missed the exact instant when the boy was hit. According to sworn testimony on October 3rd the firefight between armed Palestinians and Israeli soldiers lasted 45 minutes, of which he filmed approximately 27 minutes. What bad luck for a cameraman like Talal Abu Rahma, experienced in armed conflict, to take his finger off the button just when the figures his camera had been focused on for such a long time were shot—doctors said 6 to 9 bullets for the father and 3 for the child.

11/19/04 Nicolas Delesalle & Marc Belpois Télérama N° 2863

In November 2000, Enderlin insists heavily on the presence, in the outtakes, of very long sequences of the death throes [*agonie*] of the child caught in the shootout. According to his information there must be dozens of minutes of images of the al Duras under fire, as horrifying if not more so than what is seen in the 55 seconds of the reportage.

"'He [Talal] gave dozens of interviews, to many different medias, including Israeli channels, and the only one cited by the Mena, is the one given to an NGO not recognized by the UN, that has him making statements he didn't make,' grumbles Charles Enderlin. As for the death throes [*agonie*], in fact it does not appear in the France 2 raw footage, as might be understood from Enderlin's Télérama interview in 2000: 'I edited out the death throes [*agonie*] of the child, it was unbearable...' A misunderstanding, he says. 'The death throes [*agonie*], refers to the whole scene of the shootout. We didn't show it all. If we'd shown the whole scene it would have taken up too much space. I also had images of wounded Israeli soldiers and demonstrations in Hebron in the same sequence.'"

3/13/05 Daniel Scheiderman, The Big Blog
[*Scheiderman hosts Arrêt sur Images, a TV program that analyzes media twists. French to English summary.*]

As for Talal Abu Rameh's raw footage that supposedly demonstrates Enderlin's dishonesty... we've had it since the beginning.... Charles Enderlin gave it to us. We have viewed it over and over and all of us agree that nothing can be concluded about the death of the child. Did some Palestinian combatants overact for the camera? (We know that images are among the Palestinians' best weapons) Maybe, maybe not. But the raw footage proves nothing. You have to know how to drop an investigation when it is inconclusive.

It would have been better if Enderlin hadn't said that he edited out the "death throes" because there is no image of death throes in the raw footage; Abu Rahmeh explained that he had to stop shooting during 'dull moments' to spare his battery."

2/15/05 Cybercast News Service, Eva Cahen
"Jeambar and Leconte were allowed by the France 2 network to view an unedited master cassette of the incident...

"They also found that the first 20 minutes or so of the cassette showed scenes of young Palestinians 'playing at war' in front of the camera, falling as if wounded and then getting up and walking away.

"France 2 communications director Christine Delavennat told Cybercast News Service in an interview that none of the scenes on the cassette was staged and the cameraman and the station stood by that claim.

"Delavennat said the cameraman never retracted his claim [that the Israeli army killed the boy]. Rahma merely denied making a statement—falsely attributed to him by a human rights group—to the effect that the Israeli army fired at the boy in cold blood, Delavennat explained.

"As for the 'agony' that Enderlin said he edited out of the report, Leconte and Jeambar said it did not exist on the master cassette. Enderlin told Télérama magazine late last year that there had been a 'misunderstanding,' that he had meant to use the word 'agony' to describe the scene of the shooting of Mohammed al-Durra.

"However, in an online discussion forum for le Nouvel Observateur news magazine on Feb. 10, Enderlin was asked how he would describe the same video images today.

He replied that he would say the same things, but that in the editing process he would include footage of the 'child's agony,' raising a question once again about his previous claims. During the first edit, Enderlin said, the video in question was 'cut considerably at the time because it made the report too hard'."

N.B. I didn't limit my search to references to the total duration of the raw footage (27 minutes according to Talal immediately after the incident...he should be held to that) because I think it is equally important to point out that Charles Enderlin is constantly changing his description of what is in the outtakes. Given the intensity of the controversy that has lasted already several years one would expect that he would look at the raw footage and decide once and for all what it contains. Instead of which, he adapts his version to the question he's asked. One day the death throes [*agonie*] is the entire fire fight, one day it's really death throes. One day he edited it out, one day it isn't in the raw footage... he just meant by death throes the whole fire fight. Note also that Delevannat claims there are no staged scenes in the raw footage.

P.S.

Looking through my files, I came upon this item that I've never used in an article:

In August 2005, Shams Odeh, the Reuters stringer who was briefly crouched next to the al Duras and then ran off, was stabbed near Khan Yunis. He's the stringer whose outtakes are posted on second draft.

AL DURA FRANCE 2 COOKS THE RAW FOOTAGE
November 15, 2007

Palais de Justice, Paris, November 14th, France 2 and Charles Enderlin versus Philippe Karsenty—the appeal.

In response to an order issued by the Appellate Court for handover of the unedited raw footage shot by France 2 cameraman Talal Abu Rahma on the 30th of September and 1st of October 2000, the state-owned TV network produced an 18-minute CD, a certificate of conformity, and its Jerusalem Bureau Chief Charles Enderlin. This is the first time monsieur Enderlin has stood before the court since a series of lawsuits for defamation was initiated in September 2006. Enderlin said, in interviews and on his France 2 blog, that he was pleased to have the opportunity to display the raw footage and bring an end to years of unfair, unfounded accusations. French media have shunned the issue, but an array of international journalists and concerned citizens came to see the evidence and judge for themselves. The hearing was scheduled for 1:30 PM.

By noon, dozens of people—journalists and people connected to the al Dura affair—were gathered in the small waiting area outside the courtroom. An hour later, an impatient crowd of 50 or 60 people pressed the early birds against the closed courtroom door. Gendarmes and several individuals in civilian clothes tried to clear a path for lawyers and clients to enter through a side door. Shouting, begging, and threatening to cancel the hearing, they forced their way through the compact mass, carrying folding chairs. Judge Trébucq herself, not yet draped in her official robes, was lugging chairs like a humble servant of the law.

The crush endured. It seemed endless, it was unbearable and absolutely senseless. From time to time a gendarme emerged and scolded the unruly crowd whose voices disturbed the court where miscellaneous business was being handled. Philippe Karsenty's father who was standing next to me said "Enderlin is here." We thought he was joking. Luc Rosenzwieg, whose presence in the courtroom was essential, almost passed out. Daily Mail journalist Melanie Phillips (author of the famous Londonistan), who comes from the land of the disciplined queue, could not believe the Palais de Justice would show such disdain for citizens. Over-eager citizens who have been following the al Dura affair through the Net shoved their way in front of journalists assigned to cover the story and bring the news to millions. Richard Landes and Tom Gross, who need no introduction, did their best to shield us from the worst assaults. A tall slim pale young man with a keffieh around his neck waited, expressionless. Someone whispered: "He's from the Associated Press." Once more a path was cut through the raving crowd. Charles Enderlin arrived with a suite of lawyers and a gaggle of followers.

An enraged Serge Kovacs (France 3) full of sound and fury harangued the crowd from the rear, then got into a shouting match, in Hebrew, with Stéphane Juffa (Metula News Agency). According to our translators, Kovacs was doing a *j'accuse* on us. Enderlin is his Dreyfuss. We were the lynch mob. He was out of control. We sent a few gendarmes over to expel him.

2:15 PM-The court instructed the gendarmes to let us enter one by one, one journalist, one citizen. The ordeal was over for those of us who made it through the door. It was about to begin for Jamal and Mohamed al Dura, "target of gunfire from the Israeli positions," dixit Charles Enderlin on that fateful day.

Judge Trébucq introduces the session. "I know there are many journalists here," she says... and reminds us that it is strictly forbidden to use recording devices. Yes, but the reminder has a special flavor, something like a wink, here in France where the media are conspicuously ignoring the al Dura affair. Reading an excerpt from the cameraman's testimony under oath—"I filmed 27 minutes of the incident that lasted 45 minutes—" the judge asks why there are only 18 minutes on the CD. The seasoned France 2 journalist gives a garbled excuse, a long diversion about how they never conserve raw footage, but this subject was exceptional, so he kept the cassette in a safe. He tells how Talal Abu Rahma was allowed by the IDF to go to the Annual Congress of Press Mediators in April 2001 to receive an award. This was clearly his strategic option, and he used it throughout the screening. Verbose and evasive, he constantly diverted attention away from the image, away from the specific detail under scrutiny, away from events that occurred that day at Netzarim Junction.

So how did the 27 minutes boil down to 18? Enderlin denies that anyone ever said there were 27 minutes... and then says there was some irrelevant material that he chopped off the day after the incident.

The judge presses the point, asking Rosenzweig and Landes to estimate the duration of the footage they viewed. They both attest to more than 20 minutes... Rosenzweig remembers someone mentioning 27. Karsenty's lawyer concludes for the record: something is missing.

The raw footage was not so raw. And it was barely al Dura. If we take the cameraman's word for it, given under oath a few days after the incident, not something but everything is missing. This is supposed to be the raw footage of the al Dura death scene. What we get is raw footage of Palestinian youths throwing stones, firebombs, and burning tires at the Israeli outpost. And provoking no reaction, except for one teargas bomb. Real provocations alternate with those familiar fake battle scenes with instantaneous ambulance evacuations.

Judge Trébucq had asked Charles Enderlin to move back from center stage to a more modest position but he continued to assume the lead role, talking without interruption. Telling war stories. Making cultural interpretations. He sent his trusted cameraman to Netzarim Junction that day because seven Palestinians had been killed on the Temple Mount the day before. He expected protests.

As Charles Enderlin switched on his anchorman's voice and stonewalled, his legal team—Maître Amblard, who has been handling the cases for the past year, reinforced by a tall dashing Maître Pierre Olivier Sur and the scowling Guillaume Weill-Raynal— stood squarely in front of Landes and Rosenzweig, blocking their view of the screen.

Enderlin comments: This is what we call typical Intifada scenes. A game that's played between the Palestinian youths and the Israeli soldiers. The limits are clearly defined. That's why the kids aren't afraid, they move around casually, throw a firebomb, laugh and joke. The Israelis up to this point are firing metal bullets coated with rubber. They cause big bruises.

Ah, but we are seeing all these ambulances pulling up with hurling sirens. So Charles Enderlin explains that sometimes the bullets do penetrate, the wounds are more serious, and the Palestinians call an ambulance. Yes, the game can go on for hours, then somebody loses his nerve, shoots live ammunition, and people get killed.

Judge: What time of day is this?

Enderlin: The end of the morning. This kind of action was going on off and on all morning. I told Talal to wear a bullet proof vest, but he didn't want to... As it turns out...

The time line clicks on, the minutes go by, and Charles Enderlin, flanked by someone presented as a specialist (in images? photojournalism? the Mideast conflict?) never stops talking. Still no images of Mohamed al Dura and his father caught in the crossfire. The action is interspersed with brief interviews. Enderlin translates from the Arabic. They are protesting because Sharon went into the Al Aqsa Mosque...or defiled the mosque, or destroyed it... They are angry. This is the expression of their anger.

We hear gunfire in the background. Karsenty interrupts to say there is no sign of bullets coming from the clearly visible Israeli position. Enderlin laughs in his face. Hah! If I could get a film that shows bullets coming from a firing position, it would be a scoop.

Abu Rahma interviews a Fatah leader who speaks English. He too explains that they are angry because Sharon went into the Al Aqsa Mosque. Abu Rahma asks him how long he thinks the protest will last. Undaunted by this curious question, the Fatah militant replies that it will last until the lesson is learned (does he mean until the message is heard by the Israelis or learned by the Palestinians?) and concludes: "they want to defend al Aqsa with their blood."

The timeline reads 13 minutes 66 seconds. Enderlin explains: Talal switched off his camera and wraps it up. He had done his day's work. When he turns it on again, the real shooting has begun. Enderlin's voice is dramatic. He comments, as the camera searches. Real gunfire, Talal is trying to see where it is coming from, is it the Israeli position? No, is it the Palestinian... From the "twin towers?" The fortress?

Karsenty reminds him he said you can't see the bullets coming out. Enderlin says you can see the tip of the barrel of the gun at the window.

Suddenly everything is confused. The timeline skips from 14'20 to 17'00. We see the beginning of the al Dura news report as it was broadcast. The avocat général fiddles with the controls, the image winds back, forward. We're back at the interview. The commentary is confused. Is Charles Enderlin saying the fire was coming from the Palestinian positions?

Finally—it's not clear how—we get to the al Dura footage. And all we see is what you got in the original September 30, 2000 broadcast. It's spliced. But we recognize the details. Karsenty interrupts every few seconds to point out the anomalies. No blood. The boy is holding a red kerchief to make it look like blood. The soldiers were supposed to be firing at them for 45 minutes, the wall is intact, there are a few holes. Round holes, shot head on.

Charles Enderlin and Talal Abu Rahma have consistently claimed that the Israeli position was directly opposite the targeted man and boy. It is not true. Enderlin stands in front of the judge and says everything and the opposite about the positions. He does not reply to a single objection raised by Karsenty, raised by other analysts repeatedly over the past seven years: The father's arm is intact, he claims he was hit nine times by high power bullets, his muscles smashed, his bones crushed. No blood on his white t-shirt. Voices in Arabic shout "the boy is dead! the boy is dead!" He is sitting next to his father, eyes wide open.

Charles Enderlin standing in a French court explains: Oh, that's something cultural. In their culture, when they say "the boy is dead" they mean he is in danger of dying, that he is in a very dangerous situation, he might die. The judges smile.

We reach the end of the scene as it figured in news reports, the point where Charles Enderlin said, "Mohamed is dead, his father is critically wounded." We might ask what that means in his culture...because the scene continues for another three seconds in which we see the boy who is lying on his stomach with his hands over his eyes, turn, lift his elbow, shade his eyes, look at the camera, and slowly return to a prone position.

Philippe Karsenty interrupts every few seconds, leaps up, points to the screen, asks for a slow forward, backward, forward. The boy is moving. He is alive.

The expert steps in, points to the image, the position of the boy's foot, and declares: "A living person couldn't hold his body in that position."

Back in the autumn of 2000 when the al Dura news report first hit the screens, Talal Abu Rahma and Charles Enderlin often told how they exchanged cell phone calls during the terrible ordeal as it was happening. Talal phoned to say the man and the boy were pinned down by gunfire. Enderlin said be careful. Talal described how the man tried to protect the boy, called someone on his cell phone, tried to show the Israeli soldiers he was a helpless civilian, with a child. Abu Rahma filmed, phoned, filmed. He told Enderlin to look after his family if anything happened to him. He was ducking bullets, shielded by a panel truck, a few kids were gathered around him, seeking refuge. Bullets were flying. How many phone calls? Maybe a dozen, as they told it then. All the way up to the fatal outcome.

On November 14th, Charles Enderlin, standing before the judges, as the brief one-minute of raw footage focused on Mohamed al Dura and his father drew to an end, began that litany: and Talal was calling me as it was happening...

He would have gone on if someone hadn't interrupted him. Most likely Philippe Karsenty, making another point about the signs of life in the allegedly murdered child. Enderlin might have gone on and described the dramatic phone calls back and forth, without realizing that everyone in the courtroom saw that the raw footage focused on the al Dura incident lasted only one minute. Just one minute. How many times did the cameraman call the journalist as he filmed that dramatic one-minute incident?

And the totality of film recorded by the France 2 cameraman on that fateful day, over a period of at least 5 hours, was eighteen minutes?

The session ended. The debate continued in the marble halls of the Palais de Justice. Interviews were filmed. Information and impressions exchanged. The behind the scenes story will be reported in the coming days.

The next hearing is scheduled for February 27th 2008. My inside informer says the judges will thoroughly re-examine the entire case.

AL-DURA RAW FOOTAGE? IT DOESN'T EXIST.
November 21, 2007

On November 14, 2007, before a packed courtroom with an overflow of dozens left outside, a three-judge appellate court panel screened raw footage turned over by France 2/Charles Enderlin, plaintiffs in a defamation case against Philippe Karsenty, director of the French watchdog site Media-Ratings. Convicted in October 2006 for declaring the al-Dura news report a scandalous hoax, Karsenty is conducting a vigorous counterattack that has met with a heavy silence in France and that has repercussions in high profile international media.

Throughout seven years of controversy, France 2/Enderlin had consistently refused to show the raw footage shot by France 2 stringer Talal Abu Rahma at Netzarim Junction in the Gaza Strip on September 30, 2000, the day when twelve-year-old Muhammad al-Dura allegedly was shot in cold blood by Israeli soldiers.

The cameraman declared under oath three days after the incident that he had filmed, intermittently, 27 minutes of the ordeal, which lasted 45 minutes. Elsewhere, he claimed that he had filed a satellite feed of six minutes that day and subsequently turned over two full cassettes to his producers. Enderlin claimed he edited out the boy's *"agonie"* (death throes), too unbearable to show.

In place of the unedited raw footage filmed that day, France 2 submitted a "certified copy" that lasted eighteen minutes. Instead of 27 minutes focused on Jamal al-Dura and his son Muhammad, the document consisted of miscellaneous scenes, three brief interviews, and less than one minute of the al Dura incident. The accusation that the "victims" were the "target of gunfire from the Israeli positions" is baseless; it does not appear. There is no crossfire, no hail of bullets, no wounds, no blood. In the final seconds that had been edited out of the France 2 broadcast, the boy whose death had just been dramatically announced lifts his elbow, shades his eyes, glances at the camera, and resumes the appropriate prone position.

Reports of the boy's death resounded in September 2000 when the "al-Aqsa intifada" was revving up. The alleged child killing inflamed the "spontaneous" rage that led to an unprecedented wave of murderous Jew hatred. Today's resurrection of this supposed witness to Israeli incursion is not yet earth-shaking, but it has generated extensive coverage in reputable media. (My account of the screening, along with links to other sources, can be found [1] in the PJ Media archives.)

Neither the terse Agence France Presse release nor an authentic international buzz has been able to penetrate the French media firewall. Imagine the Dan Rather incident percolating everywhere but in the United States. Imagine Dan Rather seven years after the fake memo still enthroned as reliable reporter. Above and beyond any particular harm caused by the al-Dura news report as blood libel, broad issues of media ethics are engaged. And they concern all media in the free world.

The screening of the raw footage proved that the al-Dura news report was baseless. For seven years, Charles Enderlin has claimed that the raw footage would prove, on the contrary, that the report was accurate, authentic, verified, and verifiable. And yet he was able to stand before three judges and recite a monotonous tale of intifada as the images unfolded.

Is it possible that no one remembered what was supposed to be contained in that cassette? Eighteen minutes or 27, that's not the issue. This was supposed to be the raw footage of the al-Dura ordeal that, according to the cameraman and the boy's father—sole living witnesses—lasted 45 minutes. Talal Abu Rahma declared under oath three days after the incident that he had been at Netzarim Junction since seven in the morning, that the incident began around 3 P.M., and that, filming intermittently "to conserve his battery," he shot a total of 27 minutes of the terrible ordeal.

The France 2 stringer was filming all day long. The eighteen minutes screened in the Paris courtroom is not the raw footage of that day. And it is not, albeit truncated, the 27 minutes he himself unambiguously described. While the esteemed French journalist stationed in Jerusalem may have acted in haste when he edited and broadcast the footage for prime time news that evening and distributed the news report free of charge to worldwide media, when he received the cameraman's cassettes the next day, he had to notice the total absence of raw footage of the al-Dura scene.

In conclusion: nothing of what has been said about the incident can be seen in the 55-seconds of sole existing footage. No crossfire, no shots hitting the man or the boy, no duration of the ordeal. There is no footage to substantiate the report or the framing human interest narrative that accompanied it.

Can this be responsible journalism? Could it be so widely practiced that professionals, and particularly French media, do not consider it noteworthy? Is there no difference between a news report based on ample verifiable evidence and a news report based on an inconclusive snippet of what appears to be a clumsily staged one-minute scene? How is it possible to obtain total compliance with an unwritten law to the point that no one in French media will break ranks and give the facts about this controversial affair?

One week before the shaky Annapolis meeting, the al-Dura affair stands as a pinpoint of evidence in a vast enterprise of media sabotage. The fate of the free world hangs on our capacity to conserve a free press. Informed citizens must make life and death decisions about their own lives and the commitments of their nation.

How is it possible that a Palestinian faction (or individual or authority...we don't know who) could produce false news and inject it directly into international media without encountering the slightest resistance, while the exposé that shows that the news report does not respect any normal journalistic criteria knocks its head against a stone wall and cannot reach the general public?

This explains the somewhat disarming passion of the al-Dura debunkers, which often works to their (our) disadvantage. The issue is burning and the flames are still spreading. They could be extinguished by intelligent international scrutiny. Perhaps this requires a brilliant strategy that has not yet been devised.

— *Commentary /Contentions*

Chapter 5

THE VIDEO SHOOTING OF MOHAMED AL DURA: A LONG RANGE BALLISTIC MYTH

August 2008

September 30, 2000. Netzarim Junction in the Gaza Strip. Mohamed al Dura and his father Jamal, crouched in fear, are targets—in the words of France 2 correspondent Charles Enderlin—of gunfire coming from the Israeli positions. "Mohamed is dead," Enderlin announces solemnly at the conclusion of the 55-second video, "and his father is critically wounded." Talal Abu Rahma, the Palestinian stringer who filmed the scene, reaped countless international awards for his dramatic scoop. The world was mesmerized by this graphic icon of murderous Israeli cruelty. Palestinians honored the first *shahid* of the "Al Aqsa Intifada."

The al Dura "death" scene— a news report produced and broadcast by state-owned French television—has become the al Dura "affair," a crude fabrication, a media hoax ...and a powerful diehard myth.

Today, seven and a half years later, al Dura demystifiers— investigators, analysts, commentators, activists, lawyers & defendants, and a few rare government officials striving to bring the hoax to light—are still swimming against the current. The al Dura affair occasionally comes to the forefront—it pops up in the media, is dragged into the French courts, briefly attracts the attention of think tanks or appears on the stage of symposia—but the treatment is piecemeal, subject to the constraints of the medium or the occasion. The controversy is conspicuously ignored by French media—that should be the first concerned—and shunned by Israeli officials convinced that it will arise from the dead and smite them. Blissful ignorance of basic details of the al Dura story and its complex underpinnings is shamelessly displayed, especially by those who criticize demystifiers. And the al Dura blood libel endures, gushing Jew hatred from the immaculate living corpse of a twelve year-old Palestinian boy who posed briefly as the supreme victim of Jewish child killers.

Why is it so hard to prove the al Dura news report was staged? Why can't we present a clear concise al Dura primer that any intelligent fair-minded person could grasp, appropriate, and hold firmly in mind? Why are Israeli authorities convinced that denials of responsibility for the death of the Palestinian boy will ricochet? Why bother about the al Dura affair anyway? Isn't the damage done and irreparable, shouldn't it be left on the cutting floor of current events, one more murky affair deserving of a shrug and a pox on both your houses?

My answer is: because. Because the al Dura "murder" is a staged scene of tremendous impact that triggered a staged episode billed as the "al Aqsa Intifada" in a staged "Mideast conflict" that masks a very real global war of conquest. Why does the al Dura myth stubbornly endure? Because it cannot be countered by rational argument alone; it has to be recognized as a weapon within a broader aggressive strategy for which we have not devised a winning riposte. The al Dura hoax was an attack against the free world. Its effectiveness can be gauged by the utterly irrational dismissal of those who try to show that the "news report" was staged.

The "reasonable" stance is to accept the incident as real, the news report as authentic, the anomalies as understandable. In the same way it is reasonable to affirm that the Mideast conflict will be resolved by the creation of a Palestinian state living side by side in peace with Israel. And it is reasonable to heap scorn on President G.W. Bush for dragging his country into an unjustified war, botching it disgracefully, stubbornly refusing to admit his error and withdraw in defeat.

If everyone is so reasonable, why can't we debate these issues...reasonably?

The study elaborated herein should be read as a working hypothesis. Though my long experience as a novelist has led me to focus on the narrative aspect of the al Dura controversy, I draw on the contributions of analysts and investigators who have studied the affair from other angles. Israeli physicist Nahum Shahaf collected and analyzed a wealth of documentation—including raw footage filmed on the day of the alleged al Dura incident by Reuters stringer Shams Oudeh—that has served as a basis for all subsequent research. Stéphane Juffa and colleagues at Metula News Agency disseminated and pursued Shahaf's investigation. Amnon Lord wrote one of the earliest and most perceptive articles about the report as blood libel.[1] French psychoanalyst and author Gérard Huber published a precise, comprehensive presentation of existing evidence in an insightful book-length analysis of the affair.[2] Boston University professor Richard Landes, who originated the concept of Pallywood, brought the data into the blogosphere, posting raw footage, video analyses, and a running commentary on multiple ramifications of the affair.[3] Philippe Karsenty, director of the French media watch site Media-Ratings, sued for libel by France 2 / Charles Enderlin, has unearthed treasures of evidence and spurred Israeli officials to reconsider their inaction, as he courageously defends himself in the French courts. And we should not forget film maker Pierre Rehov who, with Alex and Toni Feigenbaum, Monique and Gérard Sander, tried in vain to sue Enderlin / France 2 in the French courts shortly after the false accusation against Israeli soldiers was broadcast.

MOHAMED AL DURA, A POSTER BOY IN REAL TIME:

When the al Dura story is dissected or defended as a news report, with the underlying assumption that the incident did in fact occur, it generates endless confusion. Charles Enderlin has mocked the very idea that the Palestinians could stage such a scene in the midst of a raging battle... conveniently eluding the possibility that the hail of bullets was no less fictional than the wounds they allegedly inflicted. Journalism, need we be reminded, is not "what might have happened somewhere somehow" but what can be reliably reported on the basis of substantial evidence. Journalistically, the al Dura shooting did not happen. The burden of proof lies not with me, the demystifier, but with the three people who brought it from the private to the public sphere: Talal Abu Rahma, Charles Enderlin, and the surviving "victim" Jamal al Dura. Their testimony on every significant detail of the incident can be shown to be false.

The al Dura story has no reality as a news report; when it is examined as a fiction, an ex nihilo creation, it suddenly comes clear.

Mohamed al Dura is often described as the poster boy of the "2nd Intifada." Indeed his image has been used to represent Palestinian children murdered by Israelis (= Jews). But Mohamed al Dura is a poster boy with no verifiable prior or subsequent existence in reality. The "death" scene filmed by a France 2 "news" photographer was staged as a poster, filmed as a poster, and is endlessly reproduced as a poster. Graphically the scene bears no resemblance to news footage filmed in environments of armed conflict. The al Dura video is utterly incongruous. It's a headshot, not an action shot. It is not news and it does not look like news. It looks like what it is: an advertisement for Jew hatred.

Strangely enough, this graphic anomaly has attracted scant attention. The al Dura video image belies everything that has been said to make the incident seem real: no duration, no hail of bullets, no direct hits, no wounds, no fatal shot, no blood... And yet media outlets systematically use the image to illustrate articles defending Palestinian stringer Talal Abu Rahma, who won countless prizes for the scoop, and France 2 Jerusalem bureau chief Charles Enderlin, who has staked his reputation on the al Dura report.

All we have to attest to the brief—under one minute—life and death of Mohamed al Dura is the poster boy image, Enderlin's voiceover commentary, and a narrative recited by the two eyewitnesses—Talal Abu Rahma and Jamal al Dura. The 59-second video is so static it might as well be a set of still photos. The narrative, uncritically repeated by all and sundry in the immediate aftermath of the purported incident, has been torn to shreds by successive retractions. Stashed out of sight of public scrutiny, it reappears furtively whenever a detail can be useful in maintaining the illusion of veracity. The al Dura story—image plus commentary plus narrative—is a sham, every inch of which has been at one time or another revealed to be false.

And yet those who expose the hoax are marginalized and those who ignore or defend it are comfortably seated in reputable media worldwide. Successive revelations that should suffice to make the al Dura news report a test case for journalistic falsification emerge, circulate in the information stream, and sink back into the ocean depths as if they had never existed. Why is this so? Because of antisemitism? Of course blood libel endures because of antisemitism, antisemitism creates blood libel, is fed by it, justifies it, makes it attractive and convincing. But the al Dura case is fascinating because it takes us beyond antisemites, anti-Zionists, self-hating Jews, mainstream journalists, mindless TV viewers, and any other significant category of individuals... The belief that it really happened is so entrenched it is almost impossible to dislodge. The normal rules of evidence do not apply.

AL DURA PRIMER

The al Dura "news report" is composed of a brief 55-second video, a voiceover commentary crafted and recited by France 2 Jerusalem Bureau chief Charles Enderlin, [4] and an elaborate narrative that gives strategic depth to the incident. (Additional raw footage of the al Dura incident filmed that day at Netzarim junction by Talal Abu Rahma theoretically exists but has not been released). The video without the voiceover commentary would be virtually meaningless. The news report initially required the extensive, enveloping narrative to give it a semblance of authenticity. But that story, which holds together from beginning to end as a plausible account of events as long as you follow it obediently without looking outside it for verification, falls apart on close examination.

Three days after filming the al Dura scene, Talal Abu Rahma took the unusual step—for a journalist—of making a declaration under oath to the Palestinian Center for Human Rights. Describing the incident in detail, he accused the Israeli soldiers of killing Mohamed al Dura and wounding his father deliberately, knowingly, in cold blood; he swore that the Israeli position was the only point from which the victims could be reached by gunfire; and he validated his claims by vaunting his credentials as an experienced war reporter.

Abu Rahma testified that the incident began with a five-minute crossfire provoked by Palestinian gunmen who fired at the Israeli outpost. The Palestinian guns fell silent but the Israeli soldiers fired relentlessly for 45 minutes, aiming directly at Jamal al Dura and his son, hitting the father at least 9 times. The soldiers did not stop shooting until they had "finally" killed the boy.

How did innocent civilians fall prey to the cruel Israeli soldiers? The narrative tells how Jamal, with his twelve year-old son Mohamed in tow, left el Bureij early that morning to see about buying a used car but couldn't make it to Jerusalem—or the car market, or the meeting place—because the main road was blocked by a demonstration or, in another version, because the market was closed. They were on their way home in a *cheroot*, the taxi stopped short of Netzarim Junction because of the heavy shooting, Jamal decided they would cross the junction on foot. Israeli soldiers sighted him and started firing. "They could see we were unarmed civilians." The man and boy took cover behind an upended concrete culvert. Jamal tried in vain to get the soldiers to stop firing.

Why was the France 2 cameraman at Netzarim Junction that day? In one version, Abu Rahma says he went to the junction at 7 that morning, expecting intifada activity because Palestinian protestors had been killed the day before at the al Aqsa mosque. In another version he says he rushed over to the junction at 3 PM when he got a call saying there were fierce gun battles. [5] Charles Enderlin says he assigned his cameraman to cover events at the junction that day. "I told him to wear a bullet proof vest, but he refused."

Abu Rahma, who had been filming since 7 AM or 3 PM, was about to pack up and go home when his attention was drawn to a man and boy huddled in fear against a wall, pinned down by gunfire. Taking partial cover behind a white panel truck (he too was in the line of fire) he filmed the 45-minute ordeal intermittently, turning his camera on and off "to conserve the battery," recording a total of 27 minutes of the 45-minute incident. He transmitted 6 minutes of footage to the France 2 studios in Jerusalem by satellite feed before leaving the junction. The shooting allegedly began at 3 PM. Mohamed, carried by a huge crowd of angry mourners brandishing portraits of the poster boy, was buried as a *shahid* before sundown that day.

The whole tragic incident was created by words—words declared under oath, dramatically related in documentaries, repeated to and by journalists at the time and ever since. The only concrete evidence that might validate those words is 55 seconds of uneventful footage. We have a paradoxical situation where unsubstantiated contradictory statements shoring up a furtive inconclusive image have created a pseudo-reality that seems immune to rational analysis. Knowing commentators disdain the staged-scene thesis without bothering to re-examine the statements that made them believe the incident actually occurred.

One example among many: an experienced journalist, after hearing my presentation of the al Dura affair, challenged me in a private conversation. "Are you claiming the boy is alive? Helen Schary Motro is a friend of mine... she knows Jamal..." [6]

I replied that I had read Motro's article and would like to contact the author. "Doesn't she realize Jamal is lying? He claims Israeli soldiers aimed at him and his son for 45 minutes before they managed to kill the boy."

"What 45 minutes? I never heard anything about 45 minutes."

Indeed, the claim that Israeli soldiers fired relentlessly at a sitting target for 45-minutes is extravagant. Dispassionate commentators prefer to replace those 45 minutes of "gunfire from the Israeli positions" with an eminently reasonable crossfire of undefined duration. They conveniently ignore details that are in fact unsubstantiated, contradicted by available evidence, and/or unbelievable. Proud-to-be-reasonable journalists swallow the story in one bite without tasting individual ingredients. Casually striking out the glaring inconsistencies of the al Dura news report as if they were innocently skipping over the rough spots, they effectively hide its intent and purpose.

The video and sustaining narrative were not composed in the interests of verisimilitude. Extravagant accusations—e.g. 45 minutes of Israeli gunfire— were purposely used to demonstrate murderous Israeli cruelty. The layout of Netzarim Junction was falsified, placing Israeli soldiers directly facing the innocent victims, when in fact their position stood at a 30° angle and a distance of 110 meters. The chronology was stretched and distorted, leaving long hours in which Jamal and Mohamed al Dura could have safely crossed the junction on foot like dozens of other civilians who milled around that day. They could have walked past the Israeli outpost and feared no evil. Their taxi could have crossed the junction in the steady stream of traffic seen in the Reuters raw footage...

One might think it was foolhardy to take such liberties with easily verifiable concrete details. But one would be wrong. From the outset and to this day, Enderlin and Abu Rahma continue to insist that the gunfire came from the Israeli position directly facing the victims; the only position facing them was a Palestinian position known as the Pita. Dozens of anomalies have been repeatedly exposed...without toppling the myth. Gérard Huber cites Abu Rahma in an interview with the Egyptian daily Al-Ahrar claiming "he filmed the soldier who killed al-Dorra leaving the area, adding that the little boy was a target of different weapons and a lot of bullets for 45 minutes." [7]

The narrative with its multiple variations was widely disseminated to add depth and credibility to the minimalist news report; when specific elements were challenged they were surreptitiously withdrawn. Two years after the incident, Abu Rahma wrote a self-serving fax to his France 2 hierarchy, claiming he had never told the Palestinian Center for Human Rights that the Israelis killed the boy deliberately, in cold blood. Enderlin later explained that Abu Rahma's testimony was obtained under duress and his accusation against the Israeli soldiers was falsified by the lawyer who took the deposition. Going a step further at the November 14, 2007 screening of a skimpy excerpt of Abu Rahma's footage, Enderlin declared that Abu Rahma, the experienced war photographer, was in a "state of shock" for three days after filming the al Dura incident.

Was Enderlin, too, in shock on October 25, 2000 when he claimed he had edited out the scene of the child's "*agonie*" [death throes], because it was "unbearable"? [8] The only footage that was cut is the last 3 seconds showing the boy, <u>after</u> he was allegedly killed, lift his elbow and look at the camera. When it became clear that no images of unbearable death throes existed, Enderlin explained that the "*agonie*" he referred to in 2000 was not the child's death throes but the entire ordeal. "We didn't show it all. Besides, if we had shown the whole scene, the report would have been top heavy.... We had other images...wounded Israeli soldiers, demonstrations in Hebron.'" 9] Sorry, monsieur Enderlin, the dictionary begs to disagree. "*Agonie* = moment in life immediately preceding death when the organism fights death."

Clarifications that are really obfuscations do not improve the story; they unravel it and undermine its purpose. If the 45 minutes are cut down to 3, on the pretext that Palestinians exaggerate, and the hail of bullets coming from the Israeli positions is toned down to a crossfire, it not only contradicts testimony from the only living witnesses, it also destroys the essential message: The al Aqsa Intifada poster boy must be killed intentionally by (Jewish) Israeli soldiers.

The narrative that "proves" Jews are child killers is largely forgotten; the video image that shows nothing of the sort is remembered and revised in the visual memory; the accusation is engraved indelibly, beyond the reach of rational re-examination; and the unsubstantiated assertions of the al Dura myth are deflected onto those who strive courageously to expose it, dismissed as "conspiracy theorists," rebuked as apologists for murder, stigmatized as obsessional or politely requested to make it simple. But they have made significant inroads, overcome tremendous obstacles, achieved modest victories, and never give up. The attempt of France 2 / Enderlin to silence critics once and for all by suing them in the French courts has backfired. Though virtually censored in French media the three libel cases heard last year generated international attention; the ongoing appeal in the Karsenty case is moving mountains. Convicted, in 2006, of defaming France 2 /Enderlin with ill-founded accusations of staging the al Dura scene, Karsenty defended his appeal with a mass of meticulously detailed concrete evidence, not the least of which was a 90-page report by a court accredited ballistics expert, Jean-Claude Schlinger, who concluded "No objective element allows us to conclude that the child was killed and his father wounded under the conditions presented in the France 2 news report. There is a serious possibility that the scene was staged." [10]

Unable to respond convincingly to a single element of Karsenty's investigation, the France 2 / Enderlin legal team retreated to the high ground, claiming that Karsenty and his ilk are out to destroy Enderlin because he reports without Manichaeism from the main lines of a complex hot-headed Mideast in which there are no bad guys and good guys. Insisting equally on the integrity of Talal Abu Rahma, who is above suspicion, counsel unwittingly defined Enderlin's role as interface between Palestinian sources and Western media. That is the question!

Whether the court judges the case on its merits and overturns the libel conviction on May 21st or takes refuge in narrow legalisms and confirms it, the al Dura affair must one day be examined in the halls of journalism and exposed to civil society on a vast international scale.

A TEST CASE FOR JOURNALISM

The unverified, unconfirmed, unsubstantiated, al Dura news report fails to satisfy the minimal standards of media ethics in democratic societies. Every reputable outlet that relayed the report should retract it because it is based on affirmations by two direct witnesses—Talal and Jamal— and one indirect witness—Enderlin—who are demonstrably unreliable.

Honest journalists check facts, verify their sources...and sometimes make honest mistakes that are corrected by internal procedures and/or exposed by competing media. Press freedom includes the citizen's right to question dubious news reports. The French court that ruled against Philippe Karsenty in 2006 placed the burden of proof on the defendant, faulted for not conducting a thorough investigation before accusing Charles Enderlin / France 2 of producing and broadcasting a hoax.

A layman exercising his democratic right to question the media was expected to convince judges who did not even ask to see the raw footage that the al Dura report was falsified and, moreover, a momentous calumny against Israel, while the professional journalist who produced the report based on flimsy evidence from two unreliable sources repeatedly advances his credentials as proof... Proof of what? That he cannot be wrong?

The courtroom is not broad or deep enough to examine the essential problem: an "incident" constructed as a myth was presented as a news story. Even when it is dismantled as a news story, the myth resists. Charles Enderlin, the self-anointed infallible journalist, treats his own report as a myth. Explaining his decision to broadcast the harsh images of the child's death, he declared "Many children die in this conflict...According to UNICEF, 176 children were killed between September 28 and October 6."[15]

In 2004, when three seasoned journalists—Denis Jeambar, Daniel Leconte, and Luc Rosenzweig—invited to view al Dura footage on the France 2 premises, questioned the veracity of the report, Enderlin justified it as "an accurate representation of the situation." Leconte and Jeambar retorted that journalism reports what actually happened, not what represents the situation...and then dropped the hot potato. Luc

Rosenzweig declared repeatedly in no uncertain terms that Charles Enderlin is a liar.

Trapped into treating the report as news because it was (mis)represented as news, demystifiers are emphatically summoned to respond to the ultimate question —is the boy alive? If he was not killed, where is he? In fact, the question is irrelevant. The boy's existence, his identity, his whereabouts before and after the film are outside the realm of journalistically verifiable information. The al Dura scene does not exist in the three-dimensional world of space-time. Graphically it is a poster. Audiovisually it is 6 wafer thin slices of video footage for a total of 55 seconds.

While some commentators prefer to let the Palestinian boy die in a crossfire, others choose to acknowledge that the al Dura news report is— or may well be—staged...and justifiably so. Gideon Levy, in a recent Haaretz article, stomps and pummels al Dura demystifiers with arguments that follow Enderlin's a posteriori reasoning. What does it matter if the al Dura scene was staged? It stands for 850 real child murders— dixit B'tselem— that do not "exist" because they were not filmed! Levy, with strong backing from his talkback choir, claims—falsely—that Israelis keep trying to prove they didn't kill al Dura instead of doing the honorable thing: confess and atone. He deliberately fails to mention that Israeli authorities began by accepting responsibility for Mohamed al Dura's death and have done precious little in the interim to establish the truth. France 2 /Charles Enderlin consistently pinpoint the absence of Israeli objections as proof of the authenticity of the al Dura report. And so far, the French courts have agreed.

How did the authors of the al Dura death scene know that hundreds of Palestinian children would subsequently die off camera? Why don't Enderlin / France 2 confess, do the honorable thing? Why don't they admit the al Dura scene was faked?

Because the al Dura death scene turns a fact—Palestinian children are sometimes killed in the conflict with Israel—into a terrible accusation— Israel kills Palestinian children. The far-fetched story parroted by Talal & Jamal with Enderlin's stamp of approval shows Israelis as heartless bloodthirsty savage child-killers who aim at innocent bystanders, harmless stone-throwers, diligent pupils doing their homework, angelic toddlers asleep in their beds. Israelis kill Palestinian children for the cruel pleasure of it, the way they killed al Dura. And that's why the fake scene is truer than truth in the eyes of these custodians of conscience.

WHERE IS THE RAW FOOTAGE?

For seven and a half years Charles Enderlin has been playing on the confusion between unedited raw footage filmed that day, raw footage of the al Dura incident, and a 27-minute stretch of half-cooked footage.

Abu Rahma told ARD producer Esther Schapira that he shot a total of two full professional video tapes (one to 1 ½ hours) at Netzarim Junction on the 30th of September.[12] He testified under oath, and repeatedly thereafter, that he filmed, intermittently, a total of <u>27 minutes of the 45-minute al Dura ordeal</u>. On occasions when Enderlin /France 2 showed the "raw footage" to the privileged few they presented a grab bag of staged scenes and miscellaneous "Intifada" activity, concluding with 6 thin slices—55 seconds— of al Dura images. Ordered by the appellate court to turn over "the unedited raw footage shot by Talal Abu Rahma on September 30, 2000," Enderlin presented a certified copy of …18 minutes. Speaking at the Center for European Studies in Boston on January 17, 2008 he reaffirmed the authenticity of the al Dura news report as attested by the 18 minutes of "unedited" raw footage presented to the court… How does Enderlin get away with this sleight of hand? Is it possible that no one, including the French appellate court judges, can remember that the cameraman declared under oath, and repeatedly thereafter, that he filmed 27 minutes <u>of the al Dura ordeal</u>?

In fact there is no al Dura raw footage. All you see is all there is: less than a minute. Everything that has been recounted about the incident—the narrative, the voiceover commentary, the testimony of witnesses—should logically disappear when we discover that for all intents and purposes the incident was not filmed. There should be no need to quibble over details now that Enderlin/France 2 have failed the final exam.

AL DURA—A STAGED SCENE IN A STAGED CONFLICT THAT MASKS A REAL WAR OF CONQUEST

This brings us to the essential question of journalistic ethics and Western strategy in a context of ill-defined atypical warfare. A phony accusation—Israeli soldiers are guilty of murdering Palestinian children—has obscured a crucial debate: why do Western media add precious credibility to Palestinian (or Arab-Muslim) myths when those stories, which I call lethal narratives, are used as weapons in a war of conquest? As we see in the case of al Dura, no matter how false the news report, the myth takes root. Operating by the tried and true method of blood libel, the al Dura myth fuels savage attacks against Jews, acts as a template for continuous accusations against Jews, creates a mindset that swallows constant lies about Jews while condoning vicious persecution of Jews, manufactures limitless weaponry in an ongoing war against the Jews and, by extension, the West. Al Dura is a staged scene in a staged Intifada in a staged Mideast conflict that masks a real war of conquest.

LETHAL NARRATIVES

Lethal narratives are not propaganda as we know it. War propaganda serves to confuse and weaken the enemy while pursuing military operations to attain military victories. Lethal narratives are in and of themselves weapons employed to defeat the enemy, conquer territory, seize power without engaging in soldierly action and all it implies in the way of training, heavy arms, logistics, financing, organization, and courage. The main thrust in what is elsewhere described as asymmetrical warfare is narrative; physical violence for all its horror is, at least at this stage, secondary though long term plans include the use of weapons of mass destruction. This war, mistakenly described as résistance or guerilla warfare, bears no resemblance to acts of courage or desperation by oppressed peoples fighting for self-determination. This is a war of conquest waged by a force determined to exercise total domination over the enemy.

The notion that the "suicide bomber" is the "poor man's weapon," paired with the al Dura myth of the Israeli child-killer, is a mass destruction lethal narrative. It places on the same ethical plane a mass murderer who deliberately attacks civilians in their daily lives and a disciplined soldier subject to civilian authorities, respectful of the rules of war. The "suicide bomber" whose aim is to kill civilians is excused "because he doesn't have F-16s," while Israeli soldiers fighting against deadly combatants are held to impossible standards of accuracy: they must never cause civilian deaths or even civilian discomfort, no matter the situation, the danger to themselves or to the citizens they are pledged to defend. American troops in Iraq are judged with the same severity while "insurgents" benefit from the indulgence granted to martyrdom operations in Israel.

The lethal narrative strategy is so effective that our populations do not realize the absurdity of their conviction that despite our military superiority we cannot defeat "terrorism." They do not recognize the massive verbal attacks constantly fired at them, outweighing isolated acts of physical violence that achieve no military victories but sap their will to fight back. On any day of the week one could locate thousands of these verbal arms caches and, if only our capacity to reason were reawakened, destroy them.

As this text is being elaborated, another staged scene—the Gaza blackout—erupts in the news. The mechanism was obvious to anyone who has studied the al Dura affair...but this time the hoax was revealed within days. Jerusalem Post correspondent Khaled Abu Toameh described Hamas officials meeting by candle light... in broad daylight. Websites posted pictures of strong Middle Eastern sun seeping through dark curtains at blacked out official Hamas sessions. Mainstream media jumped on the blackout story with delight. Finally they had dramatic images of Palestinian suffering. For months Hamas operatives had been persecuting, torturing, mutilating, oppressing, murdering Palestinians in Gaza. People were thrown from the tops of tall buildings...but public opinion does not know there are tall buildings in Gaza, and is not interested in Hamas-inflicted suffering on its own people.

The staged blackout was followed by a staged spontaneous breakthrough at the Egyptian border. The wall (who knew there was a wall on the Egyptian border?), which had been gradually pierced over the preceding months, was blasted and collapsed. Residents of Gaza flowed into Egypt and flooded back with all manner of consumer goods. Media attention was directed to the common man's plight.

A reporter on French radio described Gazans coming back from Egypt with basic necessities, such as cases of soda pop. Man-at-the-wall interviews elicited tales of confinement and deprivation. Noah's Ark images of goats, horses, cows, and camels hoisted over the collapsed wall reinforced the tale of simple folk deprived of the basic means of peasant life.

You had to go to specialized websites to find proud owners of flashy new motorcycles, stories of conflict between Palestinians and Egyptians, and cash flow statistics. Over two and a half million dollars were spent by poverty-stricken Palestinians...later corrected to account for a million in counterfeit currency. Profligate spending and a lethal traffic of combatants, weapons, and money were obscured by human interest stories.

In France, the entire operation was reported with a straight face. No revelations about darkness at noon came to dim the effect of the candlelight ceremonies, no millions of spending cited to contradict the crying poverty of Gaza. Who covered the Gaza blackout hoax for France 2? Talal Abu Rahma and Charles Enderlin! Using the tried and true al Dura method, Enderlin voiceovered Talal's footage as if he were standing just behind the camera. The story dropped out of the news when Egyptian authorities, wary of their own worst enemies who had snuck in to plague them, closed the border.

Lethal narratives operate with a high voltage emotional sting that disables rational thinking. By focusing on the suffering of everyman it mobilizes identifying mechanisms in each man: it could be me, deprived of food, electricity, freedom to come and go. The sting jolts the action out of chronology where one might ask how the victim came to be in that dire situation, to what extent he is responsible for his own distress, what might be wrong or even immoral in the strategies he devises to break out of his miserable condition. The staged scene is pure emotion, timeless and untouched by cause and effect. Only one reaction is possible: stop the ordeal. No matter how, no matter what.

A free press in free societies should present concrete facts, aim for maximum accuracy, follow important stories as they develop, add new information as it is revealed, and give citizens the raw material with which to form opinions. Honest competent journalists would detect the Gaza blackout falsification and, like Khaled Abou Toameh, tell the truth.

In a climate of healthy competition—necessary for a free press—journalists compete to get the story first and get it straight. Today, especially in France but to a lesser degree in all western nations, they are more likely to follow the leader. For each major issue, a "reasonable" analysis is accepted; every interpretation that does not respect those guidelines is dismissed as "extremist." Complacent media do not question the source of sources, and are singularly lacking in curiosity about how it was imposed. Journalists have reframed their vocation: instead of giving the facts so that citizens can draw conclusions, they use their persuasive powers to shape opinion. Puffed up with self-importance, journalists presume to solve the great issues of our day...and their favorite issue is the Mideast conflict.

This power is somewhat curtailed by alternative Net sources of information and analysis. Incidents staged after the al Dura story—the Jenin and Gaza Beach "massacres," Lebanese fauxtography, and the recent Gaza blackout—were more quickly debunked. Denounced as propaganda, bias, disinformation, these news reports proliferate, nevertheless, like drug-resistant bacteria. Could we combat them more effectively if we recognized how they function in a staged "Mideast Conflict": a genocidal war disguised as a struggle for legitimate national aspirations?

Instead of covering the conflict, the media relay lethal narratives. Beyond bias, this is a betrayal of the very definition of journalism—the treatment of events as they unfold day by day. Using the tools and constructs of scholarship, with a lesser degree of training and discipline, journalism describes in its haphazard way the ups and downs, causes and effects, actions & reactions, and underlying elements of things as they occur. Historians will treat the same material later with hindsight and sharper tools. History tells what was, journalism relates it as it is happening, and lethal narratives dictate a fabricated version of both individual events and the overall conflict.

That fabricated version, like the poster image of al Dura, is static. It is a wholesale condemnation of Israel and by extension of the Jews. In the case of Iraq, substitute Americans for Jews, the mechanism is the same. Can the *New York Times* run a full page kill-the-Jews advertisement every day, every year, until the injunction is fulfilled? No. That would be disgraceful. The *New York Times* can and does contribute massively to the pursuit of the kill the Jews (and Americans) project by lending the credibility of its prestigious masthead and type face to the lethal narratives that destabilize and demobilize our populations. And of course the NY Times is but one example among many, worldwide, including in Israel.

These methods are a smashing success. Overwhelming evidence is brushed aside, bogus explanations are passionately embraced, debate is impossible. Attacked at home and abroad, threatened with extermination, despised, mocked, trampled, forced to impose onerous strategies of homeland security on ourselves —all of this raised to the hundredth power where Israel is concerned—we are told by the purveyors of lethal narratives that we are not at war. If we are not at war, we have no right to defend ourselves. And if we are at war, it is our own fault.

Beyond buildings and civilians, the lethal narrative attacks rationality, the very foundation of Western civilization. This enormous offensive should provoke a resounding call to arms. But it is so insidious, that our very surrender becomes invisible. Citizens cannot reason about the force that is determined to destroy us. They cannot examine events in terms of cause and effect. They do not even recognize chronology. They are prisoners of the lethal narrative.

Our freedom depends on our capacity to observe events as they unfold, and to develop strategies to influence their course. Two recent episodes—the 2000 Palestinian war and the 2006 Hizbullah war—illustrate the use of lethal narrative to mask a static vision of events. The failure of the July 2000 Camp David talks was the endpoint of the Oslo peace process; if the reasoning that informed that process was valid the sincere hopes raised in 1993 would have been fulfilled at Camp David. Arafat's refusal of a reasonable offer that followed logically from all that had gone before was in effect a refusal of the process itself. In a rare moment of truth, editorialists, negotiators, and public opinion placed the onus on Arafat: He was not a statesman, he had failed his people.

Rumors of a military buildup were circulating—in closed circles – during the summer. To escape from the disgrace of a negotiated peace and save his honor as a Palestinian leader Arafat, it seemed, was preparing to seize independence by heroic military action. The rest of the world went about its business, unaware of these rumblings, unconcerned when an Israeli soldier was murdered by his Palestinian joint patrol partner, never suspecting that the Camp David fiasco was the prelude to an all-out attack on Israel. The war was staged as the "Al Aqsa Intifada." Ariel Sharon's visit to the Temple Mount on September 28th 2000 was the pretext for a chain reaction of "Intifada-type" activity, provoked and manipulated to produce Palestinian civilian casualties. On the 29th, Muslims on the Temple Mount lobbed previously stockpiled rocks at worshippers praying at the Kotel. Israeli forces intervened. Seven Palestinians were killed and many more injured. Palestinians were enflamed with rumors that the mosque had been defiled. The Al Dura blood libel, produced on the 30th at Netzarim junction, triggered a savage war of atrocities against Israeli civilians and a parallel worldwide outbreak of violence against Jews...in which the Palestinians would be portrayed as innocent victims.

The switch was total and instantaneous. Arafat's war became the noble struggle of the weak against the powerful. Israel was the aggressor. While Israeli civilians were blown to bits, Europeans marched by the tens of thousands to support the Palestinians. No superlative is strong enough to describe the obscenity of public opinion in those years, with everlasting effects to this day, and no way of being sure it will not flare up once more to fever pitch. Western populations drooled over Jewish blood and body parts while thinking of themselves as the ultimate in humanitarians. They did not dream they would soon be "enjoying" the same experience at home—New York, Madrid, London...the list is too long. They were cheering the monsters that would soon come to devour them. They were softening themselves for the kill.

And it was done with the emotional sting. The fake murder of Mohamed al Dura, less than one minute of crude footage, destroyed rational thinking about the failure of Camp David and the war that would be unleashed against Israeli civilians. TV viewers, unaware that Palestinian stringers were filming fake battle scenes at Netzarim Junction that day, were convinced the al Dura scene was shot in a war zone. The illusion is upheld to this day by commentators who defend the news report, even after viewing (e.g. Reuters raw footage) blatantly fake battle scenes filmed out of reach of Israeli gunfire while civilian traffic comes and goes unafraid and unharmed. Those who would temper the accusation of deliberate Israeli gunfire aimed at the innocent explain with a shrug that war is hell, these things happen, children get caught in the crossfire, civilians get crushed in the confusion. If only Israel would make the proper concessions, whatever they might be, the same ones offered at Camp David plus more and better, this hell of a war would finally be over. James Fallows concluded: "There would never have been a showdown at the Netzarim crossroads, or any images of Mohammed al-Dura to be parsed in different ways, if there were no settlement nearby for IDF soldiers to protect."[13]

The staged al Dura scene was a massive attack against Israel and the Jews. A single lie, the murder of Mohamed al Dura, was powerful enough to wipe out the truth of all that would follow. Shahid operations, glorified under the misnomer "suicide bombings" and further travestied in France as "kamikaze attacks," were perpetrated in full view without arousing normal reactions in public opinion. Day in and day out the perverted logic instilled by the al Dura hoax was reinforced. Palestinian children were thrown into battle and their deaths were exposed as evidence of Israeli cruelty and justification for Palestinian atrocities. The lopsided body count—more Palestinians than Israelis were killed—was held up as proof that Israel was conducting an unjust war. Enderlin uses this as a leitmotif in *The Lost Years*.[14][1] "In April 2004, three Israelis and fifty-three Palestinians were killed." (p. 238) "During the month of June 2004, five Israelis and forty Palestinians were killed." (p. 241) "In July 2004, three Israelis and 57 Palestinians were killed." (p. 243) "In August 2004, seventeen Israelis and thirty-nine Palestinians were killed." (p.244) "In Gaza, the Israeli operation continued, killing eighty-four Palestinians, including at least twenty under the age of sixteen." (p. 246) And so on until "In December 2004, nine Israelis and sixty Palestinians were killed as a result of skirmishes, targeted killings, and IDF incursions." (p. 252)

No matter how often I write about the al Dura affair, I still cannot believe how easy it was to convince the world that Israelis deserved to be hunted down in every corner of normal life and blasted to smithereens. Every time I think of those years, those months and days and hours, the taste of blood and tears wells up in my throat and my heart caves in. I wrote about it as it was happening, years ago, but I can't ever put those memories into the past. Their weight is and will always be unbearable.

The al Dura hoax, too, cannot be relegated to the past. It is not, as some would hope, "over and done with." And it is not an incident. It is an ongoing strategy that we will not defeat unless we identify it correctly: a staged scene in a staged conflict that masks a real war of conquest.

THE JULY-AUGUST 2006 HIZBULLAH WAR

From 1948 to 1973, Arab armies periodically joined together in conventional military operations with the openly declared intention of destroying the state of Israel. Repeatedly defeated on the battlefield, those forces reorganized and developed new worldwide strategies in the pursuit of the same goal. The September 2000 al Dura hoax initiated a highly effective phase of that ongoing war. Though the "al Aqsa Intifada" petered out with no clear-cut Palestinian victory it has inflicted untold damage on Israel's standing among the nations, and has indelibly inscribed Jew hatred in contemporary world culture on a sliding scale: Arab-Muslim genocidal Jew hatred is justified by Palestinian grievances, violent attacks against Jews in European countries are excused as understandable identification with those grievances though the predominantly Muslim source of attacks is obscured. Public opinion has been remarkably resistant in the United States, where sympathy for Israel is as high as 70%, but snide pseudo-scientific antisemitism flourishes (e.g. Walt & Mearsheimer), and rabid anti-Zionism is entrenched in Academia and on the far Left.

The kibitzer's mantra during the Al Aqsa Intifada War was "there is no military solution to suicide bombings," meaning "they'll never stop unless you give them what they want." In fact, Israel developed intelligent measures that drastically reduced inhuman-bomb attacks. Damage in lives lost or forever maimed can never be recuperated. Damage to the public mind, maimed by the lethal narrative, has not even been addressed. But Israel showed incredible resilience, the economy rebounded, normal life resumed.

And a new phase of the war was initiated in the summer of 2006 with the Gaza Beach Massacre hoax. This time the emotional sting was inflicted with the grief of a Palestinian girl, Huda Ghalia. The story broke with the usual fracas— a Palestinian family picnicking on a Gaza beach is decimated by a missile fired from an Israeli gunboat. The truth was drowned in the girl's hysterical run across the beach, her tears, her screams. An archive shot of an Israeli gunboat snorting fire and destruction was inserted to substantiate the claim of a deliberate direct hit aimed at pristine innocence, in the same way that Palestinian media inserted an Israeli soldier firing point blank at al Dura. The story broke on Friday the 9th of June. Reliable information from IDF sources started circulating on the Net by Saturday evening, but Israeli guilt was already established in the public mind. Meticulously calibrated IDF data and videos were brushed aside as lame excuses. The media preferred the certainties of Marc Garlasco, a bogus "Pentagon specialist" working for Human Rights Watch, who claimed the size and shape of the crater indicated it could only have been made by an Israeli shell (cf: the Israeli position is the only place from which the victims could have been hit). I myself tried in vain that weekend to pitch a debunking scoop to several outlets with which I work regularly. [15]

The Gaza Beach affair was compared with the al Dura incident in numerous articles published that week in the *Jerusalem Post*. Herb

Keinon clarified Prime Minister Olmert's statement "...past experience had shown that myths could be created that were divorced from the facts," as a reference to "Muhammad al-Dura... killed during an exchange of fire between the IDF and Palestinians..."[16] Anshel Pfeffer compared the IDF's delayed response—24-hours— that allowed the Palestinians to win their propaganda victory to past ineptitude. "It took months before the army put out an official version of the death of 12 year-old Palestinian Muhammad al-Dura, one proving he had been killed by Palestinian gunfire. By then he had become an international icon of Israel's cruelty towards children."[17] Why not go right to the bull's eye and identify the Gaza Beach hoax and the al Dura news report as staged scenes?

Accurate information about the Gaza Beach incident slowly emerged but major news sources never corrected the story; they just let it sink into the background leaving the indelible impression of another all-purpose Israeli massacre. Richard Landes, who was able to obtain the raw footage, has posted a video analysis of the ill-concealed staging on his Augean Stables website. As for the telltale crater, it doesn't exist.

Huda Ghalia did not become a poster girl, but the Gaza Beach hoax was a sneak attack that opened a new phase of violence in the ongoing war. It was followed (June 25) by a cross-border attack from Gaza in which an IDF officer and a soldier were killed, four were wounded, Corporal Gilad Shalit was abducted. On a July 12th cross-border attack from Lebanon, Ehud Goldwasser and Eldad Regev were kidnapped, five soldiers were killed in a rescue attempt, and rockets were fired into Israel all along the northern border. The abducted men are not prisoners of war but hostages, held to this day in inhumane conditions. The terms of an eventual release are impossible.

Widespread sympathy for Israel prevailed in the first days of the Hizbullah war; it was quickly dilapidated by the lethal narrative strategy. Israel's military campaign was undermined by a diplomatic initiative spearheaded by the Chirac government that surreptitiously imposed Hizbullah's conditions as the basis for a negotiated ceasefire under the aegis of the United Nations. Israel's response to a large scale unprovoked Hizbullah attack was branded "disproportionate" and the war was repackaged as a Lebanese humanitarian crisis. French media shamelessly churned out images of (Lebanese) civilian distress, feeding Chirac's incessant demands for an immediate "humanitarian ceasefire." Foreign Affairs Minister Philippe Douste-Blazy, with the willing collaboration of a slightly dazed Condoleeza Rice, engineered the disastrous UN Resolution 1701 that has left Lebanon in a dangerous impasse. [18]

Whatever the errors committed by Israel's military and civilian leadership during the month-long Hizbullah war, the conflict unfolded in the public mind as a psychodrama, a static demonstration of "Israel's disproportionate response," which was played out with the illusion of action and reaction, cause and effect, turning points, beginning middle and end. A mixture of real and staged incidents was relayed by Western media with equal credibility. Public opinion was mobilized, forged, manipulated, and re-injected to exert pressure on Israel.

As the story goes, Israel's justified retaliation against an act of war committed by Hizbullah was heartily approved by the U.S. and loyal allies, who expected the usual stunning one-week victory. Exasperated by Israel's miscalculations, botched operations, indecision, and clumsiness, Israel's friends finally invited the U.N. to step in and clean up the mess. If only Israel had done a proper job...

The lethal narrative of the Hizbullah war is: Israel inflicts untold suffering on Muslim populations, and must be punished. It is assumed that Muslims have the right to attack but Israel does not have the right to retaliate; Israel's enemies may attack civilians without causing a humanitarian crisis; when Israel's enemies are defeated, the international community must arbitrarily award them the victory they desired and deserved. The "victory" rightfully celebrated by Hizbullah in the pulverized ruins of its southern Beirut stronghold, with the triumphant Nasrallah in hiding, was the successful reiteration of the story: Israel inflicts suffering on Muslims. The UN resolution was Israel's punishment and Hizbullah's reward.

The war was a static defense and illustration of the above accusation and assumptions. If the conflict had been a proper war, Israel would have won hands down. The Hizbullah victory was obtained not by brilliant military strategy but by the staging of civilian deaths. Combatants nestled in friendly civilian territory fired at Israeli soldiers and civilians, provoking return fire and inevitable (Lebanese) civilian casualties. Armed combatants, too, were counted as civilian casualties to achieve body-count proof of Israeli guilt. Guns and rockets are understood by the general public as instruments of war. They do not understand how civilian casualties—real and fake—function as lethal weapons.

Unlike Gaza, Lebanon was open to international media during the 2006 war. Fauxtography, rather quickly discovered and exposed by Net journalists, reached mainstream media during the conflict...except in France, where it was not mentioned until the last days of the war, only to be dismissed. Even though staging was exposed, it did not stem the tide of lethal narrative. A mixture of real, faked, accidental, and deliberately provoked casualties sustained the illusion of dynamic public opinion responding decently to realities as they unfold. The "Qana massacre" – most likely staged if not simply provoked and exploited—was brought in, the same way an army brings in reinforcements, to deliver a decisive blow against Israel and raise a worldwide cry of "this has got to stop, we can't stand it anymore."

The al Dura hoax initiated the al Aqsa war, the Gaza Beach hoax launched the 2006 Hizbullah war and at this writing the Gaza blackout hoax looks like a parting shot in a looming episode of mass violence.

The January 2008 Gaza blackout was definitely staged. Amir Mizroch analyzed it as a PR victory for Hamas, facilitated by a sluggish Israeli reaction and customary hasbara-deficit: It took hours to get a shot of the Gaza switch at Ashkelon in ON position. [19]

If the blackout hoax was PR it might make sense to fight it with better PR but if it is, as I think, lethal narrative—an attack— it can't be countered with proof of good faith. You have to retaliate as in battle. In this case, Israel could have switched off the electricity, turning the carefully prepared hoax into authentic chaos. Instead, Israel got tangled up in Supreme Court decisions, the world chalked up another myth, and Hamas went on to the fake spontaneous breakthrough on the Egyptian border.

Israel's enemies do not outsmart us with clever PR, they fight with aggressive techniques that overcome rational thinking, disturb the sense of chronology, and disable the capacity to integrate new information and correct false impressions. Myth is timeless. The myth of Israeli guilt is peddled as news, the war to destroy Israel is disguised as a movement of Palestinian liberation, and the accusation that Israel stole the land has replaced deicide as justification for genocidal Jew hatred. But it does not stop there.

WHAT KIND OF WAR IS THIS ANYWAY?

9/11 /2001: The United States was attacked by *shahids* in civilian airplanes less than one year after Israel was hit with the al Dura myth. Public opinion looked on in horror as the Towers collapsed, wept in sympathy with the victims, pledged short-lived allegiance to the United States, and quickly slipped into condemnation mode. Lightening quick military operations produced radical victories, first in Afghanistan and then in Iraq. But they were not followed by peace and prosperity. They opened on to the real war, the one we do not know how to describe, to fight, to win.

Opposition to "the war in Iraq" has become a badge of honor. What war?

In recognizable wars of the past, citizens who peddled enemy propaganda were severely punished for treason. In this war of confusion, those who propagate lethal narratives are draped in honor. They present themselves as the nation's conscience, transcendent patriots who stand above base instincts, vulgar ambitions, and primitive warrior passion.

First Israel and now the whole free world is trapped in a type of warfare that uses civilian casualties as weapons; civilians are targeted as they enjoy the freedoms that are the hallmark of our civilization, enemy civilians are deliberately thrown into the line of fire or killed by their own forces, and we are accused of war crimes…by our enemies and our own citizens. Any leader who dares to give an accurate description of this war and declare a determination to fight and win becomes the focus of unprecedented irrational hatred, not only by the enemy but by his own citizens. Commentators who accurately describe our situation are smeared as extremists. The pressure is intolerable. Most people back down. Democratic leaders cannot defend their populations without a significant level of popular consent. Today, as the danger increases, our leadership wavers, our chain of alliances goes slack, and we are on the defensive. Having blamed Israel instead of recognizing that it stood on the front lines of the war that has now engulfed us, America's natural European allies now blame the United States for employing military power instead of practicing the fine art of negotiation. Europeans hide under the American umbrella they condemn, hold themselves up as an example of civility, and drape abject appeasement in the frilly pretenses of superior diplomatic skills.

Look at our situation: We live on the battlefield. Credible threats permeate our daily lives. But, since most of them do not materialize, it adds to the confusion and encourages denial. We accept with untold docility the burden of checkpoints, barriers, pat downs, long lines in airports. We leave nail files in our checked baggage because of 9/11 box cutters, take off our shoes because of a shoe bomber, do not carry liquids because a killer team planned to blow up planes with baby bottles; we take off our coats, belts, and jackets, take our computers out of their cases, pass everything through powerful machines monitored by highly stressed personnel; we apply for visas, carry biometric passports, get checked and double checked and meanwhile jihadis are crossing the southern U.S. border disguised as wetbacks or carrying Venezuelan passports. Europeans converted to fanatical Islam come and go without arousing suspicion. Plotters of our destruction hold government positions or have entry as respected advisors, oil-rich jihadis finance our universities and quietly acquire the possibility to grab control of our stock markets. We are hemmed in, ripened for the kill.

But we are not allowed to describe let alone remedy this situation. Why? Because the project of conquest is connected to a religion—Islam—and we are not allowed to say bad things about a religion. This self-censorship is reinforced by a propensity to slit the throats of those who criticize Islam. Islam, a religion that does not separate the spiritual from the political, hides behind this special protection but the state of Israel, which is the homeland of a Jewish nation whose identity is inextricably national, philosophical, and religious, is fair game for criticism, invective, defamation, calumny, delegitimization, and threats of extermination. The connection between the Qu'ran and terrorism is minimized, the connection between Israel and Judaism is inoperative to the point where it would sound ridiculous to say that it is wrong to criticize Israel because we must respect Judaism.

STAGED SCENE, STAGED CONFLICT, REAL JIHAD

We are not fighting insurgents, we are not stymied by patriotic guerilla fighters, we are not spilling blood for oil, we are not neocolonial neo-imperialist predators, we are swept up in an acute phase of jihad conquest. This jihad energy was liberated by the decolonization that left the Arab-Muslim world free to pursue its chosen goals. We are told that all human beings want to get on with life, put food on the table, be fruitful and multiply, live happily ever after. But an indefinable proportion of the Islamic world chose to resume the irrevocable obligation to wage jihad against the infidels. This aggressive option is not, as some would have us believe, a diversion of Islam from its normally peaceful pursuits, it is Islam in its immemorial, unchangeable vocation. All of the evidence points to this conclusion. Every so-called terrorist attack, from the most spectacular—9/11—to the millions of aggressions misinterpreted as ordinary crime is performed within the framework of jihad and justified by the perpetrators in the terms of jihad either directly as prescribed in the Qu'ran or transposed to modern means of expression, e.g. justifying theft, rape, and torching with thinly veiled social arguments that belie a jihad mentality with its assertion of rights over infidels. How curious to observe that the perpetrators always use jihad language and the so-called moderates always deny that Islam—the Qu'ran, hadiths, shari'a—is the authentic source of the behavior. Further, jihad is not limited to Arab-Muslim warriors. It has already spread, integrating other anti-Western movements—anarchists, anti-capitalists, black power, anti-globalists, Bolivarians, and common law criminals. This reality has crept up on us, has spread and multiplied and intensified to become the crushing menace we feel but don't dare articulate.

Jihad against Israel is disguised as legitimate Palestinian aspirations to statehood. Israel is under constant pressure to fulfill the legitimate claim—statehood—when in fact the concessions always lead to destruction of Israeli lives and property. The only concession that would be acceptable to the jihadis is total surrender. Jihad in Europe is disguised as a civil rights movement, for diversity against national identity, against discrimination for social justice. Jihad in the United States is disguised domestically as American-Muslim progress and economic success and internationally as demands for peace and justice.

People who warn of impending danger are stigmatized. People who expose the al Dura hoax are branded as extremists. Our real enemies, the ones who want to kill us, are arbitrarily declared infinitely improvable and always given the benefit of the doubt. And this insanely naïve suicidal attitude is certified Reasonable and set as the default position.

An overwhelming mass of evidence about what is happening, who wants to harm us, where they are, why they want to do it, how they do it, how they build networks, how they operate... is ignored. One little shred of false hope is weighed against all the evidence and found to be valid. And this is exactly how the al Dura affair functions. All the evidence is on one side: it's a staged scene. Six slivers of video bound up in a bunch of words is held as a truth that will not budge. All the evidence is on one side: someone is making war on our civilization. And one sliver of a word—Peace—is held as a saving grace that no truth can contradict.

As if the entire world were clinging to one little life raft.

(1) Lord, Amnon. "Who Killed Muhammad Al-Dura?/ Blood Libel – Model 2000." JCPA, Jerusalem Letter / Viewpoints N° 482, 6 Av 5762 / 15 July 2002.
(2) Huber, Gérard. *Contre-Expertise d'une mise en scène*. Editions Raphaël, Paris 2003. A synopsis with excerpts was published in English translation by World Net Daily. *Whistleblower* 12:3 March 2003 and WND.com
(3) seconddraft.org & augeanstables.com
(4) "Three PM at Netzarim Junction in the Gaza Strip. Dramatic turn of events. The Palestinians shot live ammunition, the Israelis riposted. Ambulance drivers, bystanders, journalists are caught in the crossfire. / Here Jamal and his son Mohamed are the target of gunfire from the Israeli positions. Mohamed is twelve years old. His father tries to protect him. He waves./ But another round of gunfire bursts out. Mohamed is dead, his father is critically wounded. A Palestinian policeman and an ambulance driver were also killed in this battle."
(5) interview in Kol Ha'zman October 6 2000 "I was in my Gaza City office when we received notice that there was shooting at Netzarim Junction...when I arrived there was already heavy shooting...the shots came from all over...It was terrible and I was forced to take cover inside the van."
(6) "That Boy who wore Our Hand-Me-Downs," *Jerusalem Post* October 29, 2000.
(7) Huber, Gérard. Contre-expertise d'une mise en scène. Editions Raphaël. Paris. 2003. p. 11.
(8) Télérama N°2650 October 25, 2000.
(9) "La controverse de Netzarim," *Télérama* N° 2863, November 22, 2004.
(10) Schwartz, Adi. "Independent expert: IDF bullets didn't kill Mohammed al-Dura," Haaretz, March 2, 2008. Schwartz commits the usual error of saying Mohamed al Dura and his father were caught in a crossfire between Palestinian gunmen and IDF soldiers. Further, he mistakenly states the issue as "doctored footage" before finally giving the expert's conclusion— there is a serious possibility that the incident was staged.
(11) *Télérama* October 25 2000.
(12) Outtakes of her interview with Abu Rahma for the documentary film *Three Bullets and a Dead Child*.
(13) Fallows, James. "Who Shot Mohammed al-Dura," *Atlantic Monthly* June 2003.
(14) Enderlin, Charles. *The Lost Years. Radical Islam, Intifada, and wars in the Middle East 2001-2006*. Translated by Suzanne Verderber. Other Press. New York. 2007 (original title: Les Années perdues)
(15) I did eventually publish "Blame Israel Always," *City Journal*, Summer 2006
(16) "Losing the Propaganda War," *Jerusalem Post*. June 12, 2006.
(17) Ibid. "Palestinians may have caused Gaza beach deaths, Olmert says"
(18) See my articles on French diplomacy *tcsdaily.com* and *Atlas Shrugs*. My suppositions have recently been confirmed by John Bolton.
(19) "Lights (off). Camera. Action," *Jerusalem Post*, January 24 2008.

Chapter 6

OUT DAMN SPOT:
The Al Dura affair comes back to haunt Charles Enderlin

4/19/08 It's been called the mother of all fauxtography, the biggest media hoax of our times, the most damaging image ever attached to Israel, an icon of hatred, blood libel on an international scale: the shooting of Mohamed al Dura, a 12 year-old Palestinian boy allegedly gunned down by murderous Israeli soldiers on September 30, 2000 at Netzarim Junction in the Gaza Strip. The incident, fortuitously filmed by France 2 cameraman Talal Abu Rahma, has been at the center of debate ever since. Al Dura, the poster boy of the al Aqsa intifada, has served as justification for some of the most atrocious crimes of this decade—two Israeli reservists massacred by an enraged mob in Ramallah to avenge Mohamed al Dura; the Palestinian boy's shooting spliced into the beheading video of WSJ's Daniel Pearl... Echoes of the hatred generated by the al Dura image resound to this day. The murder of eight students at Jerusalem's Mercaz Harav yeshiva is the latest in a long series of savage attacks against civilians in Israel and Jews worldwide, in revenge for some Ur-crime committed against Palestinians.

Despite conclusive evidence to the contrary, France 2 Jerusalem correspondent Charles Enderlin has never withdrawn the accusation that the boy was killed and his father wounded by gunfire "from the Israeli positions." The origin of that hypothetical gunfire is a moot question to observers who claim the whole scene was staged.

While Israeli authorities hunkered down, hoping the al Dura accusations would fade away, France 2 correspondent Charles Enderlin has staked his reputation on keeping them blood red. French media closed ranks and stifled the controversy on their home turf but it kept bouncing back internationally. Determined to silence "enemies" once and for all, France 2 /Enderlin brought defamation suits against three websites that had posted critical examinations of the al Dura report, losing one on a technicality and winning two on generalities.

But one of the defendants, Media-Ratings director Philippe Karsenty, appealed and Enderlin's slam-dunk litigation is looking more like a boomerang. Whereas the court of first resort had avoided questions that might have embarrassed the state-owned television network, Laurence Trébucq, the no-nonsense president of the three-judge Appellate Court panel, lifted the lid to see what's cooking and ordered France 2 to turn over the raw footage. The court got a stingy 18-minute excerpt, but it was enough to confirm the initial observation that France 2 stringer Talal Abu Rahma did indeed film fake battles, simulated injuries, and comical ambulance evacuations...that fateful day. And the al Dura shooting? Also staged? Or paradoxically authentic?

Evidence and closing arguments were heard at a marathon session on February 27th. Initially convicted of defaming France 2 / Enderlin without conducting a proper investigation, Philippe Karsenty presented bushels of evidence that the judge observed with rapt attention. France 2 /Enderlin brought in its Big Bertha in the person of Maître François Szpiner, former President Chirac's personal counsel. Szpiner defended the Paris Mosque in the *Charlie Hebdo* - Danish cartoons case (he lost) and was literally dispatched to represent Ruth Halimi whose son Ilan was tortured to death by the anti-Semitic "Gang of Barbarians" in February 2005.

The aggressive, abusive, sarcastic Szpiner did not attempt to defend the facts on the ground, obviously a lost cause. He saved his ammunition for underhand blows and snide remarks about "The Jew who gives money to a second Jew who gives it to the third Jew who fights to the last drop of Israeli blood." Karsenty, described with a snarl as a cross between the Shoah negationist Faurisson and the 9/11 revisionist Meyssan, has it in for Enderlin, says Szpiner, because the France 2 correspondent covers the hotheaded Mideast conflict with consummate fairness and not, as some would wish, as a fight between the good guys and the bad guys. Enderlin, in turn, vouched for his trusted Palestinian cameraman, assuring the court that if Talal had engaged in crooked reporting, the Israelis would have revoked his accreditation.

In fact, Abu Rahma's accreditation has not been renewed since 2002 because, according to Government Press Office director Daniel Seaman, he was filming staged scenes. Invited to react to this information, news director Chabot relayed the request to Enderlin who shot back with a half dozen insulting e-mails including one in English—addressed to the Foreign Press Association—identifying me as "that lady." "You are a militant," wrote Enderlin, "I expect nothing from you. You won't even mention that we won four libel suits and the *Avocat Général* recommended confirmation of Karsenty's initial conviction." In the midst of the bluster, Enderlin confirmed that the GPO withdrew accreditation from all Gaza and West Bank journalists, including Abu Rahma, at the end of 2001. Any other explanation, he threatened, is a lie.

Caught off guard during a brief recess during the trial, Arlette Chabot let off steam. "I just want this shitty affair over and done with. I want Karsenty to lose! This nutty case has been bugging me since day one." Implying that her people have no idea where the murderous gunfire came from, she assured the gentleman who had buttonholed her that she was willing to investigate everything and everyone if she could only get this shitty case off her back. What about the fact that the dead child identified as Mohamed al Dura was brought into the hospital between noon and 1 PM while the alleged shooting occurred at 3PM? Making the motions of someone who turns back a clock, Madame Chabot explained there was "some kind of time change that day in Gaza."

She had already left the premises when Philippe Karsenty stood before the court and replied soberly to the ultimate question: Why are you doing this?

"I will not give up. I owe it to the father of Daniel Pearl, beheaded with the image of Mohamed al-Dura incrusted in the video. I owe it to my parents, who taught me to respect the truth. I owe it to the Jewish people, victim of lies, I owe it to France, I owe it to history."

The verdict will be pronounced on May 21st.

— *FrontPage Magazine*

AL DURA TRIALS AND TRIBULATIONS
May 15, 2008

State-owned radio station France-Inter pre-recorded an interview with Philippe Karsenty for broadcast on May 21st. Could this mean they expect him to win his appeals case?

May 12, 2008: in Israel Shurat HaDin presents its case for the withdrawal of Charles Enderlin's and France 2 press accreditation to the Supreme Court on the grounds that the uncorroborated al Dura news report has done grave damage to the image of Israel and, more precisely, has incited murderous hatred, resulting in the deaths of many people, including the Wall Street Journal reporter Daniel Pearl. May 21, 2008, in Paris the 11th Chamber of the Court of Appeals will render its verdict in the defamation case brought by France 2 and Charles Enderlin against Philippe Karsenty, convicted by the court of first resort of defaming the plaintiffs by denouncing their part in producing and disseminating the al Dura hoax.

The September 30, 2000 al Dura news report is the most questionable broadcast of recent times. The purported shooting of a Palestinian boy and his father at Netzarim Junction in the Gaza Strip, captured live for television audiences worldwide, bears no resemblance to news. The fleeting image—approximately 55 seconds—belies the voice over commentary that carried it into contemporary history: "The boy is dead, his father critically wounded." France 2 Jerusalem correspondent Charles Enderlin claimed that day, and forever after, that the Palestinian civilians were "targets of gunfire from the Israeli position." His trusted cameraman, Talal Abu Rahma, declared under oath that Israeli soldiers fired at the hapless victims unremittingly for 45 minutes. Leaving—the video is clear on that point—some eight bullet holes in the wall that served as a backdrop for the icons of Israeli cruelty.

Under normal circumstances the bogus news report would have been rapidly reevaluated and withdrawn. But the al Dura shooting kicked off the "al Aqsa Intifada" and the accusation it framed worked as a weapon of mass destruction against Israel two months after the Palestinians rejected the offer of a peace-processed state. The al Dura blood libel transformed Palestinian humanicide bombers—who were already waiting in the wings— into noble *résistants* facing Israeli child-killers.

The video murder of the innocent Palestinian child resists rational examination because it captures a timeless accusation. Finally the Jews are caught in the act! France 2 was not there when they crucified Jesus, there was no Abu Rahma on site to film their criminal rejection of the prophet Mohamed, but al Dura the shahid is living proof of these crimes. So it doesn't matter if the scene was staged...because the accusation is True.

In this highly charged atmosphere there is little breathing room for journalistic ethics. The worldwide media that broadcast the scene have shown scant interest in the controversy it aroused. Schools of journalism have yet to give it the attention it deserves. French intellectuals who like to be known for their elevated humanism have shied away from an issue that might tarnish their medals.

But the al Dura affair has not disappeared and the attempt of France 2/Enderlin to silence detractors by taking a few of them to court in France has backfired. One of the defendants, Philippe Karsenty, convicted of libel in 2006 for denouncing the al Dura hoax and calling for the dismissal of Charles Enderlin and news director Arlette Chabot, carried the case to the appeals court. When presiding judge Laurence Trébucq asked to see the raw footage, France 2's lawyer dropped her pencil with a resounding thud. It looked like the goose was cooked. The state-owned TV channel and its eternal Jerusalem correspondent have no evidence to corroborate the al Dura news report. But the case does not hinge on the authenticity of the report.

Karsenty was convicted of defamation because he did not have sufficient evidence to back his accusation against Enderlin /France 2. The three-judge panel may uphold Karsenty's conviction on strictly legal grounds or, in virtue of extensive evidence produced by the defendant, they may reverse the lower court decision. Whatever the judgment rendered by the 11th Chamber of the Court of Appeals on May 21st, nothing can erase the effect produced when Judge Trébucq said: "Some of these staged scenes did appear in France 2 news reports."

The protagonists are not passively awaiting judgment. France 2,

Charles Enderlin, and Philippe Karsenty have been active on all fronts since the appeal was filed in the fall of 2006.

Karsenty a young investment banker and occasional politician (he was recently elected deputy mayor of Neuilly) stood up like many French Jews in 2000 to defend Israel. He created a watchdog site, Media-Ratings, to expose unseemly behavior in French media...including the al Dura broadcast. With his hallmark straight talk Karsenty accused Enderlin of defaming Israel with the al Dura hoax and Chabot of covering for him. Dragged into court, convicted of libel, Karsenty came out fighting. He has matured in the process, refined his approach, channeled his energies, and is scoring some important victories at the moment... many of which cannot yet be revealed.

While Karsenty, the amateur, gains assurance, Charles Enderlin, the pro, is flailing and stumbling. Praised—in France—as an arch-specialist on the Middle East conflict, he cobbles together notes and dispatches every few years and brings out an "authoritative" book that gets excellent reviews in friendly domestic media. Who knows if his reputation carries outside this French *huis clos* and its Israeli branch? The English translations of his books don't produce much excitement. Whether in French or English, the ineptitude of Enderlin's writing is rivaled by the consistent bad faith of his documentation and twisted analyses. His most recent production, Par le feu et par le sang, tells the "true" story of Israel's foundation by Jewish terrorists who make their Palestinian counterparts look like harmless kittens. Following this logic, the murder of Mohamed al Dura would be a natural continuation of the violent Israeli behavior that Enderlin castigates with the ardor of a disappointed lover.

Philippe Karsenty is always on the move, digging up new data, organizing Power Point presentations, showing them to skeptical or hostile people who can influence opinion, giving talks... Welcomed as a hero at a 2006 Herzliya conference organized by Richard Landes, dismissed as a crackpot by know-nothings, scorned by French journalists loyal to Enderlin's cause, scolded by friends and allies for undiplomatic flare-ups, he won't give up the fight to save the honor of the Jewish people, falsely accused of child murder.

Charles Enderlin, too, is concerned with the honor of his people. He believes he is a model of objective journalism; rising above personal allegiance to the Jewish state, he unflinchingly exposes Israel's bad deeds. This happens to satisfy a gnawing hunger in French public opinion, effectively promoting Enderlin's reputation...but his conscience is clear. No right thinking person would question his faultless reporting. The attacks come from ultra-nationalist, ultra-Zionist, ultra-rightist Likudniks who want to impose their version of the facts.

While Karsenty examines and re-examines the data, Enderlin builds and rebuilds this exclusive line of defense. Neither he nor those who defend him have ever produced any concrete evidence to sustain the accusations made in September 2000. They have not furnished any plausible explanation for major discrepancies in the video and the cameraman's testimony. Standing before black-robed judges in the *Palais de Justice* or looking into the camera of a friendly colleague, Enderlin repeats the same defense: I trust my cameraman, I know more than you about this conflict, these activists want to keep me from telling the truth.

A documentary broadcast on pay-to-view Canal + a month before the awaited verdict in Karsenty's trial used a rehash of material on 9/11 conspiracy wackos as a ploy to throw al Dura debunkers into the same meat grinder. A scene filmed at a colloquium on blood libel organized by the eminently respectable scholar Shmuel Trigano of the equally distinguished *Alliance Israélite Universelle* was transformed into a meeting of evil plotters in the style of the Protocols of the Elders of Zion. The Hebrew letters of a page from *Makor Rishon* were flashed on the screen as evidence of Karsenty's traffic with the devil. In sharp contrast with these dark forces, Charles Enderlin, playing the good guy, tells how he carefully reexamined the video—the day after broadcasting it—and checked out the scene at Netzarim Junction. Nothing amiss. So, you understand, he had to go to court to keep those activists from attacking him.

The documentary got good reviews from a few journalists who obviously know zilch about the al Dura affair. No dissenting voices. Not even a polite note of surprise that the French press hasn't been covering this seven-year controversy suddenly revealed in the Canal + documentary. The media share in Enderlin's narrative, public opinion swallows it, and those who disrupt it pay the price.

Elisabeth Levy, a talented journalist who has been hired and fired by a variety of media—trendy, conventional or highbrow—for speaking her mind, created an elegant webzine causeur.fr, where she can be her own person. She co-authored with Gil Mihaely an article on the al Dura affair and, I am told, she has been going door to door convincing influential French intellectuals that the al Dura scene was staged. However, none of them has gone public. One article by one big name might tip the balance. Why do they keep silent?

Paradoxically, they cover up the hoax to preserve their own reputations. And the unwashed mass media journalists cover it to bolster their credibility. If X or Y, who is invited to high places, should blurt out "as a matter of fact, the al Dura scene was staged," he would be instantly transformed into a wacko. If a handful of journalists began to publish informative articles on the affair, it would become obvious that the press has been sitting on it for close to eight years with shuttered eyes.

And the French court? Is it possible that the no-nonsense Laurence Trébucq might judge in favor of Philippe Karsenty and send all these chickens clucking?

Videos and power points can be viewed at seconddraft.org, and on Charles Enderlin's France 2 blog

— *Makor Rishon*

AL DURA: ENDERLIN LOSES. CIVILIZATION WINS!

May 2008

Presiding judge Laurent Trébucq of the 11e Chambre d'Appel announced the verdict in the al Dura case at 1:50 PM today. It only took her two minutes to say in her sweetest voice: Philippe Karsenty is acquitted, the plaintiffs—France 2 and Charles Enderlin—are dismissed. The French word for "dismissed" is "*déboutés*"...to our ears it sounds like they got a kick where it does the most good. French mainstream media were not there to hear the news. They left it all for a small band of courageous journalists, such as Véronique Chemla, who has been covering the trials with notable distinction (in French) for *Guysen Israel News*, a film crew from ARD German TV, reporters from *Yedioth Aharanot, Haaretz* , and *Honest Reporting* / Take a Pen, Elisabeth Levy, and of course me.

Philippe Karsenty was nearly in tears as he made his first recorded statement (for ARD)....a message of reconciliation that should be spread as widely as the message of hate carried by the al Dura blood libel. He said he had fought not only to defend his own honor, but to defend Israel, the Jews, and the free world. He hopes that his acquittal will be heard as a warning to those who have been spreading evil falsehoods that enflame Muslims and lead them to senseless violence.

The full explanation of the verdict will be available tomorrow. In the meantime the spin has started, as media that have been defending Enderlin rush to claim that Karsenty's acquittal does not mean the al Dura news report was staged. Hmmm? When Karsenty was convicted of libel last year, they all hollered whoopy, the court has ruled that the al Dura news report was authentic.

Let them spin. If you spin enough, you twist yourself to exhaustion.

Let them spin. I saw Maître Amblard, the France 2 lawyer, disappear into thin air when the verdict was pronounced.

Let them spin. Charles Enderlin already posted on his France 2 blog. He lost but he is crowing. The "headline" claims Karsenty is guilty of defamation but acquitted on good faith. So he already saw the judgment, which has not been made public? I thought it was against the law to disclose such information, but then Enderlin is a law unto himself. So what does it mean if the court does in fact say that Karsenty defamed Enderlin? To claim that a journalist produced a fraudulent news report and continues to defend it to this day is in fact defaming his honor. But if the defamation is true, his honor is truly defamed.

— *Atlas Shrugs*

HEAR YE HEAR YE BREAKING NEWS IN THE AL DURA AFFAIR

May 27, 2008

Why should Americans take note of a verdict announced in the musty halls of the *Palais de Justice* in Paris? Philippe Karsenty, convicted of defamation in 2006 for declaring in a Media-Ratings release that the al Dura news report was a hoax, a fraud, a staged scene, was acquitted in the Court of Appeals on May 21st. Pursued by state-owned France 2 and Jerusalem bureau chief Charles Enderlin, the courageous businessman cum media watchdog director, bounced back from the harsh judgment of the lower court, carrying bushel baskets of evidence. The meeting of the tireless Karsenty and a perspicacious French judge, madame Laurence Trébucq, produced an earth-shaking judgment that concerns all media in the free world...and all tainted news sources in the lands of discord.

Where is the earth when truth comes shaking? French media, which are the most immediately concerned by this judgment, have hunkered down to the point of absurdity. A few flabby spin attempts were dropped like litter on a systematically uninformed public just in case someone might realize that Karensty's acquittal is Charles Enderlin's disgrace. The 13-page Ruling is there for all to see, and it belies last-ditch efforts to claim the defamation charge endures.

The antiquated late 19th century press law offers two paths to absolution: 1. absolute proof of the truth of the incriminated statement(s) or 2. convincing proof of good faith, serious investigation, lack of personal animosity or excessive verbal violence. Acquittal on either of the two accounts is acquittal of all charges.

Not only did the court acquit Mr. Karsenty—a stunning exploit given the hefty weight of France 2 and Charles Enderlin—but the judges displayed impressive mastery of every detail of this complex affair. Instead of ignoring Judge Trébucq, French journalists should take a lesson from her fair-minded, intelligent, skillful exercise of a noble vocation.

Justice was done! It is time for justice to be applied in the realm of another vocation—journalism—whose integrity has been sorely lacking where the Mohamed al Dura case is concerned. Beyond the dramatic staged killing of the Palestinian boy that has lodged poison in millions of hearts and inspired murder and mayhem all over the world, the widespread practice in Western media of swallowing questionable material from unverifiable sources—in the Palestinian territories and more generally in the Arab-Muslim world—is targeted by the findings of the French Court of Appeals.

One could hardly accuse former President Jacques Chirac of participating in the staging of the al Dura scene. However, he immediately employed the alleged murder of the Palestinian child as a stick with which to beat then PM Ehud Barak and pressure Israel to cave in to Palestinian demands. Civilian (Palestinian) casualties served as a weapon against Israel when the Palestinians began their intifada-war in September 2000. The alleged murder of Mohamed al Dura covered the real and absolutely deliberate murder of hundreds of Israeli civilians that followed.

Chirac's France was an influential underhanded opponent of the

United States in those crucial years. The new Sarkozy government is a forceful, vibrant ally. Next month France will take its turn in the rotating EU presidency. President Sarkozy has courageously reinforced French troops in Afghanistan, he is firm in his determination to prevent Iran from going nuclear, his government is committed to stemming the influx of illegal immigrants, he is implementing a bold program of economic and institutional reform.

Contrary to the mumblings of surrender freaks, relations with Europe improve when the United States accepts its international responsibilities, including the military interventions that no other country can ensure. Nicolas Sarkozy, elected by popular enthusiasm, has been the target of unconscionable contempt in French media, much of which seeps right into American MSM. And what does this have to do with the al Dura controversy?

The French media blackout of information about this gigantic media hoax is an indication of the abysmal absence of a vibrant free press here in France. The media sleaze Sarkozy, trash Bush, and protect Charles Enderlin whose reports from Israel perpetuate the tiresome bashing that serves no honest purpose. This zombie French press silence should not be contagious. American mass media broadcast the al Dura image, participated in the dissemination of the hatred it bears. They have not even begun to examine the case, the footage, the sources.

Ladies and gentlemen of the press, the al Dura hoax makes Lebanese fauxtography look like a childish prank. It caused more deaths than 100 Mohamed cartoons. Where are you when we need you? Will the first brave journalist please stand up!

— *National Post, Canada*

AL DURA: A HOAX?
May 27, 2008

September 30, 2000, Netzarim Junction in the Gaza Strip: France 2 correspondent Charles Enderlin offers the world a front seat on the video shooting of Mohammed al-Durra and his father Jamal. Targeted, according to Mr. Enderlin's voiceover commentary, by "gunfire from the direction of the Israeli positions." A few seconds later: "Mohammed is dead, his father is critically wounded."

The France 2 cameraman, later identified as Palestinian stringer

Talal Abu Rahma, caught the child killers in the act. A prize-winning scoop!

Independent analysts and Israeli officials seeking clarification of inconsistencies in the al-Durra news report encountered stubborn resistance from the state-owned French channel and its Mideast correspondent. An Israeli army investigation concluded the gunfire could not have come from their position; independent investigators went further and declared that the incident had been staged. Exasperated by the controversy, France 2 and Mr. Enderlin sued four Web sites for defamation, won three cases and lost the fourth on a technicality. Philippe Karsenty, director of the Media-Ratings watchdog site, convicted of defamation for calling the al-Durra report "a hoax," took the case to the Court of Appeals.

May 21, 2008, Palais de Justice, 11th Chamber of the Court of Appeals: Presiding judge Laurence Trébucq announced the verdict with a delicate smile: Philippe Karsenty is acquitted; the plaintiff's claims are dismissed. France 2 counsel Maître Bénédicte Amblard blanched, shrugged her shoulders, and disappeared into thin air. Mr. Karsenty celebrated the decision as an admonition to reckless media who provoke violence with falsified inflammatory news.

An honest reading of the ruling calls into question the al-Durra myth. French media didn't bother to come to the funeral. Were they confident that Charles Enderlin would be vindicated? Did they think Philippe Karsenty, whose honor they had sullied by likening him to Holocaust deniers and 9/11 conspiracy nuts, was already dead and buried?

Mr. Karsenty's defamation conviction in the court of first resort had been celebrated as proof that the al-Durra death scene was authentic. Reactions to his acquittal, which can be counted on the fingers of one bony hand, reassert that impression. In a three-second segment at the tail end of Wednesday's primetime news, France 2 implied — with the famous al-Durra image in the background — that the report had, once again, been authenticated despite the acquittal of an — unnamed — defendant.

Playing on the complexity of the law dating back to July 29, 1881, Charles Enderlin and his allies insist that Mr. Karsenty is still guilty of defamation. The incriminated statements Mr. Karsenty made in 2004 on his Web site did damage their reputations. But the court found that despite the lack of absolute proof, the statements were nevertheless justified by the defendant's good faith, due diligence and appropriate language. The judge therefore acquitted Philippe Karsenty of all charges.

In a move unprecedented in media litigation, France 2 and Mr. Enderlin have referred the case to France's highest court (the *Cour de Cassation*), which rules solely on technicalities, not on substance.

The 13-page ruling is drafted with the same ethical and intellectual clarity exercised by Judge Trébucq throughout the proceedings. The court first establishes the principle that Charles Enderlin "...as a professional journalist reporting from Israel and the Palestinian territories for primetime France 2 newscasts...cannot shield himself from criticism; he is...[necessarily] exposed to...scrutiny...from citizens and colleagues." And then the court validates, exhibit by exhibit, the evidence that led Philippe Karsenty to question and ultimately denounce the al-Durra report.

While Mr. Karsenty submitted voluminous evidence, France 2 and Mr. Enderlin relied on an above-suspicion strategy based on the elevated reputation of the journalist, his total confidence in the Palestinian cameraman who filmed those images without the French correspondent there, and the unquestionable dignity of the state-owned television network. Their position weakened when Judge Trébucq ordered them to submit the unedited raw footage filmed on Sept. 30, 2000. They only partially complied. In lieu of "unedited raw footage," Mr. Enderlin presented an 18-minute excerpt and, for the first time since litigation began, appeared in court on Nov. 18 to oversee the screening.

Reinforcements were brought in for the final hearing on Feb. 27 — news director Arlette Chabot to bolster Mr. Enderlin, and Maître François Szpiner to assassinate Mr. Karsenty's character, comparing him to 9/11 conspiracy theorist Thierry Meyssan, Holocaust denier Robert Faurisson, and "the Jew who pays a second Jew to pay a third Jew to fight to the last drop of Israeli blood." This aggressive strategy backfired.

The court kept its eyes on the evidence. It is impossible in the limited space available here to do justice to a document that deserves line-by-line appreciation. The following examples drawn from the decision are a fair indication of its logical thrust: Material evidence raises legitimate doubts about the authenticity of the al-Durra scene. The video images do not correspond to the voiceover commentary. Mr. Enderlin fed legitimate speculation of deceit by claiming to have footage of Mohammed al Durra's death throes while systematically refusing to reveal it. He aggravated his case by suing analysts who publicly questioned the authenticity of the report. Examination of an 18-minute excerpt of raw footage composed primarily of staged battle scenes, false injuries and comical ambulance evacuations reinforces the possibility that the al-Durra scene, too, was staged. (There is, strictly speaking, no raw footage of the al-Durra scene; all that exists are the six thin slices of images that were spliced together to produce the disputed news report.)

The possibility of a staged scene is further substantiated by expert testimony presented by Mr. Karsenty — including a 90-page ballistics report and a sworn statement by Dr. Yehuda ben David attributing Jamal al-Durra's scars — displayed as proof of wounds sustained in the alleged shooting — to knife and hatchet wounds incurred when he was attacked by Palestinians in 1992. In fact, there is no blood on the father's T-shirt, the boy moves after Mr. Enderlin's voiceover commentary says he is dead, no bullets are seen hitting the alleged victims. And Mr. Enderlin himself had backtracked when the controversy intensified after seasoned journalists Denis Jeambar and Daniel Leconte viewed some of the raw footage in 2004. The news report, he said, corresponds to "the situation." The court, concurring with Messrs. Jeambar and Leconte, considers that journalism must stick to events that actually occur.

The frail evidence submitted by France 2 — "statements provided by the cameraman" — is not "perfectly credible either in form or content," the court ruled.

The landmark ruling closes with an eloquent affirmation of the right of citizens to criticize the press freely, the right of the public to be informed honestly and seriously, the right of expression guaranteed by Article 10 of the European Convention on Human Rights, a right that applies not only to inoffensive ideas but also to those that are shocking, disturbing, troubling.

The media that dramatically reported the killing of Mohammed al-Durra are deathly silent today. They didn't inform the public about the ongoing controversy, didn't attend the trials and have apparently decided to place this story into an artificial coma. As if this judgment against a colleague who placed blind trust in his Palestinian cameraman and, when called to clarify his report, attacked the questioner instead of questioning his own competence were not newsworthy?

The press corps has consistently closed ranks with Charles Enderlin. One week before the verdict was announced, pay-to-view TV station Canal+ aired a documentary seemingly concocted for the purpose of branding Philippe Karsenty — and anyone who challenged the al-Durra story — as conspiracy-theory crackpots.

Mr. Enderlin is the dean of French Middle East reporting. He has full latitude on France 2 to present his editorializing as factual news. Pointedly ignoring the al-Durra controversy, France 2 continued to give Mr. Enderlin — in tandem with cameraman Talal Abu Rahma — high-profile status on primetime news. Every few years Mr. Enderlin collects his material into another "authoritative" book on the Arab-Israeli conflict. Mr. Enderlin has been the driving force in convincing French public opinion that Israel was to blame for the breakdown of the July 2000 Camp David talks. Further, Mr. Enderlin argues that the "Al Aqsa" or second intifada turned violent because of the disproportionate repression of civilian protest by uncontrolled Israeli military personnel.

Mr. Enderlin claims ultra-Zionist Likudniks want to prevent him from reporting objectively on the Arab-Israeli conflict. He is now replaying the Karsenty case on his French State TV blog where, in the absence of the wise Judge Trébucq, he wins hands down. He claims the al-Durra controversy was fomented in response to the publication of "Le Rêve Brisée" (Shattered Dreams), where he pinpointed Israel's responsibility for the collapse of the peace process.

France Télévisions director Patrick de Carolis and the CSA — roughly equivalent to the U.S. Federal Communications Commission — have been repeatedly called by media watchdogs to intervene in the al-Durra controversy. Can they all remain deaf to the wisdom of a courageous judge who has reasserted the journalist's responsibility to serve the people and account for the way he does his job?

— *Wall Street Journal Europe*

GUILLAUME SANS CONQUÊTE

[5/28/08 "William without the Conquest." Translation of my talkback in French to Guillaume Weil-Raynal, "Al Dura Affair: a win for the real imposters," posted on Marianne 2.]

Hatred is blinding. Disappointed by the court's verdict, Maître Guillaume Weill-Raynal spills out his guts and inspires a mob of readers whose comments disgrace Marianne 2. For example: *Posted by r32: the wheel turns for everyone even for the Jews soon they are going to relive the past and we'll get a big laugh out of it in fact it already started last summer with the whipping they got from hezbollah.* Is that the best they could find to fill the abysmal lack of information in French media since the very beginning of the controversy raised by the France 2/Enderlin report, broadcast with fracas on September 30, 2000?

In the video, which is as brief as it is questionable, we do not see "gunfire from the Israeli positions," we do not see Mohamed "dead" and his father "critically wounded" [voiceover commentary by Charles Enderlin]. We do not see the boy in his father's arms, the father who looks at his son, sees he is dead and says to himself "he is a *shahid*," we do not see the dead boy who dies a second time, bleeding for twenty minutes, we do not see the ambulance that picks him up, carefully putting his intestines back into his lacerated abdomen... We see nothing of the 27 minutes of outtakes of the dramatic scene allegedly filmed by France 2 cameraman Talal Abou Rahma, nothing but 6 thin slices of film spliced together to make the 55-second news report that enflamed the world with hatred. Hatred against Israeli soldiers, Israelis, the state of Israel, and the Jews.

This hatred, expressed concrètely, does not wear off. The proof ? *Marianne* readers are proud to understand better than anyone the criteria of verification of a journalistic report. To wit: the proof of the authenticity of the al Dura report is that Israelis are savages who take pleasure in killing Palestinian children just as they killed Mohamed al Dura. Following this logic, the opposite would be equally true: if the al Dura report is a fake, is staged, it follows that no Palestinian child was killed by Israelis.

It's not logical, it's total madness. Let's look at the facts *["facts" in English in the text]*. Given the pathological incapacity to distinguish fact from opinion [*in French media*] it will be better to use the English word as a sort of flashlight to lead us out of the obscurity imposed on a beautifully clear judicial ruling.

You wouldn't know it from reading Maître Guillaume Weill-Raynal but there are an enormous amount of *facts* about the al Dura reportage. The idea that a staged scene was abusively presented as a news report by a state-owned channel—otherwise governed by a proper deontological code—was not inspired by some hatred of Palestinians but simply followed from concrete observations of the said report, subsequently confirmed by multiple serious investigations.

Of course you have the right to defend the seriously challenged news report ... seriously. It's simple: you add your *facts* to the *facts* already presented, and base your argument on the *facts*. By bringing the case to court, Charles Enderlin and France 2 were bound to respect French justice. They won in the court of first resort and lost the appeal. Curiously, a strategy conceived to end the controversy has—finally—brought it to the attention of the French public.

Pitiful readers, jumping with joy to see Maître Guillaume Weill-Raynal spew contempt on "communitarian" media that dare to cover the al Dura affair, don't you realize you've been deprived for the past seven years of information so important that it has been widely commented in the international press? Are they communitarian too? The *Wall Street Journal*, the *New York Times, Reader's Digest, Atlantic Monthly,* and still others.

The total silence of our media creates a void in which your hoax detector can blare out absurdities without fear of contradiction. He accuses Denis Jeambar and Daniel Leconte of originating—in 2004—the staged scene hypothesis. Excuse me but the personal investigation these excellent journalists mention left no traces ...unless they're taking credit for Luc Rosenzweig's essay *"Le crime médiatique était presque parfait"* [an almost perfect media crime] commissioned by *l'Express* for publication in 2004, and suddenly killed. The unbeatable Charles Enderlin explains (on his blog) that the controversy was started in 2002 by Zionists offended by the truth hammered out in his masterpiece *Le Rêve brisé* [Shattered Dreams]. In fact, the widespread practiced of staging scenes was demonstrated at the end of 2000 by the physicist Nahum Shahaf who collected a treasure of audiovisual material and factual data that has helped all analysts understand the affair.

We know, from raw footage shot by other Palestinian cameramen at the junction that day, that fictitious battle scenes were performed behind an abandoned factory out of reach of "gunfire from the Israeli positions [sic]." The fake wounded were scooped up hastily by excited ambulances, some bearing the UN logo, and taken directly into the firing line of the only Israeli position, while crowd mills around calmly, out of danger!

The best of these scenes, filmed from beginning to end, shows men in street clothes and others in uniform calmly preparing the scene at the abandonedfactory. Then, the camera focuses on a group of armed men chatting inside a room in the factory. They come out, the civilians are shooed away, the Pallywood soldiers line up against the wall and the brave *résistant* runs up to a hole in the wall and fires a round into the room that his friends just evacuated.

When that scene was shown in the 11th Chamber of the Court of Appeals, Charles Enderlin explained: "Hmmm, we don't know what he was shooting at but it must be something ... the Palestinians don't have ammunition to waste ..."

We aren't stupid. The presiding judge Laurence Trébucq isn't either. The brave combatant was firing into an empty room. No Israeli soldier in sight. Nothing in the room and, one is tempted to say, nothing in the head... because the truth had to come out one day.

Don't take my word for it. Do like real scholars, consult the available documentation, beginning with the Ruling of the 17e Correctionnel and the 11th Chamber of the Court of Appeal ...then, take a stroll on Google...preferably in English. Be sure not to miss the Wall Street Journal of May 28th.

GUILLAUME AGAIN

[Translated from French by the author. Offered to causeur.fr. Rejected.].

I submitted to *Marianne 2* a reaction to an article by Maître Guillaume Weill-Raynal published by Marianne.net.

Now I must react to the vehement ignorance of his statements published by *Causeur*.

I am in fact the author of the *Wall Street Journal* article casually mentioned by Elisabeth Lévy without attribution. Thanks to the Net you can see for yourself, along with the accompanying editorial. The Ruling is available on request at the Media-Ratings site. That way you can understand what it is all about before commenting.

Armed with vain certitudes, knowing nothing about the investigations undertaken over the past eight years by various scholars, journalists, analysts and specialists, the scolders think those who express doubts about the al Dura report are, like themselves, shooting blindly. Well, it's not true.

The debate that has been going on elsewhere for years has finally opened in France. N.B.: debate doesn't mean throwing assertions like rotten tomatoes at the adversary.

A journalistic report is necessarily based on verifiable information from reliable sources. Otherwise it's anything and everything. Why, then, demand a derogation from these basic rules for the al Dura case?

Let's take one single element: the raw footage. How much? 27 minutes? 18 minutes? Edited or not? Charles Enderlin's defenders support his version of the incident by simple reiteration, and then pounce like wild animals on anyone who questions it. Detractors point out a piece of red cloth, a glance at the camera, the source of gunfire, death throes or no death throes? They're nuts, barks the wild animal pack. What matters is that the child is dead and it's the fault of the Israelis.

What do we know about the raw footage, based on assertions from the very sources that ask us to believe Mohamed al Dura was killed and his father critically wounded before our eyes?

Cameraman Talal Abu Rahma declared under oath on October 3, 2000 that Jamal al Dura and his son Mohamed were targeted by gunfire from Israeli soldiers for 45 minutes. Of those 45 minutes he filmed 27. That's the original figure: 27.

27 minutes of raw footage? No. 27 minutes of an 80-minute al Dura scene that breaks down as follows: 5 minutes of crossfire, 45 minutes of gunfire solely from the Israeli position, 20 minutes in which Mohamed al Dura bleeds, ten minutes in which the first responder stuffs the guts of the dead child back into the abdominal cavity before taking him to Schifa Hospital.

Charles Enderlin says Abu Rahma missed the instant when the boy was hit by the fatal bullet because he had turned off the camera to spare the battery. He couldn't film the ambulance evacuation because he was changing his battery. Having testified that the child martyr spilled his blood for 20 minutes before the ambulance arrived, the France 2 cameraman is saying it took him 25 minutes to change that preciously spared battery.

The journalist and his trusted collaborator testify that the cameraman, who had come to Netzarim Junction around 7 AM, had wound up his report and was about to leave when suddenly he saw the man and the boy in distress.

Subsequently, in an interview with Esther Schapira, author of the film *Three bullets and a dead child*, Talal Abu Rahma said he had filled two cassettes that day.

Two professional cassettes of a total duration of 100 or 120 minutes would be the authentic raw footage. What has become of that footage? Either it never existed or France 2 is hiding it. The fact remains that the figures come from the main witness, Abu Rahma.

Twenty-seven minute, he says? Of what? Of outtakes? No. <u>27 minutes of the al Dura scene</u>. Truth is, during the interview with E. Schapira the 27 minutes boil down to 6. In fact there are only 65 seconds of al Dura images. Ordered by the Court to turn over all the raw footage filmed at Netzarim Junction, on September 30, 2000, France 2 only gave 18 minutes! And they try to make you believe that those who doubt the reliability of Charles Enderlin and Talal Abu Rahma are wacko crank revisionist?

They scribble two lines to justify the absence of raw footage, five words to explain away the absence of signs of wounds, a few sighs over Palestinian suffering and that's supposed to demolish serious precise investigations of every single detail of the alleged news report?

Should we modify the narrative? Make a concession on the duration: the incident only lasted a few minutes. The cameraman who boasts of his qualities as a war reporter missed everything but you have to take his word for it, it was really horrible. Concede on the source of gunfire? Okay, we lied. It's the Palestinian position that was directly facing the unfortunate victims. But we mustn't say it publicly because the Palestinians are very attached to their martyrs.

Not to worry, Maître G. W-R assures us, the child's death throes [*agonie*] are really truly there. Karsenty is mistaken. Mohamed al Dura who turns over, looks at the camera, and resumes his position...that's the death throes. Sorry, dear Maître, but there's someone more maître than you. It's Charles Enderlin! As cited by Nicolas Delesalle, & Marc Belpois, *Télérama* N° 2863 19 November 2004.

"As for the death throes, in fact they do not figure in the France 2 outtakes, as one might think by reading the interview of Enderlin inTélérama in 2000: 'I edited out the child's death throes, it was unbearable...'

A misunderstanding, explains the correspondent: 'The 'agonie' [death throes], is the whole scene of the shootout. We didn't show the whole thing. Besides, running the whole scene would have skewed the balance of the reportage. In the same feature, I also had shots of wounded Israeli soldiers and demonstrations in Hebron.'"

Let's recapitulate: the "*agonie*" (lasting 10 seconds) is no longer the shot of Mohamed declared dead who raises his elbow and looks at the camera (according to some) or else writhes in unbearable pain (according to Maître G. Weill-Raynal). The "*agonie*" [death throes], says Charles Enderlin who is never mistaken, is the whole scene of the shootout, too long and absolutely unbearable. But he did show that "*agonie!*" It's the total of 55 seconds that make up the reportage. All that's missing is 10 seconds... that, we finally understand, is no longer the *agonie*... but...the misunderstanding.

LETTER TO JUDGE TRÉBUCQ

[5/30/08 (translated from the French by the author) I could have simply left this embarrassing letter out of the book. It was private, no one knows it exists. Except for the person I sent it to, Madame Trébucq, presiding judge of the Court of Appeals that had just acquitted Philippe Karsenty. Many years later I learned from a reliable source that Judge Trébucq had ordered presentation of the raw footage because she thought it would clinch the case in favor of France 2! So much for impartial justice. Well, a bit impartial after all. After seeing the outtakes, the 3- judge panel did, however reluctantly, rule in favor of Karsenty. Looking back, I would suppose madame the Judge was more embarrassed to receive this letter than I am to make it public.]

Madame,

An intellectual feat accomplished with finesse and courage deserves recognition, all the more so when it is a feat of justice. I wanted to share with you the enclosed article published in the May 27 edition of the *Wall Street Journal* along with the accompanying editorial that shows the importance given to the Court's verdict.

In an earlier draft I had called the Ruling a masterpiece and you a heroine of the *République*... somewhat excessive expressions that we deleted without, however, erasing all traces.

I hope to have the opportunity in the near future to analyze the Ruling in detail. Impressed from the first broadcast of the al Dura reportage by the inconsistencies of the vidéo and the narrative used to situate it in the realm of reality, I am particularly sensitive to your mastery of the case, demonstrated at every step of the trial and entirely reflected in the Ruling.

Your verdict in favor of the right of citizens to be correctly informed is to your honor and to the honor of your vocation.

Would you kindly let me know if it would be possible, within the framework of your judicial responsibilities, to express yourself publicly about the case in a *Wall Street Journal* interview.

Respectfully yours,

(mme.) Nidra Poller

AL-DURA: THE TIDE IS TURNING
June 22, 2008

The keepers of the Al-Dura myth were caught off balance by the appellate court acquittal, on May 21st, of Philippe Karsenty, convicted of libel by a lower court for declaring that the Al-Dura "death scene" was staged. Had they swallowed the verdict with pained silence, the affair might have dropped back into limbo. But they went public in what looked like a desperate attempt to "settle out of court" or, more exactly, settle without the court by pleading the case in friendly media - at a safe distance from judges, lawyers, and the defendant. It began with plaintiff Charles Enderlin reheating, in the meanderings of his *France Télévision* blog, the arguments that had just been dismissed in the halls of the *Palais de Justice*. Presenting himself as the victim of a seven-year slander campaign, he demonstrated - once again - that there is no journalistic evidence to back up the Al-Dura report. If Enderlin had evidence, he would have presented it seven-and-a-half years ago, when he told the world that Israeli soldiers were heartless child-killers. He would have presented it in 2005, when he and state-owned France 2 TV sued three Web sites with the declared intent of silencing critics. If he had convincing evidence, he would have shown it to the appellate court. In fact, there is nothing left standing of the al Dura news report at the end of the 13-page appellate court ruling (a complete English translation is posted at augeanstables.com The court validated, item by item, all the evidence presented by Philippe Karsenty. This doesn't, however, keep ill-informed commentators from confusing affirmations with evidence, and reiteration with corroboration. And it didn't stop several hundred French journalists from signing "An Appeal for Charles Enderlin" in the upscale leftwing weekly *Nouvel Observateur*. Deaf to the eloquent reaffirmation of journalistic ethics stated in the appellate court ruling, they expressed dismay that the court had granted equal credibility to a scrupulous journalist working under difficult conditions and to his detractors, who - with no experience in conflict-zone reporting - were simply trying to discredit him. Here is Enderlin's defense in a nutshell: "I'm the journalist, you're a nobody. I know everything, you know nothing. If you criticize me, it's slander." Citizen-readers, overwhelmingly critical of this appeal, have greater mastery of the issues than the know-it-all press corps. The Appeal set off an unexpected chain reaction. The Al-Dura affair, which had been kept under wraps by French media, was out in the open and out of control. The Al-Dura myth-keepers are being countered by rational, unemotional arguments from prestigious personalities and a host of voices that have kept silent over the years. Spurred by the *Nouvel Observateur* manifesto, *Radio Communauté Juive* director Shlomo Malka, who had been avoiding the Al-Dura controversy, invited Alain Finkielkraut, a brilliant philosopher who always does his homework, to comment on the case. The obsessively anti-Sarkozy weekly *Marianne* published an op-ed by Eli Barnavi, former Israeli ambassador to France and a darling of highbrow leftists, who spoke out against the appeal. The tide is turning. In dragging the case on to France's highest court, as France 2 and Charles Enderlin have now done, they demonstrate disrespect for the public service they represent. There is good reason to expect that President Sarkozy will step in and ask them to clean house. Though Judge Laurence Trébucq deserves praise for her masterful treatment of the Al-Dura case, it should never have been dragged into court. Litigation places the burden of proof on the citizen, allowing journalists to play fast and loose with information. The Al-Dura hoax is the most egregious, but certainly not the only, example of complicity between Western media and hostile, tainted sources. Once the story, no matter how preposterous, is out there it is engraved in stone, and those who question it are slandered and their characters brought into question. If Enderlin's colleagues were so quick to close ranks, doesn't it suggest that they too want permission to relay unfounded accusations and hide troubling facts from the public? These same media have been sniping at a president elected to modernize French society and institutions. They use skewed news reports to make French people feel poor, miserable and frightened to death; only the Socialist program voters rejected at the polls can calm their anxiety and put this uppity president in his place. A wholly appropriate presidential reprimand of the state-owned network on the Al-Dura issue would be helpful across the board. Before the world starts laughing at 300 French journalists who decided to sink with the ship, it is time to recognize that this is a worldwide issue. Thanks to a wise judge, the French are knocking the Al-Dura affair out of the sand trap where it was doing its dirty work and exposing the lethal equations it generates: You murder our children (Al-Dura) in cold blood = our cold-blooded murder of your civilians. (*Shahid* attacks) are not an atrocity, but self-defense. We will make sure that you cannot defend yourselves without killing our children = you cannot defend yourselves. Consequently, even though your cause is just and your military is mighty, you have to negotiate from a position of weakness, accept our terms and disguise abject surrender as clever diplomacy. Result: Our hollow triumph will condemn still more civilians to death. The Al-Dura affair teaches us that it takes something stronger than *hasbara* - information - to put a stop to this perverse, murderous game.

— *Jerusalem Post*

Chapter 7

LETHAL NARRATIVES:
Weapon of Mass Destruction in the War against the West

On September 30, 2000, state-owned France 2 television channel broadcast a video showing the alleged killing of a 12 year-old Palestinian youth, Mohamed al Dura, and the wounding of his father, Jamal. The ordeal was supposedly filmed as it happened at Netzarim Junction in the Gaza Strip by a France 2 cameraman, later identified as a Palestinian— Talal Abu Rahma. France 2 Jerusalem Bureau chief Charles Enderlin announced, in a dramatic voiceover, that the man and boy were "targets of gunfire from the Israeli position." Seconds later: "Another round of gunfire. The boy is dead, his father is critically wounded." The inflammatory al Dura image triggered an outburst of murderous violence against Jews in Israel and set off the worst wave of anti-Jewish attacks in Europe since the Shoah.

Doubts raised about the authenticity of the news report were pushed aside. In fact, its impact was based <u>on the force of the accusation of child murder</u>, not on the credibility of the images or alleged circumstances. Analysts and investigators have exposed inconsistencies, anomalies, and outright lies but the French network has consistently refused to participate in an honest search for the truth. On the contrary, lawsuits were brought against webmasters of three sites that had taken a stand on the controversy or simply posted articles about it. The avowed intent of the suits was to silence critics once and for all but the case against Philippe Karsenty backfired when the media watchdog appealed his defamation conviction. In May 2008 the appeals court ruled in his favor.

But the al Dura hoax clings stubbornly to the public mind. My extensive experience with this thorny issue, which began with a letter to the editors published by the International Herald Tribune in October 2000, led me to the broader question of "lethal narratives," a term I coined to describe a formidable weapon that interferes with the rational thinking that is essential to Western civilization. In trying to understand why people could not reason about the al Dura news report I came to see how the same method of lethal narratives kept them from reasoning about the Arab-Israeli conflict, the war in Iraq...and global jihad.

Global jihad, like the Qur'an itself, is timeless and uncreated. Pressing forward or hanging back according to circumstances, it remains focused on the ultimate objective of bringing the entire world into a state of submission to Allah. The Khomeinist revolution that led to the establishment of the Islamic Republic of Iran marks the contemporary revival of jihad conquest. Khomeini lived like a head of state in exile at Neauphle-le-Château France for a year before his triumphant return to Iran in 1979. Three decades later Iran is developing nuclear weapons to fulfill its vow to destroy Israel and exterminate the Jews. The al Dura hoax, presented by France 2 as a legitimate news broadcast, prepared the way for worldwide acceptance of genocidal Jew hatred.

The fleeting video—less than one-minute—of the al Dura incident does not meet the minimum requirements for a news report. The visual contradicts the audio, the backup story is full of contradictions, the eyewitnesses are found to be liars, and Charles Enderlin, the France 2 journalist who lent credibility to the report filed by his Palestinian cameraman, has never provided a shred of corroborating evidence. On the contrary, voluminous evidence shows that the France 2 / Palestinian production was a crudely staged fake.

And yet the poster-style image of Mohamed al Dura crouching behind his father is indelibly engraved in the public mind. Among the innumerable uses of the al Dura image by jihadis, we will cite an Osama bin Laden recruiting video and the filmed beheading of WSJ journalist Daniel Pearl in which the al Dura scene is interspliced as justification. Weren't we told that Guantanamo is a major recruiting tool? So, if bin Laden latched on to the al Dura incident to recruit for 9/11, he must have known Guantanamo was in the cards. This a posteori reasoning sounds ridiculous but, as I will explain, lethal narratives obliterate notions of chronology, cause and effect...the very logic that is essential to Western rationality. Charles Enderlin justified the hasty airing of the al Dura video by the fact that so many children were killed in the conflict. But the staged al Dura shooting preceded—and actually kicked off—the military onslaught launched by PA leader Yasser Arafat two months after the failed Camp David talks where he turned down the offer of that state without which, we are told, Palestinians cannot become peaceful. *Shahid* operations— misnamed suicide attacks—killed over a thousand Israeli civilians, maimed 5,000, and brought grief to tens of thousands of families.

Why was it so easy, 60 years after the Shoah, to commit atrocities against Jews and get away with it? The staged death of Mohamed al Dura, a twenty-first century international blood libel, justifies the real cold-blooded murder and planned annihilation of Jews. But, we are told, ten times more Palestinians than Israelis were killed. And we are asked to believe that tens of thousands of Muslims killed in Iraq are victims of America's war, fomented by the despised George W. Bush. These lopsided body counts serve to justify Muslim attacks on our civilians.

The victims are not "collateral damage," they are weapons used by cowards who do not fight soldier to soldier, who hide in bunkers and deliberately provoke civilian casualties to delegitimize our cause. Yes, the ostentatiously displayed bloody bodies—preferably of children— are weapons in the hands of cowards.

BEYOND PROPAGANDA

We hear that the Palestinians are good at PR and propaganda. That Israel is losing the war of words and images. We are told we must use our smarts, improve *hasbara* (information), counter dis- and misinformation. And meanwhile, global jihad advances inexorably, widens its scope, conquers territory. And we cannot even convince people in the free world that we are—whether we like it or not—at war. The very opposite is happening. The United States of America, a great military power with a tradition of defending freedom and fighting to victory, is now governed by a president who lulled them with a "pretend we're not at war" campaign. This unmitigated disaster is tragically underestimated in most quarters, even as the consequences befall us. With a purveyor of lethal narratives at the helm, the ship of state is sailing full speed into the arms of global jihad.

We are told that our magnificent armed forces cannot win an asymmetrical war against "insurgents, militants, guerilla fighters, national liberation warriors..." This is ridiculous. Poorly-armed ill-trained jihadis who brutalize the civilians that fall under their sway and are incapable of fighting soldier to soldier can win only if we tie our own hands behind our back. If we fight to win, they will lose. Meanwhile they soften us up with lethal narratives...while advancing their nuclear weapons programs.

Our enemy is united in the umma, submissive to sharia law, waging jihad by every means possible on every level of our societies and we react piecemeal to each incident, separating every theater of war, imagining every Iranian proxy as a distinct entity with specific grievances that should be addressed compassionately.

The Palestinians strike Israel, get battered, and run crying to international opinion. It always works. In July 2000, world media placed the blame squarely on Yasser Arafat for refusing the 2-state solution offered by then Prime Minister Ehud Barak with the blessings of President Clinton. Two months later the lethal narrative kicked in. "Palestinian children are being killed...in cold blood, like Mohamed al Dura." Ten times more Palestinian casualties than Israeli casualties... the new definition of unjust war. That cockeyed narrative explained away the most atrocious, extensive, inexcusable violence against Israeli civilians. When the Israeli army finally moved forcefully to put an end to that killing spree, we were served the Jenin massacre hoax. In June 2006 the Gaza Beach massacre hoax was staged to justify the subsequent cross-border attack in which several Israeli soldiers were killed and Gilad Shalit was abducted. Three years later Shalit is still held hostage under inhumane conditions. Where are the champions of the Geneva Convention? The Israeli soldier was not captured in action, he was kidnapped within undisputed Israeli territory.

Where are the two-state solutioners? On July 12th, Hizbullah attacked from Lebanon. Rockets were fired into Israel all along the border. Several Israeli soldiers were murdered, Ehud Goldwasser and Eldad Regev were abducted and later killed or left to die. Two days after the Israeli riposte to an unprovoked Hizbullah attack, then French President Jacques Chirac declared a humanitarian crisis in Lebanon and demanded an immediate ceasefire.

Despite conclusive evidence of staged news—the famous "fauxtography"— the narrative of Israel's disproportionate response and wanton killing of Lebanese civilians prevailed. The dubious Qan'a massacre—provoked or fabricated—brought international opinion to a paroxysm of empathy with the Lebanese, Hizbullah included. French foreign minister Philippe Douste-Blazy danced Condoleeza Rice into UN Security Council Resolution 1701 that handed Hizbullah virtual control of Lebanon.

Accusations of deliberate killing of civilians arise wherever we act to defend ourselves. Recent reports that 140 Afghan villagers were killed in a raid by U.S. forces were followed by a series of unconfirmed unverifiable details and the inevitable photos of hastily covered bodies. Investigators risked their lives to go into enemy-held territory rife with snipers in an effort to find out if the dead were 100% civilians, Taliban-sympathizers or, perhaps, unfortunate victims led into the area by the Taliban precisely to be targets of the provoked air strike. How can we prove that U.S. military personnel are not ruthless murderers who deliberately aim at helpless villagers for the pleasure of killing women and children? Meanwhile the Taliban enforce sharia with savage methods and no one investigates.

Jihad fighters in Iraq, Afghanistan, Pakistan, Somalia, and Gaza are transformed into hapless civilians when they die in battles that they provoked. When they are captured, as in the case of the Guantanamo prisoners, the lethal narrative strategy turns them into prisoners of war protected by the Geneva Convention, quasi-citizens deserving of due process, or oppressed minorities deprived of their civil rights. Our moral integrity cannot be judged by the way we handle ruthless fighters who do not respect the laws of war.

They have their own laws. Fighters dress as civilians, attack civilians in their own and in the enemy camp, live among civilians, keep their women and children with them in the heat of battle, deliberately attack from residential areas to provoke counterattacks that will kill civilians, display bloodied mutilated corpses—civilian or military, who can tell—as weapons in the lethal narrative strategy. This month, Taliban in Pakistan shaved their beards, dressed in neutral clothes, and slipped in among the refugees fleeing their brutal rule and trying to escape the crossfire of hypothetical battles with regular Pakistani forces allegedly rooting them out.

Instead of comprehending the overall situation we are dealing case by case with endless examples and persistently attributing our own criteria to an enemy that is playing by utterly different rules. This not only jeopardizes our self-defense on the ground, it subverts the very rationality that defines our civilization and preserves our precious freedom. Logic is not an affectation for intellectuals. It is our light, our backbone, our invincible weapon.

FROM THE AL DURA BLOOD LIBEL TO THE SURRENDER OF AMERICAN POWER

The staged al Dura death scene has been analyzed, investigated, and exposed by, among others, Israeli physicist Nahum Shahaf, Israeli journalists Amnon Lord and Stéphane Juffa, French author and psychoanalyst Gérard Huber, World Net Daily journalist Daniel Kupelian, German TV producer Esther Schapira, Boston University professor Richard Landes, and French media watchdog Philippe Karsenty. Shortly after the al Dura report was aired Tony & Alex Faigenbaum, Monique & Gérard Sander, and Pierre Rehov tried to sue France 2 for false accusations but the French court refused to hear the case. Since winning his appeal in May 2008 Philippe Karsenty has been showing his streamlined convincing presentation of the al Dura hoax to influential people, small groups, and large audiences all over the world. I myself have written extensively about the al Dura affair in *Commentary Magazine*, the *Wall Street Journal, Jerusalem Post, Makor Rishon, National Post*, and *PJ Media*.

My experience with irrational reactions to elucidation of the al Dura hoax led me to formulate the concept of lethal narratives. The video has been dissected millimeter by millimeter. There is so much documentation that hardly anyone can absorb and assimilate it all. When an informed analyst presents an exposé of the al Dura myth—in person or in the media— objections are inevitably raised by people who know close to nothing about the affair. Their memories of the original news broadcast are faulty and they have never even heard of the background stories that were put out at the time and then withdrawn piece by piece as their blatant falsehood was exposed. People feel free to defend the al Dura myth by repeating baseless assertions and flimsy arguments thoroughly demolished by meticulous investigators.

Invited to present the affair to a Paris bar association workshop, I thought that lawyers would be interested to know that the testimony of the sole witnesses to the alleged shooting—the Palestinian cameraman and the surviving victim, Jamal al Dura—is demonstrably unreliable. Isn't that how lawyers try to get at the truth? The witnesses and the journalist who produced the news broadcast endlessly repeat an obviously concocted story that doesn't hold water. Nothing they say is corroborated by the video evidence. Every detail of their account clashes with other elements of their story. As I spoke to the lawyers, the iconic al Dura image appeared on a screen—Jamal al Dura and the boy crouched behind a concrete culvert, their features twisted in a melodramatic grimace. I said, "There is nothing shocking about this image..." Before I could go on to explain how the voice-off commentary transformed a patently staged and static image into a heart-rending story, a gentleman called out from the audience. "Yes it is shocking! The death of a child is always shocking!"

Well, you'd rather have this lawyer defending your opponent than yourself in court. But then again, in a French court he might win.

Debunkers of the al Dura myth are attacked with ignorant, snide objections and aggressive ad hominem arguments. The sheer weight of the evidence is thrown in one's face as proof of dubious credibility, and the fact that this affair has dragged out for nine years—because of the refusal of France 2 to cooperate—is held as proof that the debunkers are cantankerous fools who don't know when to stop. Current France 2 news director Arlette Chabot, who found the al Dura affair on her desk when she took over in 2004 and has had the decency to partially re-examine the evidence, complained: "These people ask questions, we reply, and they ask more questions."

That used to be called investigation!

Why not just drop the issue...after all this time? Isn't it over and done with, too late to correct even if the news report was falsified? Far from over and done with, the al Dura hoax is still active and virulent. The falsified cold-blooded murder of the Palestinian youth is still injecting its poison into the bloodstream of potential shahids eager to use their bodies as weapons to kill Jews. The al Dura blood libel provoked and justified the murder of Israeli civilians and attacks on Jews worldwide. This massive contemporary injection vivifies and intensifies the eternal systemic Islamic Jew hatred. Genocidal Palestinian violence is not inspired by suffering and despair. It is not a reaction to Israel's "violation of international law." It is not a forceful way of requesting a two-state solution. It is sheer unmitigated boundless hatred.

Vibrantly alive in the Arab-Muslim world, half-forgotten elsewhere, the al Dura blood libel is a factor in the passive tolerance of Ahmadinejad's genocidal determination backed up by Iran's looming nuclear capacity. Global jihad meets feeble resistance in societies softened by lethal narratives. The forces of evil get traction by attacking Israel and the Jews. As the target widens to include the full range of "infidels" the faulty reasoning that justified atrocities against Jews remains in place...as planned. And the second-level victims find themselves defenseless, because the Jews were in fact their shield and not the cause of Muslim anger.

In the current controversy over alleged torture of US prisoners, the Bush administration has been compared to the Inquisition. The comparison is misplaced. We the people of the free world are in fact subject to a jihadist variation on the Inquisition. We are attacked militarily and then accused of misdeeds, crimes, and sins. Hostages from our camp are tortured, burned alive or beheaded, their humiliation and pain are exhibited in unbearable videos...and we are accused of illegal uncivilized behavior. Ill-conceived apologies from our side are pocketed with no benefits for the apologetics; and we are pressured for new, deeper, wider, more radical apologies. The screws are tightened. Our crimes fall into a bottomless pit. We are in a dither, running to answer for each accusation, getting further and further from the simple truth that would save us:

We are at war. Our enemy wishes to destroy us. We must fight back.

This is not an over-simplification. It is not a frivolous personal opinion. It is the conclusion that is reached when one gathers all relevant evidence and organizes it logically. Rational thinking leads to this conclusion. We cannot defend our freedom if we do not maintain our capacity to think rationally. Our overwhelming military advantage is undermined when we succumb to stories of our own sinfulness. As we see in the current debate, self-defense is no longer accepted as justification for the harsh interrogation methods that the situation imposes. And when we treat our jihadi prisoners with kid gloves and tender loving care, the hypocritical moralizers immediately find something else to condemn. Self-defense is not even a category. It doesn't enter into the equation because this controversy is not taking place on the plane of reality but in a mythological domain created by lethal narratives in which there is no distinction between war and peace, friends and enemies, options and necessities...

Let us look once more at the al Dura myth and see how it operates. It begins with an emotional sting—the death of the Palestinian youth "targeted by gunfire from the Israeli position" (dixit Charles Enderlin). The video of this scene, which lasts less than one minute, is so patently false that it cannot stand up to the barest objective examination. Remove the voice-off, take away the emotional sting, lift the incident out of the context of the Arab-Israeli conflict, and the broadcast would be the laughing stock of 21st century television. The scene is so obviously fabricated that many who defend the al Dura story admit as much and then go on to justify it as a faithful illustration of the "situation." The situation being the death of Palestinian children caught in the conflict? No! The situation illustrated by the al Dura video is the <u>cold-blooded murder of Palestinian children by heartless Israelis.</u>

Compare this to waterboarding. The emotional sting=Americans are meting out torture. Torture is wrong. This wrong must not only be discontinued and punished, it must be rubbed like salt into the wound of our evil hearts and souls. That accusation is not substantiated by rational argument but by repetition. Instead of a rational debate on the ethical dilemmas raised in the context of a new kind of warfare waged by jihadis who explicitly reject our laws, including the laws of war, we are battered with this damning accusation. And we are told, from the highest places, that our inexcusable mistreatment of prisoners jeopardizes the safety of our own military personnel that will be—what can you expect?— mistreated in turn. How can such an outlandish statement be made in public? There is not a shred of evidence to substantiate it, there are tons of evidence that contradict it, but in the mythical world of lethal narratives, as we saw with the al Dura hoax, we do not look at the evidence. We do not verify statements. We do not make ethical clarifications. We dash from one emotional precipice to another. Look at how violently they attack us! Isn't that proof of the wrong we have done?

Chronology is reversed, cause and effect are disconnected, details are tossed around like confetti instead of being rationally articulated. The broad picture is never outlined, we never get down to the essentials, there is no sense of priorities. The preposterous becomes accepted wisdom. Those who contradict it are slandered and marginalized. Take [Mark] Silverman's snide, arrogant, ignorant, and baseless article about this symposium [in the Tennessean]. Set aside the fact that the people speaking here have investigated, analyzed, and studied more than Silverman could ever comprehend if he did knuckle down and make a serious effort. He doesn't have to get serious. All he would have to do is wrest himself out of the grip of the lethal narratives he parrots. He doesn't agree with us about Islam? Fine. But why can't he debate the issues like an adult? Because the notion of blasphemy has crept into our society by every door and window. Normal critical faculties are stymied by sharia precepts that have been surreptitiously knitted into the fabric of our societies by a combination of seduction and intimidation.

Preposterous accusations are pumped into the information stream and purified as they move from the source to the relays—academics, opinion-makers, politicians, community organizers—that deliver them in the trappings of normalcy. The raucous blood-curdling shouts of pro-Hamas foot soldiers storming through European cities were hidden from view of the general public by media that deliberately refrained from reporting on them. Later, the "Death to the Jews, Death to Israel" theme reappears in deceivingly civilized newspaper articles about the moderate Mahmoud Abbas who has courageously, against great odds, prepared his society for peaceful coexistence. But, the story goes, as long as Israel pursues the expansion of settlements that eat away at territory that should be "returned" to the Palestinians, chances are slim of finding a peaceful solution to a conflict that has endured for sixty years.

The notion of a Mideast conflict caused by Israeli usurpation of Palestinian lands is a lethal narrative concocted to disguise Islamic determination to eliminate the Jewish State and kill the Jews. Our enemies state their real aims and purposes in no uncertain terms. And there is no valid evidence of the imaginary desire for a state that supposedly explains away every evil committed by Arab-Muslim forces for the past sixty years. The "illegal war in Iraq" that has caused such deep misunderstanding between the U.S., our European allies, and the Arab-Muslim world is another lethal narrative that serves to deprive the free world of its military might and leave us vulnerable to conquest.

Time is running out! We are falling behind. We have lost so much ground that if this were a conventional war with soldiers on battlefields it would be obvious that our backs are to the wall. We will either wake up and fight our way out, miraculously, or resign ourselves to defeat.

Time is running out. The once proud once free United States of America is baring its breast to a ruthless enemy and whispering "take me!"

But...

Democracies are not suicidal. Healthy forces of self-defense will mobilize and prevail. Thinking straight is a prelude to victory.

New English Review Symposium
5/30/09 Nashville, Tennessee

UN ENFANT EST MORT [A CHILD IS DEAD]:
We're not invited to toast Charles Enderlin's definitive al Dura production

10/06/10 Ten years after the blockbuster "Killing of Mohamed al Dura" film was brought to the world by Charles Enderlin under the aegis of state-owned France 2 TV, the book version is about to hit the shelves...with a whimper. Why?

No one can forget the dramatic "news broadcast" that placed the "dead child" at the feet of viewers worldwide, unleashing waves of Jew hatred on a scale not seen since the Shoah. *A las cinco de la tarde...* 3 PM... shootout at Netzarim Junction... Mohamed is twelve years old... one last burst of gunfire...the child is dead..." Blood libel on a planetary scale. The brief—under one minute—video shot at Netzarim junction in the Gaza Strip on a day of anger organized by Israel's enemies and dutifully relayed by Western media, has been astutely analyzed, exposed as a fake, dragged into the French courts, defended by Enderlin's hierarchy and the majority of his French colleagues... What is left to be said?

My email request for a review copy left unrequited, I phoned the don Quichotte (French for Don Quixote) publishing house to ask if I could stop by and pick up a copy. The receptionist—who is apparently also press attaché, editor, publisher, and Enderlin's bodyguard—replied that it would be impossible. Might I be on a blacklist, guilty of having written extensively about the al Dura hoax? Declining her offer to mail a copy that would arrive, if ever, a week after the October 7 release, I inquired about the launch. Not that I expected an invitation...

There will be no launch, no book party, no press conference, no pride and joy. After all, a child is dead.

I jokingly remarked that I was jealous of Pierre Haski who has already reviewed the book for the *Rue89* website. "We made a very restricted distribution of review copies. I don't know why you think you should have received one." I defend my reputation: "I'm one of the few journalists based in France writing for English-speaking media."

True. I've written about the al Dura affair for, among others, *Commentary* and the *Wall Street Journal*. Which is why I didn't get a review copy and find myself in even hotter water as this curious conversation comes to a boil. "Will you be posting information," I ask, "about public appearances, TV and radio broadcasts...?"

"No we will not! I know very well why you ask me for that information! No! We are not going to publicize his public appearances!"

Phew. The phone is burning. I honestly don't know why she thinks I should know why she knows I want to know. It's only later that I realize she thinks I might turn up to assault monsieur journalist Charles Enderlin... with a legitimate question. In a world hooked on PR where writers and publishers will die for a bit of high profile publicity, this quixotic publisher seems to be terrified that some uncontrollable element might dare to express an opinion about the untouchable book.

"Actually, I would just like to know so I won't miss the programs."

"He was on *Les 4 vérités* [*France 2 TV*] this morning."

"*Très bien*. I'll catch it online."

Quatre vérités means more than "4 truths"; it's the whole truth. On this episode of the whole truth show, Roland Sicard serves Charles Enderlin like an impeccably polite waiter in a posh restaurant. Sicard swallows whole whatever his colleague Enderlin offers to plug the holes in the al Dura story. It's worth watching, even if you don't understand a word of French. [pluzz.fr/les-4-verites-2010-10-05-07h45]

They actually begin with a rerun of the al Dura "death scene" originally aired at prime time on that fateful September 30, 2000. Sicard innocently asks how the report became controversial. Monsieur journalist Charles Enderlin calmly explains how, two months after the incident, Israeli army officials concluded that the gunfire more likely came from the Palestinian position. Curiously enough, says Enderlin, one of the two experts on that commission had declared only two days after the broadcast that it was a staged scene.

In urbane tones—several levels below the dramatic voiceover that convinced the world of the deliberate murder of a Palestinian child by Israeli soldiers—Charles Enderlin tells how the absurd notion that the killing was a staged scene became internet buzz, eventually picked up by—unnamed— personalities, and finally blossomed into a full blown conspiracy theory. Upon which, with a paradoxical dose of mockery, France 2's eternal Jerusalem correspondent unwittingly describes what happened that day:

Conspiracy theorists would have us believe that 24 hours after the start of the Intifada, Palestinians brought together hundreds of people to play act, the boy and his father play acted, the scene in the Jordanian hospital was faked and the blood seeping from the father's wounds was ketchup. "Francis Ford Coppola in Gaza! Harumph."

It's true: Dozens if not hundreds of Palestinians were organized to play act combat scenes — totally out of firing range of Israeli soldiers, complete with fake injuries and comical ambulance evacuations. All of this was captured on raw footage from Reuters and other agencies whose Palestinian fixers, including Talal Abu Rahma, can be seen filming these vignettes.

Did Enderlin ever doubt the sincerity of his cameraman? Of course not. Talal has worked with France 2 for years. He won several prizes for this reportage. Following a request for clarifications from monsieur Enderlin, the Shin Beth cleared the cameraman of all suspicion: "He's white as the driven snow. He doesn't belong to any anti-Israel organization."

Timidly taking the initiative (perhaps he was told to ask one tricky question) Sicard wonders if the al Dura controversy is more intense in Israel or France. Enderlin replies with a yes, no, yes, no, adding that there is also a campaign against him in the United States. Then, waxing philosophical, he sums up the "war of images" theme: "When an image makes trouble for Israel, Israel makes trouble for the image."

The strategy is transparent. We can expect to see it employed in Enderlin's book and reflected in forthcoming friendly reviews and interviews. It requires an iron grip on all elements of this staged debate in which every detail must be kept slightly out of focus. Counting on the real or feigned ignorance of the journalistic class and the impossibility of making dissenting voices heard in mainstream French media, every question will be placed just far enough beside the point to maintain the overall blur. No precise detail of the meticulous investigations that have exposed the al Dura hoax will ever be mentioned. No precise objection will ever be answered. Questioned about the authenticity of the video, Enderlin and his handmaidens will always reply with attacks on those who question it. He will lump them together as conspiracy theorists even as he weaves <u>them</u> into his very own conspiracy theory.

Falsehoods about the falsified killing of a young man portrayed as a child, the better to accuse Jews of blood libel, will be smoothed like butter on Enderlin's bread. Any one equipped to call him on these falsehoods will be pushed aside and dismissed. Elisabeth Lévy [causeur.fr] asks when Charles is going to explain himself on the "death throes." "He said he edited out the death throes, it was too horrible to show. But in fact there is no footage of death throes." Journalist François Gross snaps back: "They don't save all the raw footage."

False, of course. They did save the raw footage. Enderlin testified, under oath, that it was kept in a safe. He turned over (some of it) in compliance with a court order. Lo and behold, there is no raw footage of the al Dura death scene. Nothing more than the snippet aired on September 30th and forever after. Everyone knows by now that the so-called death throes are in fact the few seconds where the boy, allegedly dead, moves and looks at the camera. Further, Enderlin claimed some years later that the "death throes" are the whole incident from beginning to end (allegedly 45 minutes), the complete footage (allegedly 27 minutes). But why should François Gross possess such useless information?

Officially there will be no launch of *Un enfant est mort*. For all we know, a lovely cocktail party will be held behind closed doors, in the presence of a smiling Talal Abu Rahma and an aggrieved Jamal al Dura. Champagne and petit-fours, knowing winks and pats on the back. Worldly smiles and blasé sighs. But I'm not invited and neither are you.

What surprises me, actually, is that the book will be sold on the open market. Knowing the methods of the al Dura affair, I would expect it to be restricted to True Believers. Will I have to prove my good faith when I walk into a bookstore tomorrow and fork up 18 euros for the ultimate smokescreen?

— *Makor Rishon*
— *New English Review*

ENDERLIN, CHARLES. UN ENFANT EST MORT
October 2010.
[Un enfant est mort/ Netzarim, 30 septembre 2000. *Don Quichotte Éditions*] On the 10th anniversary of the dramatic al Dura news broadcast, Charles Enderlin, Jerusalem correspondent of state-owned France 2 TV, has published his defense of the controversial video that was broadcast hours after the alleged shooting "from the Israeli position" of a Palestinian child and his father at Netzarim Junction in the Gaza Strip on September 30, 2000. "The boy is dead," announced Enderlin in voiceover, "and his father is critically wounded." Mohamed al Dura instantly became the poster boy of the "Al Aqsa Intifada" and, simultaneously, the focus of controversy. Enderlin is blamed by some for hastily relaying the unfounded accusation that Israeli soldiers intentionally shot a Palestinian child. Others maintain that the French-Israeli journalist passed off a crudely staged Palestinian fabrication as a piece of legitimate journalism.

Presenting himself as the victim of a growing number of believers in a "Palestinian conspiracy theory," monsieur Enderlin has unwittingly crafted a springboard text that exposes his own twisted arguments and questionable motives. The tone is petty, petulant, and disingenuous. He usurps the nobility of his adversaries by citing, in an epigraph, Jean Jaurès in praise of the search for the truth and the courage to tell it. Blithely declining responsibility for the exploitation of the al Dura "murder" by extremists (e.g. the beheading of Daniel Pearl), the France 2 journalist blames his critics for everything from affronts and persecution—for example, the unfair treatment of his daughter when she passed her *baccalauréat* orals— to death threats against him and his family.

The argument can be summarized as follows:

The al Dura broadcast is impeccable news reporting. The two eyewitnesses—France 2 cameraman Talal Abu Rahma and the aggrieved father,

Jamal al Dura—are above suspicion. Minor contradictions in their testimony or in the video report should be chalked up to the grueling conditions of armed conflict. There is no legitimate reason to criticize the report. Consequently, anyone who expresses doubts about its authenticity is guilty of disgraceful partisan motivations or stupid belief in conspiracy theories. Talal, Jamal, Palestinian authorities and medical personnel have always told the truth about the incident. The Israeli army—systematically guilty of bungled operations and disproportionate violence against Palestinian protestors—issues cynical communiqués to cover up its misdeeds. Yasser Arafat was unjustly blamed for the failure of the July 2000 Camp David negotiations. The Intifada was a spontaneous popular uprising, not a premeditated coordinated PA attack against Israel. Media that publish articles sympathetic to the "conspiracy theory" are right-wing, neo-conservative, opposed to peace, and sympathetic to the "colonization movement." Doubts about the al Dura video are deliberately fabricated by "communitarian" Jews to undermine the reputation of Charles Enderlin whose objective reporting challenges their one-sided parochial view of the conflict. These Jews want to prove the Palestinians are not partners for peace, so they claim the al Dura scene was staged to incite Palestinian violence. None of the experts cited by critics of the al Dura report are qualified; only the specialists cited by Charles Enderlin are worthy of the title. Many analysts have reached conclusions about the controversial report without giving Enderlin, Abu Rahma, or Jamal al Dura the last word. Accusations of media bias against Israel are unfounded. Israel has only itself to blame for its ever worsening image.

As the bodies of Palestinian victims of "disproportionate Israeli force," pile up from page to page, Charles Enderlin shoots down his critics with a barrage of insults. Lesser known targets of his ire are dismissed as crackpots spewing nonsense on "communitarian" websites of ill repute, while high profile intellectuals, diplomats, scientists, and journalists are roundly scolded for swallowing the conspiracy theory. *Commentary, Atlantic Monthly, Jeune Afrique, the Wall Street Journal, International Herald Tribune, Weekly Standard*, and Fox News are thrown onto the garbage heap along with online outlets such as *Metula News Agency, Guysen Israel News, AtlasShrugs, FrontPage Magazine*... And there's the rub!

Charles Enderlin doesn't seem to realize that the names, numbers, and prestige are stacking up against him. And if there's a conspiracy theorist in the lot, it is monsieur Enderlin himself. The writers, thinkers, and officials he discredits are not united in an ignoble campaign to destroy Charles Enderlin's reputation; they are inspired by the honest conviction, based on ample evidence, that the al Dura news report is flawed or an outright fabrication. He dismisses us (I am proud to be included) as naïvely misled by material we can't understand (raw footage shot by other cameramen on that fateful day) misinterpreted by dubious sources and analyzed with ulterior motives. But his own fragile arguments are built on shaky testimony from two sources—Talal Abu Rahma and Jamal al Dura—contradicted by doctors at Shifa Hospital, and undermined by ludicrous statements from three or four journalists allegedly present at Netzarim Junction that day.

Un enfant est mort is the work of a nose-to-the-grindstone journalist who lacks the inner voice of a writer who hears his own words, revises, refines, and shapes a coherent whole. Monsieur Enderlin, who pretends he has [p. 123-4] "... no problem with critics who wonder what happened that day at Netzarim. But we have been insulted, we've been called liars," insults everyone who dares to disagree with him.

Repeatedly showing himself to be an intellectual lightweight, he throws verbal rocks at his critics, haughtily discredits their experts, and then gives another hoax, the June 2006 Gaza Beach "massacre," as an example of Israeli trickery. The army investigation that concluded Israel was not responsible for the attack, he says, was invalidated by an— unnamed— Human Rights Watch expert... who happens to be Mark Galasco, recently unmasked as an expert collector of Nazi memorabilia. The France 2 journalist, borrowing from a shoddy Canal + (French pay-to-view channel) "documentary," gives the "elders of Zion" treatment to a symposium on the theme of blood libel organized by a distinguished academic, Shmuel Trigano.

Unable to explain away the facts attested by Dr Yehuda David, who operated on Jamal in 1994, monsieur Enderlin scolds the surgeon for revealing private medical records. Are we, then, to swallow garbled explanations from doctors at Shifa Hospital and conclude that Dr. David is lying when he testifies that Jamal al Dura's scars were inflicted when he was slashed and stabbed in Gaza in 1992 and not, as he now claims, by Israeli gunfire in September 2000?

Un enfant est mort is the latest in a series of retellings of an al Dura tale elaborated to accompany the incident and repeatedly revised over the years. Here, as in earlier attempts, the pseudo-elucidation of the facts chokes on two bones: duration and intention. Jamal and Talal repeatedly insist on a 45-minute duration for the alleged ordeal, whereas the total al Dura footage runs for approximately 52 seconds. This leaves a credibility deficit of approximately 2,648 seconds between the 45 minutes that measure the cruelty of Israeli soldiers relentlessly firing on a sitting target and the 52 seconds of furtive images of the man and the boy. Here is how Enderlin explains the curious absence of raw footage of the actual al Dura scene:

[p.55] "During the 45-minute crossfire [sic]...Talal did not film continuously; as a good news cameraman he filmed Jamal and Mohamed al Dura in 5 takes of nine to twenty-nine seconds, at intervals impossible to determine. He was at the end of a tape and his battery was wearing out."

The astute cameraman, who knew from the instant he spotted the man and boy cringing against a wall that he had to make his battery last until the end of a long sequence, missed every bullet that allegedly hit the victims, including the final fatal shot. He could not film the twenty-minute (or, in another version, one-hour) agonizing wait before an ambulance could evacuate the wounded...because he was changing the battery. Is this why he felt the necessity to testify under oath, three days after the incident, to the Palestinian Center for Human Rights? Israeli soldiers, he declared, murdered the boy and wounded the father intentionally, in cold blood. After the five-minute crossfire, Israelis fired directly at the boy and man for 45 minutes without interruption, says Abu Rahma, specifying that he filmed 27 minutes of the fusillade. As an experienced war photographer he could attest the Israeli outpost was the only position from which the boy and the man could be hit.

For years Charles Enderlin and his hierarchy have been trying to smudge this troublesome testimony. Monsieur Enderlin has no qualms today about omitting the "intentional, in cold blood" parts and pretending the cameraman simply said he thought the gunfire came from the Israeli position. How often do experienced war photographers supplement their reports with testimony under oath?

Having swept a mountain of incongruities under the rug, Charles Enderlin explains [p.197] that certain people are trying to "sink" him because he contradicts official propaganda that demonizes Yasser Arafat and blames him for refusing Ehud Barak's so-called generous offer of a Palestinian State at Camp David in July 2000. Israeli officials, he claims—against all evidence—try to discredit the al Dura report because it shows them as they are: trigger happy, dishonest, and careless with Palestinian lives. Partisan Jews, he says, embarrassed by the misdeeds of the Israeli army, moan and groan about so-called biased media coverage of the conflict, and raise the specter of "blood libel" in order to accuse Europe and its media of anti-Semitism.

Why, after the exposure of so many manipulative media fakes—Lebanese fauxtography, the Jenin massacre, the Gaza blackout—would a seasoned journalist, backed by his hierarchy, colleagues, and government (Charles Enderlin was awarded the Légion d'honneur this summer) persist in defending a flawed news report that should never have been broadcast? Why do so many people still believe the report is authentic, while still others, half-heartedly admitting the scene is a fake, defend it "because Israeli soldiers killed so many children off camera?"

"This factual sober narrative is written in the style of the major investigations that have earned Charles Enderlin, here both actor and witness, a reputation as an internationally acclaimed specialist of the Israel-Palestine conflict." This is how the book jacket packages the muddle of discrepancies, loose ends, ad hominem attacks, and distortions of a self-serving document that unwittingly reveals the key to the al Dura hoax.

The first clue is in the title: *Un enfant est mort*, a child is dead, the unmitigated pathos of a generic universal tragedy divorced from circumstances. A child is dead. Don't ask questions. React with emotion to the emotional blow. How do we know Mohamed al Dura was shot by Israeli soldiers that day? We know because his death is so terrible. Is his father telling the truth? How could he not be trustworthy? Look at his terror, his desperation, his grief. Did Charles Enderlin, perhaps...maybe...it does happen...make a mistake? Was he fooled by his cameraman? Impossible. He's internationally acclaimed.

The "cold-blooded murder of Mohamed al Dura" is the flimsiest and, at the same time, the most damning indictment of Israel and the Jews since the Shoah. Charles Enderlin claims that we want to demolish the al Dura news report because it illustrates and confirms an objective analysis of Israel's responsibility for prolonging and intensifying the conflict.

The opposite is true. The overarching narrative of the Arab-Israeli conflict is elaborated along the same principles as the al Dura blood libel. The Oslo Peace Process, the 2006 Hizbullah war, the Cast Lead operation, the Mavi Marmara incident, the construction of homes for Jewish residents of disputed territories, all the clashes, incidents, decisions, and background are reported with the same disregard for facts and appeal to emotion that marks the al Dura "death scene."

Recognition that the al Dura news report does not respect the minimum standards of free-world journalism could be the first step in restoring rational, factual, enlightened analysis of the Arab-Israeli conflict and its connection to a worldwide conflict with Islamic jihad. This is why some of us are devoted to exposing the hoax, and others cannot relinquish it.

— *Scholars for Peace in the Middle East*

A RETOOLED LIBEL

[page references in parentheses]

30 September 2000, Netzarim Junction in the Gaza Strip. State-owned France 2 TV airs footage of the allegedly fatal shooting, in real time, of a Palestinian youth and the critical wounding of his father, "targeted by gunfire from the Israeli position." The news report, distributed free of charge to international media, created the icon of the Second Intifada, Muhammad al-Dura.

Ten years after the controversial al-Dura news broadcast triggered – and helped justify – a worldwide onslaught of anti-Jewish violence, Charles Enderlin, the France 2 Jerusalem correspondent who produced the report, has published a book-length defense in which he portrays himself as the victim of far-right, ultra-Zionist Likudnik conspiracy theorists determined to undermine his role as a speaker of Middle East-conflict truth.

Dramatizing the threats and insults he endured at the hands of these enemies, the journalist minimizes the atrocities committed in the name of the shahid al-Dura (37). Although the Jerusalem correspondent acknowledges a radical increase in anti-Semitic acts perpetrated in France from October to December 2000 (43) [1] attributed by "several sociologists...to non-politicized, non-Islamicized youths of immigrant origin," he refuses to accept responsibility for the (mis)use of the incident: "If a journalist were expected to anticipate the subsequent use of his report by extremists, it would amount to unacceptable self-censorship." (99)

Does such a defense also cover a false report or an outright hoax? A journalist who knowingly or unwittingly validates a staged scene deliberately fabricated as an incitement to violence bears a heavy responsibility. A reader with no personal malice toward Enderlin would expect to find in this book a coherent defense of the al-Dura report that would put to rest all doubts about its authenticity. Instead we are offered an accumulation of pseudo-factual details, remodeled to accommodate the inconsistencies that have been revealed by researchers over the past decade. Anyone familiar with the affair will recognize the text as one more in a series of elastic reconstructions of the background story that interested parties have used to shore up the al-Dura video.

A FABRICATED DEFENSE

This amplified revisionist version of the al-Dura myth is enhanced with journalistic name-dropping to show that Enderlin has access to important people who trust him. The credentials of Talal Abu Rahma, his trusted cameraman who filmed the incident, are burnished beyond all plausibility. Israeli authorities, we are repeatedly told, say he is "pure as the driven snow." By contrast, monsieur Enderlin pours contempt on every writer, thinker, journalist, specialist, public official, or simple citizen who dares to cast doubt on the authenticity of his al-Dura "news report."

A detailed exposé of the way *Un enfant est mort* refurbishes the al-Dura report would be counterproductive; it would only sustain the illusion that we are dealing with an event that actually occurred. One or two examples of glaring aberrations should suffice to discredit the journalist and his cameraman.

The allegation that Israeli soldiers deliberately and knowingly fired at the man and boy for an uninterrupted forty-five minutes upholds the image of Israeli soldiers as murderous. But it goes against common sense. Why would it take soldiers forty-five minutes to hit a clearly visible sitting target? Enderlin peppers his book with vivid accounts of various occasions in which merciless Israeli soldiers allegedly mowed down innocent Palestinian civilians. For some reason, however, he now retrospectively tempers his cameraman's assertion that the soldiers could see Jamal and Muhammad al-Dura. "I was not convinced; I asked him to express this doubt when he testified the next day before the Palestinian Center for Human Rights." (17)

Apparently undaunted, Talal testified on 3 October that the Israeli soldiers wounded the man and killed the boy deliberately, in cold blood. Equally undaunted, Enderlin says his cameraman's testimony was improperly elicited and incorrectly transcribed. This is ludicrous. Talal Abu Rahma and Jamal al-Dura repeated the accusation of cold-blooded murder on the airwaves, on the internet, in documentary films, at political meetings, in fact wherever they went, for years on end. And this begs another question: why did the cameraman feel the need to testify under oath three days after filming the incident?

For years Enderlin led us to believe that the raw footage shot that day at Netzarim Junction held clinching evidence. Finally on 14 November 2007, when eighteen minutes of videotape were viewed in a French court, it turned out that Talal Abu Rahma had captured less than one minute of the al-Dura scene. There is no raw footage of the alleged forty-five-minute ordeal, nothing but the montage of six thin slices that made up the original broadcast, plus another pinch of film depicting the child's nonexistent "death throes."

For Enderlin the seasoned journalist, this lack of footage needs no explanation. If you don't understand, he says, it shows you know nothing about war reporting. He affirms with similar nonchalance that the Palestinian general, Ossama el-Ali, picked up all the spent shells – which would have proved the origin of the gunfire – on the day after the incident, and told Talal to keep it quiet (52). One could go on pointing out discrepancies forever, and Enderlin would presumably come up with a new incoherent explanation or *ad hominem* attack for each detail in an endless dance.

THE ENDURING EFFECTS

Since the al-Dura myth has nothing to do with facts, it cannot be undone by factual arguments. Perniciously introduced into the news stream as though it were a piece of – albeit imperfect – journalism, it cannot be undone until it is removed from that usurped position. The effect of the blood libel was both instantaneous and enduring. In a few brief seconds it seared into the collective consciousness a quintessential Jewish guilt for which the only rightful punishment is extermination. The al-Dura image awakened something deep and primitive in the human mind, triggering the age-old mechanisms of an ongoing genocidal narrative: Jews as iconoclasts, Christ killers, murderers of the prophets, a poison in the bloodstream of the human race. These deadly accusations are tragically facilitated by a Jewish sense of responsibility or guilt. The al-Dura blood libel operates on a level that is beyond the reach of rational reexamination. The effect is indelible.

Factual demonstrations enlighten some people individually but do not touch the immensity of a blood libel. [4] If the al-Dura shooting had been a news report broadcast by conscientious media, it would have been withdrawn long ago. If it were simply biased journalism, it might be too late to put it through a disinformation wringer and set the record straight. This has long been the position of Israeli authorities, convinced that no rectification would ever be accepted by "international opinion," and wary that attempts to clear Israel's name would only reinforce the accusation of merciless child killing.

Blood libel stokes visceral Jew-hatred in Arab-Muslim populations already steeped in scriptural and historical anti-Semitism, and inures the wider population to the attacks it incites. The atrocious slaughter of Israelis that began in the immediate aftermath of the al-Dura broadcast – human beings torn limb from limb in restaurants and buses – was too often condoned by international opinion as a reaction to Palestinian distress. Synagogue burnings and attacks against Jews in Europe were attributed to the resonance of Palestinian suffering in Arab-Muslim immigrant communities. Nothing was savage enough to shock hearts and minds under the influence of the lethal blood-libel narrative.

The al-Dura blood libel can be judged by its fruits: a relentless cycle of attacks against Israeli civilians, an international wave of anti-Jewish violence unlike anything seen since the Shoah, an endless series of lesser blood libels swallowed with shocking gullibility and perversely fostered by condemnation of Israel's slightest gesture of self-defense.

During the first two years of the Second Intifada, "everyone" knew there was no way to stop the "suicide bombers," glorified as the poor man's weapon of mass destruction. After the Park Hotel massacre of Passover 2002, Israeli forces went on the offensive and wiped out the jihadi nest in Jenin. A massacre! Palestine sources claimed five thousand dead. "Everyone" was outraged. The body count was reduced to five hundred, and finally settled at a bit over fifty, most of them armed combatants. And yet the "Jenin massacre" endures.

Israel began construction of a security barrier. Casualties on both sides were drastically reduced, but it is regarded as a "wall of shame." The unilateral withdrawal from Gaza left an "open-air prison." The Cast Lead operation launched late in 2008 to stop incessant rocket attacks from Hamas-controlled Gaza was "disproportionate force." Jihadis on the *Mavi Marmara* - a "humanitarian" mission to break the naval blockade of Gaza – were foiled and Israel was condemned. Almost no gesture of self-defense is acceptable to the warped collective mind. On the scale of threats to humanity, the building of homes for Jews in disputed neighborhoods is rated far above the development of Iranian nuclear power avowedly aimed at Israel's annihilation.

Charles Enderlin, of course, is not the mastermind behind this scheme; he is a cog in the machine. Acclaimed in France as an international authority on the Middle East conflict, he periodically publishes laborious books that read like a compilation of a journalist's daily notes. He claims that his detractors use the al-Dura controversy to subvert the impact of his scrupulously objective analysis of the conflict. "I trouble [them] because my books and documentary films contradict official propaganda and, first and foremost, the demonization of Yasir Arafat, accused of refusing the Palestinian state generously offered by Ehud Barak at Camp David in July 2000."(197) The author insists to this day that the Second Intifada was a spontaneous popular uprising, not a campaign planned by Arafat and his cronies. He paired up with Robert Malley (now an adviser to President Obama) to write articles denouncing the Camp David offer of a "Bantustan" state that no respectable Palestinian leader could accept.

The systematic condemnation of the state of Israel is not media bias, not sophisticated Palestinian PR, not blithering anti-Semitism; it is war. It is a strategy of contemporary jihad. Unable to defeat Israel militarily, its enemies are trying to destroy the state by a blitzkrieg of specious arguments and lopsided analyses. Now as in the past, blood libels unleash murderous violence. But the designated victims today are not defenseless Jews grabbed from their shtetl, stripped, and shot on the rim of mass graves. The sovereign state of Israel with its exemplary army stands between Jews and genocide.

In this slim volume crafted to put fresh makeup on the al-Dura myth, Charles Enderlin stubbornly pursues his engagement in the battalion of journalists who disdain the honest demands of their profession and reach for the higher vocation of resolving the "Middle East conflict"...over our dead bodies.

(1) Based on figures released by the then interior minister Daniel Vaillant, nine violent anti-Semitic acts were reported in 1999 compared to 116 in the period October-December 2000, with an additional six hundred "acts of intimidation."

— *Jewish Political Studies Review*
23:1-2 (Spring 2011)

Chapter 8

THE MUHAMMAD AL-DURA HOAX
AND OTHER MYTHS REVIVED

On September 30, 2000, a day after Yasser Arafat launched his war of terror, euphemized as the al-Aqsa *intifada*, state-owned France 2 Television broadcast a news report, filmed by a Palestinian cameraman, of the fatal shooting of a 12-year-old Palestinian identified as Muhammad al-Dura. The dramatic voiceover commentary by the station's longtime Jerusalem correspondent, Charles Enderlin, described how the boy and his father Jamal were pinned down by Israeli gunfire at Netzarim Junction in the Gaza Strip. The father pleaded frantically with the soldiers to stop shooting, to no avail. "A last burst of gunfire," intoned Enderlin, "the boy is dead, his father critically wounded."

The bloodless images of Jamal and Muhammad al-Dura were instantly seared into the public mind. Distributed free of charge to international media, repeated endlessly like a raucous war cry, the Dura video provoked anti-Jewish violence in Israel and, on a scale not seen since the Holocaust, throughout Europe. The al-Jazeera television network, founded in 1996, was boosted by exploiting the Dura death scene.

Recognized almost immediately as a staged scene by astute observers, denounced by others as an unfounded accusation against Israeli soldiers, the Dura video has been analyzed, investigated, dissected, exposed, taken to court, attacked, defended, exploited, and debated for almost ten years. As it turned out, the Palestinian cameraman Talal Abu Rahma, who has won countless prizes for the video, captured less than one minute of the dramatic scene that lasted, according to his sworn testimony, for forty-five minutes. Forty-five minutes of uninterrupted gunfire "from the Israeli position" left the man and boy miraculously intact as far as one can gather from looking at the video. Contrary to what the world has been led to believe, there is no raw footage of the scene. And, contrary to what might be expected, this and other equally embarrassing revelations have left the Dura myth, to all intents and purposes, intact.

REINVENTING A LIE

In his latest attempt to silence critics of the controversial broadcast, Enderlin recently published a book-length defense of the original allegations, *Un Enfant est mort* (A Child is Dead), followed by the dateline *Netzarim, 30 septembre 2000*. The France 2 correspondent, systematically presented in France as an internationally acclaimed expert on the Arab-Israeli conflict, is virtually unknown in the rest of the world, except perhaps for his role as producer of the "Death of Muhammad al-Dura."

Enderlin likes to scold critics of the broadcast by saying they have never set foot in Gaza and know nothing about war reporting. In spring 2011, riled by complaints in "communitarian" (i.e., Jewish) media about the failure of national media and, more particularly, the state-owned France 2 TV channel, to cover the blood-curdling slaughter of five members of the Fogel family in the Itamar settlement on March 12, 2011, the professional journalist treated critics to a lecture on his blog on how a newscast is composed. "I wish I could report all important events," he wrote, "the horrible Itamar crime, the tragic death of Palestinian adolescents killed last year by an Israeli strike on Gaza (... for which Benjamin Netanyahu apologized), rockets that fall regularly in the south of Israel." A news director, explained Enderlin with a touch of exasperation, must allocate limited air time to a flow of incoming news. Priorities are set according to "well-established criteria." With thousands dead from earthquake and tsunami in Japan, "the world's third largest economy," there was no room to cover "what happened in Itamar." The next day, he added, a short item was squeezed in on the consequences of the murder (i.e., anticipated settler violence). Until the culprits were arrested, opined the seasoned journalist, the attack could not be qualified as a terrorist assault. [1]

No such doubts about the identity of the culprits had tempered Enderlin's enthusiasm for the Dura video, aired within a few hours after its filming. No "well-established criteria" had weakened the conviction of his dramatic voiceover commentary: The boy was killed and the father wounded by gunfire from the Israeli position. Today, readily admitting that the Dura scene was exploited by, among others, the killers who beheaded Daniel Pearl the France 2 correspondent asserts his right to unrestricted liberty: "If a journalist were expected to anticipate the subsequent use of his report by extremists, it would amount to unacceptable self-censorship."[2] Does the Dura broadcast respect any well-established journalistic criteria? Reliable sources, corroboration, fact-checking, general credibility, coherence? Does the video actually correspond to the incident as it was reported? Was the original report modified by subsequent input? Does the journalist honestly address questions raised by serious investigators about the veracity of the report? The answer is no, no, and again, no.

Though fed into the news stream, the Dura report was not produced as news. What was it, then? Sloppy journalism? Crafty Palestinian propaganda? Perhaps a new form of street theater: a staged killing to represent the very real "murder" of Palestinian children, year in year out, at the hands of merciless Israeli soldiers? Or, more gently, a staged representation of the real killing of Palestinian children caught in the crossfire of an endless conflict? These and similar hypotheses fly in the face of the testimony of the sole eyewitnesses—Talal Abu Rahma and Jamal al-Dura—and the France 2 correspondent who brought the incident to the world's attention.

Careful study of the literature shows that no credible defense of the Dura scene as a legitimate news item has ever been formulated. Arguing the case that they brought before the French courts as plaintiffs against media watchdog Philippe Karsenty and other defendants, Enderlin and the France 2 hierarchy were unable to furnish any new material evidence to prove the video's authenticity. Likewise, in his recently published *Un*

Enfant est mort, the author rehashes the original narrative, twisting and tweaking here and there to cover with new inventions some of the glaring anomalies exposed by his detractors.

Here is an example of the method and its madness: What became of the spent shells left at the feet of the victims, which would furnish irrefutable proof of the source of the alleged forty-five minutes of uninterrupted gunfire? The France 2 cameraman Abu Rahma, who has repeated in countless interviews the enveloping narrative that gave substance to his brief non-graphic video, was no match for Esther Schapira of the German broadcast network ARD, who caught him in a convoluted explanation of the disappearance of the spent shells. First, he told her that the Palestinian general Osama al-Ali had the bullets, to which she argued that she had footage of the general denying that he had the bullet casings. Abu Rahma stumbled, then admitted that France 2 had them, breaking into an irrepressible smile of pure deception.[3]

Now Enderlin sets the record straight: "If Esther Schapira had bothered to ask, she would have learned that the Palestinian general Osama al-Ali went to the site early in the morning after the death of Muhammad al-Dura to examine the barrel and, so doing, he put the stone back on top of it, as it was in the France 2 video. He also gathered all the spent shells and asked our cameraman not to tell anyone."[4]

Is this the work of a responsible French-Israeli journalist and his loyal Palestinian cameraman? Is no one shocked or embarrassed by this confession? Did the dozens of French journalists who signed a petition in defense of Enderlin, victim, in their eyes, of conspiracy theory whackos backed by a communitarian lobby, read this passage? Did the journalists who served Enderlin a microphone on a silver platter in so-called interviews to promote this book ever read that passage? Or would they argue: "In case you don't know it, journalists have a right to protect their sources." Their colleague, Enderlin, demeans every individual, newspaper, magazine, or online media that has dared to cast doubt on the authenticity of the Dura incident.

BLOOD LIBELS AND GENOCIDAL INTENTS

Muhammad al-Dura, alleged victim of merciless Israeli soldiers, was reportedly twelve years old; more of a youth than a child. What is the connection between the world-shaking news of his death and the eerie journalistic silence that veiled the murder of a 3-month-old Jewish infant, Hadas Fogel, on Sabbath eve? The baby's throat was slit so far she was nearly decapitated. Two of her brothers were slaughtered like animals in their beds. Their mother and father, who tried to protect the children, were stabbed to death. The bloodied, stabbed, slashed corpses lay in pools of blood. The Dura video, by contrast, displays no signs of violence, bodily harm, or untimely death. The sensation of violence is induced by the voiceover commentary, by the grimaces and gestures of the alleged victims, and guttural cries from unseen observers within range of the microphone attached to Abu Rahma's camera.

One might ask with feigned innocence why the picture of a man and boy bearing absolutely no signs of physical assault would stir the collective soul of humanity to its utmost depths while the vicious bloody slaughter of three young children and their parents—coupled with the heartbreaking portraits of family members when they were still alive and full of light—seems to provoke an embarrassed shrug.

Stripped of its context and significance, the slaughter of the Fogel family was apparently handled by newsrooms as a onetime crime whereas the Dura incident, enhanced by a crudely fabricated narrative that escaped critical examination, was raised to the highest media power. Is there a connection between the unfounded certainty about the identity of Dura's killers and the artificial doubts about the murderers of the Fogel family? Yes, if there is a connection between blood libel and genocide.

The twenty-first-century blood libel branding Israelis as child-killers, like the earlier version that accuses Jews of killing non-Jewish children for ritual purposes, is intractable to factual evidence. Deconstruction of the Dura myth encounters a cascade of problems: Only a tiny minority of the general public has the slightest knowledge of the case. That tiny minority of informed, convinced, discerning observers can at best enlarge its circle by small increments, leaving essentially the whole world still believing that a Palestinian child was deliberately shot by Israeli soldiers. Those who are convinced by the mass of concrete evidence to the contrary rarely figure among the population that will commit genocidal acts based on or reinforced by the blood libel.

Though scriptural and historic Islamic anti-Jewish bigotry would suffice without the Dura incitement to fill certain hearts with murderous rage, the Dura blood libel, indelibly engraved in the public mind, interferes with the perception of a rising genocidal wave. Blood libel incites and excuses genocidal attacks on Jews whether they are the slaughter of the Fogels, *shahid* operations (misnamed "suicide bombings"), rocket attacks from Gaza, or the promise to wipe Israel off the face of the earth. One way of disguising genocidal attacks is to treat them like common crimes. Was the Fogel massacre soft-pedaled because of an overabundant news flow or was it kept out of view precisely because it reveals genocidal intentions?

A similar mechanism operated in France to cover the true nature of two atrocious murders of Jews. The Sébastien Selam murder was literally attributed to one third jealousy, one third insanity, and one third anti-Semitism. The twenty-seven defendants in the kidnapping, torture, and murder of Ilan Halimi were tried behind closed doors in the court of first resort and again in appeals court. Attempts to expose the true nature of these killings have been decried as Jewish hypersensitivity, tribalism, self-interested exploitation of suffering, manipulation of the judicial system by pressure groups, and shameful resort to primitive vengeance.

These and other acts of gratuitous, unmitigated cruelty were committed in a context of explicit genocidal intentions that are willfully ignored or denied. By contrast, the alleged killing of Muhammad al-Dura is readily accepted though framed by a ludicrous narrative. Cameraman Abu Rahma and the surviving victim, Jamal al-Dura, insist that Israeli soldiers deliberately shot at the defenseless civilians for forty-five minutes until they had critically injured the man and killed the boy. Insisting adamantly that the gunfire came solely from the Israeli position, they claim the soldiers could clearly see the target. One can imagine that television viewers believed they were watching the scene from the same vantage point as the soldiers, who saw it in a close-up, as it appears in the video, looking more like a poster than a news clip.

Soldiers do not need forty-five minutes to hit a sitting target at close range. Obviously embarrassed by this detail, commentators seeking to show that critics of the Dura story are wrong-headed often replace the forty-five minutes of uninterrupted gunfire with a more credible crossfire. Blithely contradicting the two eyewitnesses, they create a more palatable version of the incident for Western consumption while tacitly admitting that the Dura report is for some reason excluded from factual analysis. [5]

Whether one prefers forty-five minutes of relentless gunfire aimed at the man and boy, or forty-five seconds of crossfire, Jamal al-Dura's wounds combined with his grief at losing his son are given as evidence of the veracity of his testimony. The wounded man wrapped in bloodied bandages was filmed on his hospital bed the day after the incident. He has dramatically described the wounds, bullet by bullet. His scars were displayed on several occasions, most recently in a film made by Abu Rahma for screening at a semiprivate press conference organized by then-news director of France 2, Arlette Chabot, in 2004 when two mainstream journalists, Denis Jeambar and Daniel Leconte, came close to exposing the Dura broadcast as a staged scene. Those wounds are now at the center of a libel suit brought by Dura against journalist Clément Weil-Raynal and the Israeli surgeon he interviewed, Yehuda David, as well as Serge Benatar, editorial director of the *Actualité Juive* weekly, who published the interview.

David has testified under oath that the scars exhibited by Jamal al-Dura were not inflicted by gunfire in September 2000; they were inflicted by knives and an ax wielded by fellow Palestinians who attacked Jamal in 1992. David did reparative surgery, successfully restoring the patient's use of his right hand. On April 29, 2011, Weil-Raynal and David were found guilty of public defamation of Dura. [6] The text of the decision is incoherent, illogical, and peppered with contradictions. The defendants have appealed.

In the meantime, Metula News Agency—one of the major sources of investigation and analysis of, in their words, the "Netzarim Controversy"—reexamined a passage in the video.[7] As he describes how a bullet pierced his right hand, Jamal waves a report from the Jordanian hospital where he was treated several days after the alleged shooting. A zoom on the document shows that Jamal was treated for a gunshot wound to the left hand. In fact, a close look at the Dura "death scene" reveals that Jamal's right hand was deformed in the first image, shows no signs of additional damage at the end of the brief video, and looks exactly the same today as it did before it was allegedly pierced by an Israeli bullet.

Charles Enderlin asks, rhetorically, how Palestinians could be so clever as to stage the Dura scene in the middle of a fierce gun battle. But raw footage shot at Netzarim Junction shows that "fierce gun battles" were also staged that day. While men and youths attacked the Israeli outpost with rocks, firebombs, and burning tires, fake battle scenes were filmed in another part of the junction, out of range of the Israel Defence Forces outpost.

Many staged scenes and Israeli atrocity hoaxes have been launched and eagerly consumed by the Western media in the past decade. Abu Rahma and Enderlin relayed the Gaza blackout hoax in 2008. The term "fauxtography" was coined for the method used in the 2006 Lebanon war. The Dura scene is particularly resistant to demystification. The emotional investment elicited by the incident extends far beyond the core population of anti-Zionist anti-Semites. This is due, some would argue, to the dramatic construction that draws the viewer into identification with the father, said to be desperately trying to protect his son. Then, in a brief lapse of time, less than one minute, the helpless father is said to be critically wounded, and his child is dead. Viewers feel that they should have jumped in and saved the child.

The vast majority of articles devoted to the Dura affair begin, notably, with a visual memory of the scene (e.g. "the boy dies in his father's arms") induced by testimony from the two eyewitnesses but contradicted by the concrete reality of the video.

A recent incident in the Libyan capital of Tripoli shows how journalists can, if they so desire, exercise healthy skepticism when invited to cover staged scenes. Reporters were shown damage allegedly wreaked by a coalition strike on the home of a prosperous, well-dressed gentleman. Furniture and personal belongings were topsy-turvy, but there was no sign of an explosion, breakage, or soot. The alleged victim argued that his home was not a military target: "The children were doing their homework." A reporter, displaying missile fragments in the garden, points out the absence of signs of an explosion on the site. The crater, which was apparently dug for the occasion, does not correspond to the munitions displayed as evidence. Other television reports on mass funerals or wounded civilians taken to hospital were accompanied by levelheaded warnings: "None of this can be verified. We have no way of checking this information. The wounded were perhaps used by Qaddafi's forces as human shields; they may be soldiers disguised as civilians."

All of that lucidity should also be retroactively transposed to Israel's 2009 Cast Lead operation in Gaza. The same manipulations were practiced by Hamas without evoking the appropriate skepticism. (Richard Goldstone has just admitted that his report was based on faulty information, to which Jeffrey Goldberg commented: "Well, I'm glad he's cleared that up. Unfortunately, it is somewhat difficult to retract a blood libel, once it has been broadcast across the world."[8] Obviously, and regrettably, staged news, parroted agency dispatches, falsified documentaries, and sloppy journalism are common fare. When, however, Western media serve as facilitators for hostile forces engaged in geopolitical operations aimed at radically transforming the international balance of power, they cannot be shrugged off as the petty misdemeanors of mass communications. Israelis in particular and Jews in general are the target of the Dura blood libel, but it does not stop there. Other "lethal narratives" are funneled into the news stream with exquisite ease.

MYTHS AND DOUBLE STANDARDS

Viewers have been presented, since December 2010, with what the world media has termed the "Arab Spring." Though the footage in this case is not staged, it is subject to highly selective editing and transformed by way of narrative into a spontaneous uprising of freedom-loving democrats throwing off tyrannical rulers in certain Arab-Muslim countries. Western governments are expected to align themselves with the popular uprising at the speed of television coverage: Anchormen and women, who identify with the crowd in this or that liberation square, set the pace, and Western leaders appear to follow suit. European heads of state scramble to outrun President Obama with imperious demands for immediate compliance. The targeted autocrat is told to abdicate. His misdeeds are splashed across the screen; his foreign investments are frozen; his crony capitalism is denounced; his wife is vilified, and his opponents are portrayed as Internet savvy, cosmopolitan, secular, charming, young professionals who would fit in with one's dinner party guests tomorrow evening.

This young Facebook-Twitter image is pasted over the somewhat grimy reality actually captured by television cameras. Soothing words flow from the mouths of journalists determined to deny the reality of Star of David graffiti, women in *hijab* (Islamic head covering), men with Islamic beards, shouts of *Allahu Akbar* (Allah is great), row upon row of prostrate men praying in the "secular revolution" square, man-in-the-square interviewees promising to destroy Israel, Muslim Brotherhood figures waiting in the wings, confusion, connivance, danger, violence, and sexual assault.

Spring blossomed with the "Jasmine Revolution" in Tunisia. In the space of three days, commentary went from, "What Islamists? There are none!" to "The dictator ben Ali had excluded many groups, including the Islamists, from the political arena" to "Of course, the Islamists, like other parties, will assume their rightful place in the democratic process."

Step by step, country by country, in what was supposed to be an entirely positive, virtually unstoppable momentum, the conflicts become more violent, culminating at this writing in the Libyan adventure—armed intervention by a hastily concocted, essentially untenable coalition that includes, or included, the Arab League.

Western journalists and reporters, like gawkers at a country fair, run from one show to the next, rarely looking back to report on retrograde forces gobbling up freedom-lovers or newly-liberated nations spilling out refugees. Over 20,000 have landed in Lampedusa since January 2011, and thousands more are on the way. Jews are harassed in Tunisia; Copts are persecuted in Egypt; Shari'a is poised to replace the arbitrary rule of the dictator with an implacable tyranny.

The question is not, "How could we have known it would turn sour?" Nor can one conclude that, come what may, democracies should always act to defend a popular uprising even at the risk of paving the way for a new autocracy. The question is rather: What will become of democratic countries if they abdicate their international relations and defense to a consortium of the United Nations and international opinion?

The power balance in the Middle East is undergoing a radical transformation that touches Western vital interests, not the least of which is the security of Israel. Old-fashioned national sovereignty is nearly as unpopular as the Oriental potentates pushed out of their palaces and into a black hole. Democratically-elected leaders committed to defending the welfare and security of their citizens are now expected to prove their integrity precisely by ignoring that responsibility. A crowd with slogans and banners is instantly awarded the title of "humanity," and everything done to satisfy their demands is "humanitarian." Of course, the citizens of democracies should be inclined to welcome liberation movements against tyrannical rulers, but it is absurd to actively support movements that may well shift the international balance of power toward greater tyranny.

CONCLUSION

And what does all this have to do with the Dura hoax? The answer is: far too much for comfort. As suggested above, the staged Dura death scene was conceived by forces hostile to Israel and Jews and made credible by the Western media that relayed it. Though the video and its narrative are crude, the prestige of Enderlin and the French television network have protected it from the profound reexamination that could eventually remove its sting. Similarly, the restructuring of the Middle East, which could ultimately deliver free individuals, groups, and nations into the hands of our enemies, is prettied up by the Western media that, hand in hand with official discourse, makes one believe this change harbors no danger. Citizens of the free democracies are enticed into trusting the United Nations, which has in fact lost its integrity, instead of counting on their democratically-elected governments and national sovereignty.

Finally, who is that international community with its international opinion enthroned like bloodthirsty spectators of gladiatorial combats, empowered to give the thumbs up or thumbs down? Is it not the dumbstruck viewer convinced that this Palestinian child, a "target of gunfire from the Israeli position," could escape death if only he would come to the child's rescue?

In a parallel inversion, jihad conquest justifies itself as a defense against aggression by infidels who refuse to accept the dominion of Allah and comply with Shari'a law. The Palestinian child is not a real victim of real bullets; he is the symbol of that "aggressive" refusal to submit to Islam. The murderous rage unleashed against Jews in response to that symbolic aggression reveals its genocidal intent. The fury is now aimed at Christians in Muslim lands, at Americans and Europeans on their own soil. Panic strikes the embattled citizens of our lands—not at the thought of this merciless jihad, but panic at any attempt to discern it, describe it, defend against it.

Israel is not the victim of a double standard; it is the target of no standard at all. The reasons for this are profound and cannot be limited to anti-Semitism. The fear and trembling provoked by the crudely fabricated Dura scene is the misdirected terror instilled by genocidal forces bearing down on citizens of free democracies. These citizens are the helpless child cringing in fear. No matter how honestly that force designates itself, how clearly it shows its face, how vast the territory it covers, how frankly it expresses its intentions, the frightened child seeks comfort in accusing himself of his imminent destruction.

[1] Victor Perez, " Charles Enderlin nous prend pour des simplets » : Victor Perez Blogspot, Mar. 25, 2011.
[2] Enderlin, *Un enfant est mort*, p. 99.
[3] Esther Schapira, dir., *Drei Kugeln und ein totes Kind*, Mar. 18, 2002, ARD Network (Germany).
[4] Enderlin, *Un enfant est mort*, p. 52
[5] Larry Derfner, "Rattling the Cage: Al-Dura and the Conspiracy Freaks," May, 28, 2008; Gideon Levy, "Mohammed al-Dura Lives on," *Ha'aretz*, Oct. 7, 2007.
[6] Véronique Chemla, May 31, 2011
[7] Metula News Agency, March 23, 2011
[8] Jeffrey Goldberg, "Judge Richard Goldstone Never Mind," *The Atlantic*, Apr. 2, 2011.

— *Middle East Quarterly   Fall 2011*

ATTACKING ISRAEL WITH GENOCIDAL INTENTIONS

July 2012

Abstract

De-legitimization of the State of Israel is the current episode in a persistent genocidal project aimed at the Jews and, more profoundly, at the values inherent in Judaism and shared by civilized societies. Skirting the shame attached to anti-Semitism after the horrors of the Holocaust, contemporary advocates of the genocidal plot are given free rein to attack Jews by a combination of severe criticism of the State of Israel and well-meaning plans for its geopolitical future, i.e. the peace process. Ugly lies – the Jews stole the land from the Palestinians, Israel is an apartheid state – function like the age-old charges that justified persecution of the Jews as Christ killers. Beautiful lies — the two state solutions that everyone knows – echo the proto-legalistic measures that gradually deprived European Jews of their rights, their strength, their resources and capacity to resist deportation and extermination. Americans, misinterpreting as a repetition of the 1930s the rise of violent anti-Semitism in Europe at the dawn of the twenty-first century, are unprepared to deal with a parallel rise in Muslim Brotherhood forces within the US. As brutal Islamic Jew hatred boils in an Arab-Muslim world revolting, reforming, and submitting to sharia law, the Obama administration conducts a policy of the outstretched hand and blindfolded eyes that leaves Iran free to develop the ultimate genocidal weapon. Israel is the bulwark, not only for

Jews but for the free world. Clear thinking, uncompromising discourse, and resolute action – at the risk of being labelled extremist – can stop the genocidal project and, working backward, disarm the lies.

From the first stirrings of Judaism to the present day the war against the Jews has been pursued with variations in methods, scope, and intensity. It would be foolish to sum up in a few sentences the brilliant work of a host of thinkers who have analysed this process and examined its underlying causes. We can no more ignore their thought than rest on their conclusions. We have to integrate their wisdom into fresh thinking based on the contemporary situation. What stands in the way of an early twenty-first century genocide of the Jews? Compared to the previous genocide, Jews today are healthier, wealthier, and wiser. Honest human beings the world over are sincerely horrified by the Shoah and more or less aware of the dangers of a repetition. The democratic nations in which the Diaspora lives in relative peace and prosperity are well-armed to defend themselves against attack and the Jews against potential exterminators. But all of these safeguards would crumble if not for the State of Israel.

Therefore, one could say with near scientific precision that the State of Israel stands between the Jews and a twenty-first century genocidal plot. How clever, then, to labour away at destroying Israel while denying the slightest anti-Semitic intentions. The range of weapons is limitless. The combinations are devilish. A peace process seasoned with Intifadas, martyrdom operations coupled with invocations of international law, humanitarian flotillas armed to the teeth, rocket attacks in tandem with UN recognition bids, and of course the construction of a tight-knit international network of sympathizers extending from the grassroots to the halls of power. While Israel's neighbours pound away at its existence, Muslims in Europe and the Americas blithely attack Jews to 'avenge' their Palestinian 'brothers'. Again, freedom to harm Jews has been granted along with immunity from the anti-Semite label. Domestic and foreign enemies of the Jews collaborate to conduct attacks that terrorize large populations into granting whatever is demanded in the name of Islam, Palestine, peace, and adulterated civil rights. The leavening agent of this recipe is a compound of the good obtained by a reverse chemistry that transforms the moral lessons of the Holocaust into the amoral values by which Jews can once more be pursued and exterminated.

In the name of the good, Jews can be harassed on university campuses, elbowed out of professional and commercial activities, vilified in lowbrow and highbrow media, abandoned to thugs and murderers and, conversely, glorified if they outspokenly reject Israel. Cartoonists win prizes with Nazi style caricatures where Jews are recycled as Israelis. Arab-Muslim intellectuals are invited to speak in high places and given tenure in prestigious universities for justifying the persecution of Jews identified as Israelis. Outreach operations promote the narrative that Jews, Christians, and Muslims are mutually guilty of/victims of prejudice. Idealists wave the co-exist banner. People of all colours and creeds can live together harmoniously as long as the Jews turn their backs on the outlaw state of Israel – under its present government, of course. The genocidal plot aims to divide and conquer: divide Diaspora Jews from Israel, Israeli Jews from their government, Israelis living inside the green line from 'colonists', and so on.

Here and there, the 'evils of Zionism' give permission to break the post-Auschwitz taboo and stir up old-fashioned anti-Semitic stereotypes. The hue and cry against Wall Street speculators and billionaires are emblematic targets of Jew hatred that would be unleashed if the bulwark of Israel were ever to collapse.

Nevertheless it is counterproductive to label as 'anti-Semitism' the will to destroy the State of Israel by all means possible and impossible. On the one hand this old vocabulary that we have not been able to update leads to outdated reactions and outworn strategies; on the other, it drags into dead-end debate with a new kind of enemy that will swear to the heavens and to the end of time 'I am not an anti-Semite'. Furthermore, with or without the hyphen, the term implies that it has something to do with being against Jews. Does it?

Yes and no. The genocidal plot is not a reaction to the evil deeds or noble acts of Israel or the Jews, but to the notion of the good upheld by Judaism. Ironically, the irrepressible impulse to commit genocide without hindrance from the prohibition inscribed in Judaic values leads to the hatching of genocidal plots against the Jews. In common language this would be: get out of my way so I can really do what I am falsely accusing you of doing.

This brings us full circle to the comprehensive programme – the will to destroy life – of which the destruction of Israel by specious arguments is an essential but partial element. Only when we have perceived the outer reaches of this project can we understand and combat its concrete on-the-ground manifestations. Otherwise we assume a defensive position that feeds the animosity directed against us. Rather, we should take heart from the fact that the genocidal plot is not moving forward as quickly as planned. Neither armed invasion, nor shahid operations, nor subversion, nor BDS (Boycott, Divestment, Sanctions), nor the combined forces of the United Nations General Assembly have come anywhere near to defeating Israel. Israel is flourishing. The genocidal plot persists, however, in a hair trigger configuration: an Iranian nuclear weapon over Israel's head, and a detriment to all humanity. We have to dismantle it.

What should be done with the specious arguments used to attack Israel? They are no more valid than the ones used to attack the Jews over the centuries. And yet we seem to be fooled every time into answering lies with facts. Not that the facts are worthless. On the contrary, they are helpful to those who defend Israel, the Jews, and civilized values. When used, however, to counter the destructive lies they paradoxically give weight to the accusations. Reasonable arguments inadvertently imply that there might be some truth to the accusation, and lead to quibbling over details. Since the accusers have no scruples, they will twist every single detail, constantly adding weight to the lie, never answering any objection, never conceding a point, and eventually slamming a door in the Zionist's face: 'It's impossible to discuss anything with you, you're an unconditional supporter of Likud and the colonists. So what's the solution? Do you want to kill all the Palestinians?'

The lies – I call them 'lethal narratives' – have kinship with earlier versions of Jew hatred: 'Israel stole the land from the Palestinians' functions in the same way as 'the Jews killed Christ'. No number of historical documents, deeds, multi-coloured maps, or population statistics can make a dent in that argument because, like the Christ-killer accusation, it is essential, not circumstantial. 'Stole the land' defines Israel. It does not stand upright as a three-dimensional reality which one could examine by going behind it, around it, underneath it.

'Israel is an apartheid state' does not mean that Israel treats Arab-Muslim-Palestinians like South Africa treated Blacks. It means the Israelis, who are intruders, can be forced by BDS to hand over power to the rightful inhabitants of Palestine. A few years ago a French journalist reporting from Israel translated a shabat elevator for haredim into an apartheid elevator reserved for Blacks. The whole rubbish heap of Israel apartheid charges is of the same low quality, and its long term success is not guaranteed. Israel Apartheid Week (IAW) was nipped in the bud this year in France. The major event, a colloquium scheduled at the Université de Paris 8, a hotbed of Palestinianism a stone's throw from the skyscrapers of La Défense, was cancelled by the president, Pascal Binczak, on the grounds that the organization could not ensure public order on campus and did not respect the 'intellectual and scientific independence of the university where the pluralism of scientific and critical approaches and free analytic debate must be seen as intangible academic obligations'.[1] Efraim Karsh penned a head-on collision for the IAW slander convoy.[2]

The 15 April 2012 Flytilla was grounded, provoking outrage on the French BDS site Europalestine.org, where the intention to defeat the 'illegitimate' state of Israel is broadcast in every way, shape, and form. When the Bienvenu en Palestine operation was thwarted, the organization accused European airlines, police, and military of collaborating (as in 'Vichy collaborators') with the Israeli secret services to deny them their rights – to go to Bethlehem and inaugurate a school. The movement invents international laws to condemn Israel, flouts French law that prohibits their anti-Israel boycotts, and denies the existence of international law that allows sovereign nations to require visas, establish no-fly lists, and requires airlines to repatriate unwanted passenger at the airline's expense. Duly informed that their reservations were cancelled, the Flytillistas publicly promised to cause trouble at the airports, then shrieked when met by law enforcement. Their real intention is to erase Israel's borders and strangle its sovereignty by inventing a sovereign Palestine whose borders can be defined by will or whimsy. The geopolitical fait accompli of the designation 'Palestine' is reinforced by the excitement it offers, as if it were a new sexual organ promising unspeakable orgasms.

These ugly lies are best countered with the contempt they deserve. Much progress has been made in this direction over the past 12 years. Israel is increasingly skilled at deflecting barrages of inflammatory allegations. The more Israel shows itself to be indifferent to false charges – responding sharply in international instances, deflating ludicrous accusations with lively humour [3] repelling stunts like the Million Man

March to Jerusalem, fighting back against 'humanitarians' armed to the teeth, exposing the hypocrisy of UN organizations – the less harm they can do. Though they will always subsist in the shadows, morph into endless variations, sustain the image of Israel as the Bad Guy, and stand ready to poison the atmosphere and justify violence against Jews when the occasion arises.

Ugly lies are a danger but beautiful lies are far more dangerous and difficult to counter. Ugly lies are the meat and potatoes of mean people who want to do bad deeds. They don't really care about Palestinians; they aren't really shocked by the plight of Muslims; they have no noble values to honour. But beautiful lies are a treasure held dear by masses of well-meaning people. Anyone who dares to challenge the beautiful lie of the peace process risks being relegated to the margins of public discourse, branded 'extremist' by some, accused of war crimes by others, shunned by prestigious colleagues and editors. Why should commentators or political leaders bring opprobrium on their heads by declaring that the two-state solution is just as false as 'Israel is an apartheid state' or 'the Jews killed Christ'? Since there is no chance of a Palestinian state being established in the near future it may seem easier to give lip service to the two-state solution and get on with one's career. This isn't cynical. It's a strategic choice. But I will argue that it is harmful.

The purpose of the peace process is to make war against Israel by demonstrating that Israel doesn't want peace. The term 'peace process' is a semantically self-justifying trick that confounds 'peace process' with the ways that peace can effectively be made in the real world. It follows that if Israel won't accept the terms of the process, then it is the obstacle to peace. That failure is the success of the process. The proof is that Palestinian rejection of the process is not defined as an obstacle but as further justification for placing the blame on Israel. By virtue of the peace process, certain Jewish neighbourhoods are declared to be illegal because they are located in 'occupied' territories. International law is invoked like a pagan god to bellow flames on the illegal occupiers and reduce them to ashes. Those who accept the principle of a Palestinian state living peacefully side by side with Israel on secure borders are considered to be moderates. Ostensibly free to debate details, modalities, and timing, they are in fact sucked up into 'the solution that everyone knows': retreat to the 1967 borders adjusted by land swaps, division of Jerusalem, and solution of the refugee problem. The more obvious it has become that none of this could, should, or will happen, the more the solution is reiterated. Another massive block of affirmation that cannot be examined from all or any sides.

What is the role of the peace process in the twenty-first century genocidal project as compared to the earlier version, the Shoah that we have recently commemorated? It functions like the series of proto-legalistic measures that gradually stripped European Jews of their rights, their strengths, and their capacity to resist extermination. How many people would have obeyed the laws and decrees if they knew where they were being led? Register as a Jew or you'll be arrested, leave your profession, turn over your company to an Aryan, turn in your radio, pick up your Jewish badge and sew it on your clothes or you'll be jailed, stay out of the parks and libraries, come with us or you'll be shot... Every step was legalized; the documents drafted in beautiful old-fashioned bureaucratic penmanship are lined up on the walls of Holocaust Memorials like the sharp teeth of man-eating beasts.

Today's equivalent measures are: respect international law, end the illegal occupation, surrender your sovereignty and life-saving protection, create the Palestinian state that will exterminate you, don't make us attack you, do it to yourselves.

Heads of state who have no desire to see the Jewish people exterminated periodically promise to roll up their sleeves and get the peace process going. They assure us that this time the solution that everyone knows will finally prevail. Jews who definitely do not want to be massacred or see their Israeli brethren exterminated reiterate their devotion to the peace process and, too often, grab Israel by the ear and scold it for not making the painful concessions that will, as everyone knows, bring peace.

Does this mean that Jewish survival depends on convincing the multitudes that the peace process is in fact a war and the friendly criticism of Israel fosters a genocidal project? How? What hasn't been tried yet? How do we break the stranglehold? Deny that there is a plot to exterminate the Jews and all the humanism seems to fall on the other side of the equation. You sound heartless if you say you don't want a Palestinian state. You sound alarmist if you say Israel is facing an existential threat and Jews everywhere will be in danger if Israel can't resist. You sound pretentious if you say the survival of the free world depends on Israel.

European Jews of the World War II generation are often torn between gratitude for the decisive American intervention that defeated Nazism and disappointment with the failure, in their eyes, of American Jews to pressure their government to specifically target the killing machine, to bomb Auschwitz. In fact, Jews in those days were not far removed from their greenhorn origins, subject to domestic anti-Semitism, quota systems, and other forms of discrimination. Now comfortably rich, powerful, and well-integrated, many American Jewish citizens, leaders, and donors seem to take pride in their 'independence' from Israel. They believe that gay marriage, abortion rights, and redistribution of wealth are the crucial issues of our times, the moral slide-rule by which we should be judged. Eschewing partisan support of Israel, they reach out to defend Muslims, designated as victims of prejudice and discrimination.

While Israel's score in popularity polls soars in the United States, voters chose a president whose hostility to Israel was already revealed during the Democratic primaries, later demonstrated in the Cairo speech, and repeatedly displayed in policies and attitude thereafter. The president's popularity among Jewish voters is reportedly still flying high, undisturbed by a foreign policy that belies his claim to 'have Israel's back'. (The phoney street talk betrays the speaker.) The disparity between the popularity of Israel and enduring support for an anti-Zionist president demonstrates once more the complexity of the genocidal plot. Americans love Israel in a t-shirt kind of way. What becomes of this puppy love when, as it seems, citizens and their representatives are unable or unwilling to influence the administration's bizarre approach to Iran – an outstretched hand and blindfolded eyes? Iran is given all the elbow room it needs to develop the genocidal weapon par excellence, the *New York Times* leaks Israeli war plans like a divinely ordained blabber, and Israel's best friends speak in enigmas: an Iranian bomb would be a disaster, an Israeli attack will be a catastrophe. Or vice versa.

How did we, at this crucial time, lose America? From the first Democratic primaries, at the end of 2007, the protective shield formed around the candidate Barack Hussein Obama was respected by mainstream and, with rare exceptions, alternative media. Criticism of the candidate was muted, understated, or censored. Reliable information about Obama's anti-Zionist ideas and friends was suppressed by the mainstream and diluted by the alternatives. The tyrannical mode was in place from the very beginning. No one wanted to offend unconditional Obama supporters among the readership and benefactors. Everyone was afraid of being called a 'racist'.

The rise of anti-Semitism in Europe in the past decade was misinterpreted as a replay of the 1930s and 1940s. Europe was going rotten again. Jews should immigrate en masse to the United States. Not to Israel? No, they considered Israel too dangerous. Europe was finished, collaborating once again with the Nazis, this time in an Islamist version. The images were telling: torched synagogues, battered rabbis, smashed windows, murdered Jews, swastikas. While attention was focused on the fall of Europe into its final episode of anti-Semitism, Muslim Brotherhood front organizations in suits and ties were weaving their web in the vast United States of America. Today, Jewish organizations are swimming like little fish into the nets cast by CAIR (Council on American–Islamic Relations) and its multiple front organizations. Paradoxically, the tons of garish anti-Zionist garbage dumped in Europe since September 2000 has mobilized some European Jews, particularly in France, to greater vigilance and stronger defence of Israel, while the honeyed chants of the Brotherhood are lulling American Jewry into self-destructive outreach and cosy ecumenism. (Not to suggest that we are totally immune to this kind of thing.) It is not a question of transatlantic competition but of lucidity. The misconception that the United States is a refuge today as it was in the days of Nazism weakens support for Israel and lulls American Jews into a false sense of security. If an analogy must be made, could the US be compared to Germany in the 1920s?

Above and beyond the ugly lies and the beautiful lies is the ultimate lie: blood libel. The Jews as Christ-killers are child-killers (Christ as the child of God). The Muhammad al-Dura scene broadcast by state-owned France TV on 30 September 2000, has functioned as blood libel on an international scale in the age of instant mass communication. A fabrication purporting to show a Palestinian youth killed in real time by Israeli soldiers opened the floodgates to a torrent of Jew hatred buoyed up by and justified by merciless criticism of the state of Israel. The Dura controversy has come forward once again in France, in the aftermath of the 2012 murders at Ozar Hatorah school in Toulouse. Muhammad Merah's declaration that he was avenging the killing of children in Gaza was mentioned, among other information, but did not resonate as it would have just a few years ago. France 2's Jerusalem correspondent Charles Enderlin, responsible for the Dura broadcast, has as usual leapt to his own defence and reiterated against all evidence the accusation that the boy was killed and the shots were fired from the Israeli position. Filmmaker Pierre Rehov, who was one of the first to contest the Dura broadcast, reminds us in a forceful open letter to Charles Enderlin that he interviewed the Israeli soldiers who manned the checkpoint on the day of the alleged incident.[4] They happen to be Druze. It does not make them any the less Jewish child-killers for the blood libel.

The polite dismissal of Israel by a cocktail of harsh criticism, snide remarks, inflammatory images, twisted documentaries, EU statements and UN resolutions is amplified by a chorus of crude Jew hatred from an Islamic world in a state of paroxysm. The revolt or reform (as in Salafist return to the origins) billed as the 'Arab Spring' is a retrograde movement leading to the domination of parties with different names and similar platforms based on the imposition of sharia law. Accomplished with elaborate scenarios in the Maghreb and Mashrek and brutally in sub-Saharan Africa it has met with determined resistance in Syria, where Bashar Assad's forces have killed an estimated 11,000 Syrians, most of them civilians.

The international community that stamps its feet and throws its weight around when Israel is involved has by turns entreated, pleaded, summoned, ordered, requested Assad to put an end to the killing. The hallowed United Nations expressed all forms of consternation, named an emissary, brokered a truce of sorts, and is now sending in unarmed blue-helmeted observers. Turkey reprimanded, the Arab League finger-wagged, the ECOWAS (Economic Community of West African States) threatened to send troops and President Assad is still there, doing what comes naturally. No one expects him to respond to human rights arguments.

Why would we be defeated by an enemy that is militarily, technologically, and intellectually weak, disorganized, and torn with internecine strife – an enemy that wherever it exerts its dominion has nothing good to offer its people? The only way we could be defeated is if we act as if the decision is not in our hands. We will not prevail by stretching our necks to the outermost reaches and convincing the inveterate Jew hater to change his ways, but by reaching inside ourselves and forging the utmost conviction of our right to live and prosper, forging it with such fire and light that it gradually ignites those closest to us and in an ever widening circle reaches the misguided.

The lightning speed of information offers advantages that no other generation enjoyed. The lapse of time between the premise and the conclusion is so brief the facts are in, the tricks are unmasked, the pros and cons worked out in real time in concrete reality; we have the discourse, the debate, and the consequences in a bit more than a tweet. That's why we can do what has not been done before. We have a nation, a land, an army, and the information needed to stymie the genocidal plot.

What will calm the ardour of the genociders is not painful concessions, apologies, admissions of guilt, bending over backward to mollify critics, giving 10% credit to ugly lies and heart-sinking validity to the beautiful 'everyone knows the solution' lie; no, what throws ice-cold water on the genociders is when Israel stands firm, strikes when attacked, and strikes pre-emptively when existentially threatened, fulfilling the promise of a land of refuge and fulfilment for the Jewish people and throwing the hatred back where it came from, back to the dark hearts of those who want to kill Jews so they can destroy humanity. Western civilization is not lost, it is staggering. As Jews we have a responsibility to defend ourselves so that free people everywhere can rediscover the courage to defend their freedom and highest values. That is the upright humanitarian position that reaches out to all decent human beings. It is not the phoney outreach posture of throwing ourselves into the jaws of the purveyors of sharia.

Clean up the static and the blood-curdling cry rings out loud and clear: Kill the Jews! Some think it is nothing but background noise. It's a question of fine-tuning.

1. "Communiqué de la direction de l'université Paris 8 Vincennes – Saint-Denis," 2/17/12.
2. Efraim Karsh, "The Middle East's Real Apartheid," *Jerusalem Post*, March 5, 2012.
3. Latma TV, "Benjamin Netanyahu's letter to the Flytillistas," jpost.com.
4. jssnews.com April 19, 2012

— Israel Affairs,
Volume 18, Issue 3, 2012

MEMOS TO COGNITIVE WAR COLLEGE

12/17/12 INTRODUCTION: the following is a summary of arguments I have developed since September 2000 and will present in a collection of my articles on the (al) Dura [*for various reasons I am trying to get rid of the "al"*] affair to be published this spring. In the face of the irrational resistance to cogent arguments that, I believe, would be easily accepted if the subject of the hoax were not so highly charged, I have sought to understand this resistance and change my approach, broadening the scope of my analysis and deepening my perception of the obstacles to enlightenment. The concept of "Lethal Narratives" grew out of that experience. Why do people cling to their belief in the veracity of the "al Dura news report"? Why do they persist in defending Charles Enderlin? This goes far beyond any cohort—the France Télévisions hierarchy, card-carrying jihadis, ideologically driven journalists, gullible idiots, anti-Zionist anti-Semites—to encompass the majority of any group we might encounter anywhere.

LETHAL NARRATIVES: Lethal narratives are a crucial element of 21st century jihad strategy. The al Dura hoax is not just a lethal narrative, it is blood libel; we will be mindful of both of these qualities in our attempts to effectively expose the hoax. The "Mideast Conflict" along with its variations—Arab-Israeli, Israeli-Palestinian, or territorial conflict— is a lethal narrative that disguises the jihad against Israel. Charles Enderlin and his numerous supporters cannot let go of the Dura hoax because it is the knot that holds together the myriad strands of the Mideast Conflict hoax. Once that knot is sliced, the whole narrative starts to unravel.

The Dura hoax is not a single incident among thousands of others. It isn't over and done with too long ago to fish up and correct. It is the key to developing a new offensive strategy that will finally get the upper hand in the war that is being waged on Israel and the Jews.

PURPOSE OF THE "AL DURA NEWS REPORT": To stimulate and justify genocidal Jew hatred: This was immediately successful. Israel was blamed for bringing upon itself the shahid operations of the "2nd Intifada" instead of being recognized as the target of war crimes and atrocities.

To justify the use of dead Palestinian children—real, fabricated, accidental, self-inflicted or recycled—as a weapon in the jihad against Israel and the West: A smashing success from September 30, 2000 to date.

International opinion (another lethal narrative) granted Israel the right to self-defense on the first days of the Pillars of Defense operation (2012). Then, like drug addicts, journalists returned to the opium dens of Gaza and started shooting up on dead children. This was followed by frantic calls for a ceasefire, and concluded with Palestinian victory celebrations.

THE "AL DURA NEWS REPORT" IS NOT JOURNALISM: Journalism, good, bad, or sloppy, is reporting on something that happened. The Dura incident didn't happen. There is nothing but the report. The under-one-minute video broadcast is not an excerpt from any reality extended in time and space beyond itself. But people believe something happened, believe the broadcast fits into the category of "journalism." Debunkers unwittingly treat the object of their analysis as journalism, pointing out the many ways in which it falls short of acceptable standards. There can be no end to the quibbling over details. No matter how much you win, you lose.

Why do people think the incident happened, why do they think they can form reasonable opinions on exactly how it happened? Not from looking at the video. Nothing happens in the video. It is an almost static poster, a clumsy advertisement pieced together from 6 slim bits of footage, signifying nothing. It is the voiceover commentary and the enveloping narrative that give the illusion of a dramatic incident occurring before one's eyes.

THE PREPOSTEROUS 45 MINUTES: The cameraman and Jamal insist that Israeli soldiers fired relentlessly at the man and boy for 45 minutes. Enderlin unashamedly confirms or avoids this element as it suits him, according to the circumstances. The claim is utterly preposterous to any right-minded human being, and absolutely necessary if the hoax is to serve its purpose. The boy cannot be killed in a crossfire. He must be the victim of merciless Israeli soldiers. So why can a serious journalist like James Fallows get away with inventing a crossfire? The invention of the crossfire in fact creates a separate, acceptable al Dura hoax for reasonable people, and leaves the preposterous 45 minutes for extremists. Instead of weakening the impact, this doubles it. It allows reasonable people to hang onto the whole Mideast Conflict narrative with its main dish and trimmings, while leaving the extremists undisturbed to use their version, as Mohamed Merah recently did to justify the savage murder of Jewish children and a teacher in Toulouse.

THE NON-EXISTENT 27 MINUTES: Talal claims he captured 27 minutes of the 45-minute ordeal. He goes so far as to explain why the 55-second video looks like it was shot in real time: the various frantic gestures were repeated at intervals throughout the 45-minutes in which the man and boy were pinned down by a hail of bullets. Again, this is utterly preposterous. Talal claims he turned his camera off and on in order to conserve the battery for the whole sequence. How did he know how long the sequence would last? Even so, unlucky cameraman, the battery died just as he was about to get the scene where the boy is fatally shot. And it took more than 20 minutes to change it. So he missed the part where the boy bled to death and the ambulance driver who was trying to rescue him was shot dead as well.

But it turns out that the 27-minutes of al Dura footage does not exist. The images do not appear in the 18-minutes of outtakes turned over to the Appellate court in the Karsenty case, and they do not figure in the 9 minutes that were spliced out.

THERE IS NO RAW FOOTAGE OF THE AL DURA SCENE: All you see is all there is. Less than a minute. Footage that is not plucked out of a reality that was extended in time and space. Footage that was hastily cobbled together. Even calling it a hoax is giving it too much credit! Why does this not matter to a French court, French and international media, and most people everywhere?

There is no raw footage because there is no incident. It is not a news report because there was nothing to report. But it created a hole in the head of the public mind. Because they swallowed and regurgitated this fraudulent manipulation, highly qualified journalists can't recognize a child killed in Syria and recycled as a victim of the Israelis in Gaza. They tremble with emotion over the obscene image of an Egyptian ambassador planting a kiss on the forehead of a child killed by a Hamas rocket and edified into a victim of an Israeli missile. And their senses were too numbed to do justice to the Jewish children murdered by Mohamed Merah.

A "KILL THE JEWS" POSTER WAS FED INTO THE WESTERN NEWS STREAM. How can we get it out of the news stream and back where it belongs as a lethal narrative, a weapon of mass destruction?

A mountain of anomalies, discrepancies, and incongruities has been piled up but the death of Mohamed al Dura still keeps shining on the top of the heap. Debunkers— like Israelis, Jews and Zionists in general— are always on the defensive. That's what happens when you don't recognize a war that is being waged against you. 21st Century jihad is a new form of warfare and a new type of jihad.

I am confident that people will catch on in time, and that exposure of the (al) Dura hoax will contribute largely to that enlightenment. If we haven't already figured out how to convince them, shouldn't we look for new angles, new light, new arguments?

12.19.12: The Dura hoax is the key to the 2-state solution hoax

2-state solution? The question is not the 2-state solution. People are free to say they are for it or against it, it changes nothing. The reality is that the 2-state solution has not happened, not since it was established in the 1947 UN declaration and certainly not since the launch of the Oslo peace process. If, as everyone knows, 2 states are the solution, then everyone would have to explain why, every time they are offered, the Arab-Muslim-Palestinian side says NO.

In reality, the 2-state solution is a bridge to nowhere that no one would take seriously today. In fact, no one does. But the 2-state solution serves a purpose: blaming Israel for the fact that it is not a solution. It wasn't offered soon enough, nicely enough, quickly or slowly enough and, worse, the state that is offered is not good enough. No matter how it is composed, there is always something wrong with it. One might, then, admit that what is wrong with it is that the Arab-Muslim-Palestinian camp is playing jihad and there is no room for any state of Israel on the map.

This is, to everyone who knows, unacceptable. So Israel must be blamed. And that is why the Dura hoax is so important. It allows Israel to be blamed for the crime of crimes: infanticide. It was a flash of blinding emotion that wiped out the truth that Arafat had turned his back on the best 2-state proposal anyone could offer. (Best until Olmert one-upped it and even that was not good enough)

—*Input for the aldurahjournalism.com project directed by Richard Landes*

DEBATE BETWEEN PASCALE BONIFACE AND MEÏR WAINTRATER

12/18/12 organized by J Call / Peace Now, Centre Bernard Lazare

Pascal Boniface, founder/director of IRIS think tank, allegedly advised the Socialist Party, in preparation for the 2007 presidential race, to forget about Jewish voters and cultivate its Muslim clientèle.

Meïr Waintrater, former editorial director of *l'Arche*, wanted nothing to do with the al Dura demystifiers. The one time he consented to publish an article related to the affair, he introduced it with an editorial demurral. Listening to his Peace Now reasoning in last night's debate, I understood more clearly than ever why he wouldn't touch the Dura affair.

The debate was centered on the possibilities for Israel-Palestine negotiations in the aftermath of the Arab Spring, the upgrade of Palestine's status at the UN, and other changes in the Middle East. Both debaters and the moderator uttered the article of faith: everyone knows the solution... two states roughly divided along the '67 lines with land swaps, a sovereign Palestine, a secure Israel...

Everyone knows, so why hasn't the deal been clinched?

In fact, isn't the "everyone knows solution" exactly what was offered at Camp David in the summer of 2000? The Dura blood libel and the jihad-intifada that ensued is the Palestinian response to that offer. Something worse than no!

The discourse and attitude of Pascal Boniface in the course of the debate is edifying. Presenting himself as a friend (if not of the Jews, certainly of the Jews in the audience, assumed to be convinced peaceniks), he delivers in bits and pieces a perfect plan for our extermination. And it won't be his fault—he is a friend—it will be our fault. He is a friend of Israel. Not, of course, of the current government. (And not of any recent government either) A friend of Israelis who are for peace and against the Occupation.

Boniface—remember, he is the head of a think tank focused on international strategies—was certain in 1993 that peace was irreversible. Now he admits his error. And now there's Hamas. Hamas is a reality, the Israelis have to talk to Hamas, the taboo can't hold anymore, you don't choose your enemies, you have to make peace with your enemies. The situation has worsened, Israel's image is degraded, the world has changed: the West no longer has the monopoly on Power. Israel should accept its place in the region [*i.e. not act as an intruder*] and make peace.

The conflict has become a focus of international attention. It stands at the core of relations between the West and the Muslim world. Accusing people who criticize Israel of anti-Semitism is unwise. He describes at length an incident where his son tells him he has a friend who is going to do a 2-week apprenticeship at IRIS. He would like to introduce her but she is Jewish and says Boniface is anti-Semitic. In fact she did her two-week stint, saw that all kinds of people, including Jews, work at IRIS.

Jews should take care not to let this conflict create a rupture between Jewish and non-Jewish French people. The CRIF is too powerful. The whole roster of French politicians from left to right comes to the annual CRIF dinner [*implying they come to get their marching orders*]. Waintrater interrupts to disagree on this point but Boniface insists. Oh yes, the CRIF is powerful. The CRIF of Nice was unhappy with my column in *Nice Matin*. They put pressure on the paper, the column was dropped.

Boniface says: I understand the fear of the Jews. I speak to the UOIF [*French branch of Muslim Brotherhood*]. I'm criticized for that but I think one should go everywhere, talk to everyone. I tell the UOIF they should say "Israel" not "the Zionist entity." I tell Blacks they can't compare the Shoah to the slave trade, because the Shoah was a genocidal project. But that was in the past. And you have to transmit this message to your fellow Jews. The Shoah was in the past, it's over. When the president of the CRIF compares terrorists to Nazis, that's wrong. [*Prasquier made this comparison after Merah executed three Jewish children in Toulouse.*]

Boniface opines: The most dangerous faction in the US is the Christian Zionists. They don't want Darwin taught in the schools, they own guns... AIPAC backed Romney but 70% of American Jewish voters chose Obama [*suggesting they are more intelligent and well-balanced than AIPAC*]. The conflict (Israel-Palestine) is not religious, it's territorial and political. Religion is instrumentalized... on both sides.

Pascal Boniface reiterates his complains of being persecuted, shut out of the media because he is critical of Israel, and concludes: Let me be clear about one thing— I don't put the Occupied and the Occupier on the same level. The solution has to come from the Occupier. The strongest party is the one that has to give in.

Before the Q & A session, Boniface was affable, urbane, friendly. But as soon as people started asking questions he became irritated, aggressive, and defensive. Author of a book entitled *A-t-on le droit de critique Israël?* [*do we have the right to criticize Israel?*], he himself does not accept the slightest criticism.

A woman respectfully, almost tearfully, reacted to his warning that relations between Jewish and non-Jewish French people would be blocked if the Jews kept being paranoid and complaining about anti-Semitism. She garbles the question, asks how he could say "relations between Jews and French people"... Jews ARE French... Boniface jumps at the chance to throw the question back in her face and denounce it as a precise illustration of how he is persecuted. He scolds her, she backs down.

A distinguished gentleman tries to explain that the question—do we have the right to criticize Israel—is skewed; it implies that the "lobby" will pounce on you if you dare to criticize Israel. Boniface was determined not to understand. His face darkened, he blew the man off once, twice, three times until the questioner gave up.

On several points—the CRIF, the imprescriptible right of the Jewish people to a homeland, the legitimacy of Jewish fear of violent anti-Semitism, the tenor of Abbas' speech to the UN General Assembly—Waintrater expressed a difference of opinion. Boniface did not slap him down but never really accepted to debate the issues. However, he constantly talked about the need for keeping the dialogue going.

Recap:

When we pare away details and look at the skeleton of Boniface's thought it is revealed as a recipe for disaster.

There is no genocidal threat. Therefore, when Jews complain about anti-Semitism they are being paranoid, they alienate themselves from society. Israel's existence is not threatened. It simply has to end the Occupation, accept the rules and regulations imposed by the majority in the region, forget about leaning on Western power, make peace with Fatah (on their terms) or find itself facing Hamas and forced to make peace on their terms. The conflict isn't religious, so Islamic Jew hatred in France and in Israel is not a factor and certainly not a cause. Jews should not try to influence domestic or international authorities. Good Jews in France avoid *communautarisme* (clannishness). Good Jews in Israel are for Peace and against the Occupation.

Chapter 9

AND MOHAMED AL DURAH BEGAT MOHAMED MERAH...

January 4, 2013

The fabricated murder of Mohamed al Dura has not lost its sting. Produced and broadcast by state-owned France 2 TV on September 30, 2000, the staged scene of the "death of a Palestinian child targeted by Israeli gunfire" has replaced "Christ killer" as a founding myth for genocidal Jew hatred.

The latest act of revenge took place in Toulouse last March when the French-Algerian jihadi, Mohamed Merah, slew a teacher, Jonathan Sandler, his two sons Aryeh and Gavriel, and seven year-old Miriam Monsonego. Merah, who had previously murdered three French paratroopers and critically wounded a fourth, filmed his exploits with a camera strapped to his chest. After shooting Jonathan Sandler and his sons outside the school, Merah burst into the courtyard, chased after Miriam, grabbed her by the hair, and shot her in the head. Reports of this gesture, which provoked comparisons with Nazi killers, shocked decent people in France and beyond.

Subsequently we learned that Merah had concocted a video medley of dead Palestinian children (everyone is a film maker today) that served as an introduction and justification of his deed. According to my sources, the al Dura blood libel is featured in Merah's rogue's gallery of Israeli (= Jewish) crimes. A YouTube posting identified as a video Merah sent to al Jazeera is recognizable as the original al Dura clip. The Dura-Merah connection is discussed in countless articles, videos, and debates; some denounce the al Dura hoax for incitement to genocidal Jew-hatred, others citing it as an explanation of Merah's distress.

Another aspiring Jew-killer, Yann Nkusa, awaiting trial in the case of the homegrown "Cannes" jihad cell dismantled in October, reportedly treasured a medley of dead Palestinian children. For all we know, it might be the same one Merah used. Global media, too, are hooked on the child-killer drug. To illustrate Israeli atrocities during the Pillars of Defense operation in Gaza they recycled dead Syrian children, victims of domestic accidents and misfired Hamas rockets, and Hamas combatants transformed into innocent babes... Yes but, reasonable people will argue, children are killed in this war. True. Palestinians deliberately put children in harm's way, zealously teach them to seek death as *shahids*, and use them as weapons in an aggressive war against Israel. Israeli soldiers do not deliberately kill children. The al Dura myth was crafted to prove they do.

Does this explain why Charles Enderlin and France 2 relentlessly pursue those who point out the obvious? The "news report" is a fake. Philippe Karsenty, who has been going through the judicial wringer since 2005, will be back in Appellate Court on the 16th of January after his 2008 acquittal was overturned by the highest court. Why this merciless pursuit of an honest citizen who, in the words of Enderlin himself, was acquitted simply on the grounds of good faith? The court did not rule that the "news report" was a fake but only that the defendant had given proof of due diligence in criticizing a document that is, in fact, subject to doubt.

As Merah's killing spree reminds us, the al Dura myth is fuel for genocidal Jew hatred. Is that what they want? The courts that rule with cockeyed values, the French journalists lined up like wooden soldiers in defense of comrade Enderlin, the commentators worldwide who defend a crudely staged report without ever bothering to delve into the facts?

Does it explain why, despite conclusive evidence that the scene was staged, the al Dura myth stands its ground and continues to do its heinous damage?

The journalists, the judges, the commentators, and the variously duped don't have to be anti-Semites. Then, why would they cling to a tainted object that repeatedly and verifiably provokes murderous attacks—that they declare to be unacceptable—against Jews? The sole function of the al Dura myth is to establish quintessential Jewish guilt... so that, when the genocide gets under way, it will be the fault of the victims, Israelis in particular and Jews in general... and, beyond that, our Western world.

The France 2 cameraman Talal Abu Rahma, who won a slew of prizes for his handiwork, reports that Mohamed al Dura and his father Jamal were pinned down by Israeli gunfire for 45 minutes. No crossfire. Israeli soldiers, he declares, mercilessly fired military weapons at an unarmed sitting target for 45 minutes, critically wounding the father, until they finally managed to kill the child. The incident was so crucial for what would follow—in fact, a Palestinian jihad operation peddled as an intifada—that the self-defined seasoned war reporter testified the next day under oath to the Palestinian Center for Human Rights: Israeli soldiers committed cold-blooded murder. Before his eyes.

Unfortunately he was not able to capture any of it on film.

There is nothing about the al Dura scene that isn't grotesque, ludicrous, and slipshod. The 55-second video- shot heard round the world bears no resemblance to news: six slivers of sloppily filmed and mounted footage form the kernel of an enveloping narrative—too long and winding to be summarized here— that collapses from the first line. The cameraman, the surviving "victim," and the France 2 Jerusalem correspondent, Charles Enderlin, who packaged the whole thing, alternatively show, hide, swear on, withdraw and multiply details, adapting the truth to the circumstances. And the slick card sharks have been getting away with it for eleven years!

In a feat of counter-engineering, the construction is sustained by the weight of the accusation—Jews are merciless child-killers—not by any concrete evidence. This is why the impossible 45-minutes of gunfire aimed at the innocent victims is inextricably joined to the narrative and why so many commentators choose to ignore it. One single detail proves the whole thing is false. But if it is false, what else falls apart? The intifada, for example. Just this week Suha Arafat calmly explained how her late husband Yasser planned the intifada after the failure of the Camp David talks that summer. So, the "intifada" wasn't triggered by Ariel Sharon's "provocative" visit to the Temple Mount. But it was deliberately sparked by the staged "death" of Mohamed al Dura. Notice the resemblance with the September 11th anniversary attack on the US outpost in Benghazi. There, too, a narrative of a spontaneous popular protest against an insult to Islam was concocted to cover for a jihad operation. And look how far we have come: it is the U.S. government that peddled the narrative!

How is it possible to lie blatantly in full view of the information-flush 21st century? How can Charles Enderlin persist in accusing Israeli soldiers of concentrating their gunfire on a Palestinian boy for 45 minutes when the al Dura video has been dissected millimeter by millimeter revealing that it is full of faked sound and fury? Who sent Susan Rice network-hopping to prattle about the disgraceful anti-Islamic video that triggered the protests that degenerated into violence that led to the unfortunate demise of Ambassador Stevens? The president put it clearly: the future does not belong to those who diss' the prophet. Videos of the battered ambassador dragged through the streets were circulating widely as Secretary Clinton puckered her dimples and thanked the courageous Libyans who tried to rescue our ambassador.

From Netzarim Junction in the Gaza Strip to Benghazi in an Arab Springtime'd Libya we see the same stubborn determination to confuse our citizens and disguise the nature of the war being waged against us. On 9/11/01, one year after Israel was attacked by the fabricated child martyr, the United States was attacked by civilian airplanes turned into weapons.

What, then, can we expect from the French judges convened to rule, once more, on the narrow issue of defamation in the Karsenty case? One more show trial? Or an honorable *prise de conscience* of their responsibility?

— *Dispatch International*

FRENCH JOURNALISM DROWNS TRYING TO SAVE CHARLES ENDERLIN
January 31, 2013

The honor of French journalism reached new depths on January 16 with one more absurd hearing in the lawsuit brought by France 2/Charles Enderlin against Philippe Karsenty, convicted of slander in 2006, acquitted in 2008, thrown back into Appellate Court after the highest court (*Cour de Cassation*) rejected the 2008 judgment on a technicality. Karsenty is accused of slander for declaring on his media watch blog in 2004 that the "death of Mohamed al-Dura" broadcast by France 2 on September 30, 2000 is a hoax, a fake, a staged scene. The state-owned channel, he wrote, should fire Jerusalem correspondent Charles Enderlin and news director Arlette Chabot.

The contested news report accuses Israeli soldiers of deliberately shooting at an unarmed Palestinian man and boy for 45 minutes with the express intention of killing the "child". "Cold blooded murder," in the words of cameraman Talal Abu Rahmah. Though the dubious news report has been reduced to shreds by serious investigators, citizen Karsenty is, in the eyes of the law, guilty of slander. He may be acquitted if he proves good faith, due diligence, appropriate language, and absence of personal animosity. Yes, the commoner who denounces an apparent journalistic manipulation is expected to conduct an extensive investigation while the journalist who influences public opinion on a grandiose scale does not have to prove due diligence or absence of animosity to the subject of the report, namely the Israeli soldiers in the outpost at Netzarim Junction in the Gaza Strip that day.

The press release issued by the journalist's union on the eve of the trial, urging colleagues to come en masse to defend Enderlin, was apparently a rhetorical gesture; three showed up briefly, none actually covered the proceedings. But they made their point: The distracted reader would conclude that Karsenty has been dragging Enderlin through the courts for the past eight years.

Last week's hearing was an accurate reflection of the skewed notion of journalism, justice, and reality that prevails in this pitifully unfounded lawsuit. The three-judge panel, rather smirky as Karsenty set up a large-scale model of Netzarim Junction (where the killing of al-Dura is supposed to have taken place), gradually got drawn into the defendant's encyclopedic demonstration of the anomalies, discrepancies, aberrations, fabrications, contradictions, absurdities, and falsifications concocted by Palestinian jihadis and validated by Western media. The so-called death scene is examined from every possible angle. No trace of wounds, no blood, the wall that serves as a backdrop to the cringing man and boy is intact, no signs of injury or death. The boy – pronounced dead in a voiceover by Enderlin who was in Ramallah when the scene was filmed in Gaza – squirms, shades his eyes, looks at the camera.

So much for the due diligence of the honest citizen. When it came time for the tip top professional to present his version of the facts the machine broke down. For a full twenty minutes, Enderlin and his lawyer Maître Bénédicte Amblard, fiddled with the video, trying to get their act together. Sound, image, forward, backward, nothing worked. When the show did finally go on, it was a replay of several newscasts with Enderlin's reports on the incident, followed by the spin film made in 2008 to "enlighten" the Appeals Court, and the show & tell video of Jamal al-Dura displaying his scars. This was a perfectly coherent demonstration of the plaintiff's strategy: the news report is infallible because Enderlin and Abu Rahmah are infallible. The defendant's critique is inadmissible because he relied on second hand information from "militant" sources instead of going to Gaza to interview Jamal and visiting the hospital in Amman where he was treated. Enderlin, who proudly claims to know everything there is to know about war reporting, reminds the court that this is not CCTV stuff, these are images captured in the heat of battle. Yes, but … Enderlin's newscasts are filled with snips and snaps of staged scenes that the court had just discovered, complete with their making-of, in Karsenty's Power Point. These Pallywood productions have been available on the Net for years.

Philippe Karsenty called three witnesses; Enderlin, as usual, called none. Esther Schapira, producer for the German public network ARD, and author of two documentary films on the al-Dura case, went to Israel in 2001 to get the story-behind-the-story of soldiers who shot a child and a father who couldn't protect his son. But due diligence led her to question the authenticity of the news report. Though France 2 and ARD are both members of a pan-European group, Charles Enderlin was aggressive and uncooperative. He refused her request to see the master tape of Talal's film, saying he would only show it if there was a court order. He threatened to sue her if she claimed the report was falsified. "I was shocked," said Schapira. "For a journalist, every question is open to question." She calmly expanded on her reasons for concluding that it is highly unlikely that Israeli soldiers killed Mohamed al-Dura, but "didn't want to accuse anyone of lying or fabrication, I didn't have the smoking gun".

Dr. Patrick Bloch, a surgeon specialized in combat wounds, testified to the obvious fact that the man and boy in the video were unscathed. He showed gory images of exit wounds that every war correspondent would recognize. Ballistics expert Jean-Claude Schlinger confirmed that the wall behind the alleged victims was not pulverized, as it would have been by 45 minutes of uninterrupted gunfire from military weapons. The handful of bullet holes on the wall were fired straight on, and could not have come from the Israeli position.

But there's the rub, and the *Avocat Général* (a sort of state's attorney but not really), Jean-François Cornaille de Vallray, wrapped it up concisely: the Court is not asked to rule on the "historic truth" but simply to judge the defendant within the limits of the good faith definition. Will the verdict turn against Philippe Karsenty for defending himself with documentation that was not in his hands when he wrote the incriminating article? Were the presiding judge, Jaques Laylavoix, and his two colleagues impressed by the eloquent reasoning of Karsenty's counsel, Delphine Meillet and Patrick Maisonneuve? Might the judges rule against France 2/Charles Enderlin for failing to lift a finger to corroborate the – obviously dubious – news report? Or will they harken to the trembling plea of Maître Amblard, begging for mercy for her client, Charles Enderlin, whose only fault is telling the truth about the "Middle East Conflict"? The verdict will be announced on April 3.

Whichever way the judicial wind blows, French journalism has disgraced itself. Beyond the personal failings of Charles Enderlin stands the arrogant refusal of his colleagues to face the evidence and publicly acknowledge what they privately admit.

— *Dispatch International*

ISRAELI GOVERNMENT DOWNS THE AL-DURA MYTH

May 29, 2013

French court has again postponed verdict in scandalous case

There is abundant concrete evidence that two men hacked a British soldier to death in Woolwich on May 22. There were eyewitnesses to the attempted beheading. The immediate aftermath was filmed from every angle by multiple devices. One of the perpetrators, Mujahid (ex-Michael) Adebelajo, starred in an on the spot amateur video produced at his demand. Waving his blood-soaked hands, still clutching a knife and a cleaver, he justified his act religiously – citing the Sura Al-Tawba, "we must fight them as they fight us" – followed by the usual jihadist political garbage. Most news media deleted the Koranic citation but the uncensored version is available at a click on the Net. The jihad murder of drummer Lee Rigby is an incident, not a baseless news report.

There were more people at Netzarim Junction in the Gaza Strip on September 30, 2000 than on Wellington Road in Woolwich on May 22 but no one saw the alleged al-Dura incident (the supposedly deliberate killing of a young boy by Israeli soldiers). A dozen professional cameramen had been filming scenes from early morning. Their raw footage shows Palestinians brazenly attacking the Israeli outpost with rocks, firebombs, and burning tires. Elsewhere, out of range of potential Israeli gunfire, they played mock battle scenes with fake injuries and comical ambulance evacuations. At one point armed Palestinians briefly fired live ammunition.

But the alleged victims, identified as Jamal al-Dura and his son Mohamed, were not caught in the crossfire. How do we know? Because Jamal and the France 2 cameraman Talal Abu Rahma, the only one who filmed the al-Dura scene, swore that gunfire coming solely from the Israeli position was deliberately aimed at the unarmed civilians for 45 minutes until they "finally" killed the boy and critically wounded his father. The cameraman claims he filmed 27 minutes of the incident. But all he has is a one-minute 6-strip patchwork video, broadcast by state-owned France 2 TV with a dramatic voiceover by Jerusalem correspondent Charles Enderlin. The so-called news report is so crude and clumsy, it defies description. The enveloping narrative, which deserves equal or more attention than the slapdash video, is adequate proof that Talal Abu

Rahma, Jamal al-Dura, and Charles Enderlin are not trustworthy.

The sensational child-killer accusation triggered a wave of atrocities in Israel and attacks on Jews worldwide. It stands as an abiding indictment against the Jewish state, no less poisonous than the Christ-killer charge of olden days. Once a pretext for genocidal hatred takes hold, it is almost impossible to release its grip. The al-Dura myth – forged in the space of a few seconds, on television, in the 21st century – was swallowed by a worldwide supposedly media-savvy population.

Now, thirteen years after the fraudulent news report was first broadcast, an Israeli government commission named by then Vice Prime Minister Moshe Ya'alon, under the direction of Yossi Kuperwasser, director general of the Strategic Affairs Ministry, has examined the evidence and presented its conclusions in a 36-page report.[1] As reluctant Israeli officials had warned in the past, this gesture opened the floodgates, releasing tons of the very filth that has fed and sustained the al-Dura myth to this day.

The nadir of journalistic skullduggery is exposed in a secret Facebook group, the Vulture Club, which reportedly has some 3,500 members.[2] Their vicious outhouse reactions to the Kuperwasser report are but one step removed from the published articles where they clean up the language and claim to be objective. Journalists in high and lesser places – *Ha'aretz, le Monde, UK Telegraph, rue89*, to mention a few – and their commenting readers have outdone themselves in ferocity, while the sincerely uninformed opt for polite skepticism. The defining feature of these reactions is virulent ignorance. Not daring to examine the evidence, they grab at one or two details and, with no contradictor in sight, present them as absolute confirmation that France 2's al-Dura report is authentic and its critics are extremists. I challenge them to a public debate. They will come on like rabid dogs and slunk off with their tails between their legs.

Working since September 2012, the commission examined evidence from a wide array of investigators, analysts, specialists, journalists, military personnel, and simple citizens before concluding in measured terms that the al-Dura "news report" is baseless. There is nothing to support the claim that the man and youth were "targets of gunfire from the Israeli position" and, in fact, nothing in the video to supports the claim that they were hit by any gunfire at all.[3] Further, the report measures the disastrous effects of the al-Dura incitement to hatred. The authors remind journalists of the importance of respecting their own professional codes that include due diligence, fact checking, correcting errors, and accepting criticism.

The al-Dura scene is a video, not an incident.

Where in the free world would a journalist and TV channel drag people into court for expressing doubts on the veracity of a news report? And then insist that only "an impartial international commission" can settle the issue? What should strike the alert mind is not the fact that the Israeli government took thirteen years to weigh in, but that French media and officials have been stubbornly defending a hoax for over a decade.

Skeptics should be reminded that a French Appellate Court acquitted Philippe Karsenty of defamation in a lawsuit brought by France 2 and Charles Enderlin. *Dispatch International* has learned from a reliable source that the presiding judge in that case thought France 2 would clinch a decisive victory if the raw footage were made available. After viewing the evidence the three-judge panel was honest enough to conclude that the defendant had grounds for publicly questioning the authenticity of the "news report".

The latest bounce back of the case was heard in January, 2013. The verdict, initially promised for April 3, then postponed to May 22, has now been set for June 26. What does this signify? Are the judges torn between the truth and the consequences (of condemning France 2 and Charles Enderlin)? Were the courts under pressure from the previous administration? From this administration? Either, both, or neither? Or has the al-Dura affair become *une affaire d'Etat*?

Mohamed Merah justified his execution of Jewish children in Toulouse as revenge for the killing of Palestinian children in Gaza. This is why the Israeli government decided that the al-Dura blood libel would not fade away; it must be countered. The instant blowback in all its smuggery will not have the last word. Intelligent voices are now coming forward to accredit the government report and the serious research on which it is based.

The bloody hands of the jihad killer in Woolwich are a logical extension of the bloody hands of the jihad killers in Ramallah who butchered two Israeli reservists in October 2000 – to avenge the "murder" of Mohamed al-Dura. In its evening newscast on May 22, when SkyNews was already showing Adebelajo's hands dipped in blood, France 2 devoted 15 minutes of prime time "news" to a languid feature on 3 French converts to Islam, religion of peace, harmony, tranquility, spirituality, fulfillment. Three days later a bearded man came up behind a French soldier patrolling at La Défense in Paris, slit his throat, and got away, though two policemen were with the soldier. The killer missed the carotid artery. That soldier will survive.

And we too will survive – if we heed the voices of integrity, trust the clear-minded, and exercise due diligence.

[1] plo.gov.il/English/Media Center
[2] freebeacon.com/vultures
[3] See, for example, Appendix 3: "Statement by Lieutenant-Colonel (res.) Nizar Fares, commander of the IDF position at Netzarim Junction on September 30, 2000"

— *Dispatch International*

THE AL-DURA BLOOD LIBEL AFFAIR:

July 2013 interview with Nidra Poller by Jerry Gordon [abridged]

Gordon: We are interviewing a frequent collaborator for the New English Review who has been widely published. She has a recent work of fiction, *Karimi Hotel and Other African Equations*. She has been published in such outlets as the *Wall Street Journal Europe, The American Thinker, National Review On-Line and Commentary Magazine*. She is currently the Paris correspondent for *Dispatch International*. Welcome, Nidra Poller.

Poller: It's good to be here, Jerry.

Gordon: You are about to publish a collection of your writings on probably one of the major blood libels committed during the course of the 21st Century. I am referring to the Al-Dura affair. You have covered this as a writer based in Paris since its occurrence 13 years ago. How did you get interested in this topic?

Poller: At that time ...after Ariel Sharon's visit to the Temple Mount (September 28) was used as a pretext for starting a campaign of violence against Israel... I was writing fiction... I never considered myself a journalist. I had been living in Paris since 1972. I had a nice life. That day, there was a sea change. As if I was torn out of the community. Being a writer and student of history—my undergraduate major— I started a writer's notebook. I didn't have television when the Al-Dura report was broadcast, I read about it in print media. My immediate reaction as a writer was: the coincidence is too heavy. That can't be. Somehow a cameraman was on the spot when this terrible thing happened? So I never had an emotional reaction to the image and, being a writer of words, not a specialist of image, I've never been fascinated by the image. I've always seen it as full sound and fury signifying nothing.

I wrote about it right then in my notebook. (*Notes from a Simple Citizen*). And that's how I gradually started to do journalism. In a letter published in the *International Herald Tribune* [Nov.2000], I wrote that Israelis are not child killers, Jews are not child killers... I recognized it as blood libel.

Gordon: When did you meet some of your colleagues in the course of your writings on the Al-Dura affair and begin to understand the enormity of this crime committed against Jews as well as the world?

Poller: Well I think, without flattering myself, that I explained right away how it was being used: First they say we're child killers. Then they say the children are not in the front lines of the demonstrations. That meant the Israelis were going out and finding the children under their mothers' skirts and killing them. Then—in the space of a few days they said yes, the children are out there. They want to conquer Jerusalem and there is no way we can stop them. I wrote about the al Dura image off and on in the following years. I think it was in 2002, 2003, that I started to meet people investigating it. My colleague Véronique Chemla introduced me to Stéphane Juffa of the Metula News Agency. I met the late Gérard Huber when he brought out *Contre-expertise d'une mise en scène*. I knew it wouldn't get any attention in France. I translated excerpts and summaries, and gave them to David Kupelian who published them at WorldNetDaily. Later I met Richard Landes. I introduced him to Gérard Huber and others. I worked with him as he was going back and forth between Paris, Boston, and Israel. I met Israeli physicist Nahum Shahaf and spent hours at his home viewing footage. I have worked with many people active in this investigation. At the same time I developed my own approach, based on the concept of "lethal narratives."

Gordon: Why has it taken the Israeli government 13 years to come out with an official report on the Al-Dura affair?

Poller: I go to Israel as often as possible and I've been witness directly or indirectly to this discussion in the government. I understand why they hesitated. When the government report did come out it provoked hatred, terrible comments from readers in the media. The idea was—how can Israelis think they're not guilty just because their government did a report? Many government officials thought there was nothing to be gained from bringing this up; the image would go around again. People would say the same thing again. It would be a loss. There was a lot of hope that the thing would just die down. So many other lies were told about Israel in the meantime. I can see their point of view. They're not only trying to protect the Israeli population but Jews all over the world. Their kids go into the army. Everyone knows people that were killed or maimed in terrorist attacks or military actions. Honestly, if I were the Israelis I would say look, you guys in France take care of this. It is your television that did it. Israelis are careful about not suppressing press freedom. Anyway what could they do? Throw all the journalists out? Then there are the ways of government bureaucracies: If one person thinks they should do a report, someone else will think they shouldn't, and it gets pushed aside. When it was placed in the hands of Bogie Ya'alon and Yossi Kuperwasser, nothing could stop them. We have to give credit to the people who worked on the Israeli report, the input the government has had over the years. We should give credit to Danny Seaman who stood up right from the beginning. Many times Enderlin threatened to sue him. Danny said, Go ahead and sue me.

Gordon: One of the central figures in this drama is Charles Enderlin, the producer who carries both an Israeli and a French passport and was also friendly with some of the Israeli leaders at the time. I am referring specifically to Ehud Barak and Shimon Peres. Did that have an effect on how Israel reacted at the time?

Poller: Yes. People respected Enderlin and didn't dream he would do such a thing. You see, on the one hand, we have the evidence that the video is a fake. (There'll be more than two hands). On the second hand we have evidence that Enderlin continues to defend the video 13 years later. He does it by lying and distorting and counting on help from his friends who are not very ethical. Now on the third hand we have the Barak government thinking they could stop the violence by diplomacy, without aggravating the situation. When Enderlin called the IDF spokesman he said, "I have some very damaging video and you better admit your guilt, otherwise it's going to be even worse." At every stage in the chain of events somebody made a mistake and it was hard to go back. They tried. General Yom Tov Samia who was, I believe, head of the Southern Command at the time, did an investigation and concluded the gunfire couldn't have come from the Israeli position. Enderlin called it a whitewash.

Gordon: The forensic evidence indicated that it was virtually impossible for the snipers at the Netzarim crossing to even hit Mohammed al-Dura and his father Jamal who were secreted behind this concrete object. In fact there was a Palestinian military official who scouted the area after this film was done and started picking up "spent cartridges." Was that an indication of something being played out?

Poller: The story of the spent cartridges is comical. Enderlin explained: "Esther Schapira thought she caught Talal in a lie. Well, she didn't bother to ask. We could have told her the general picked up the spent cartridges and told Talal not to say anything."

Think about it. A state-owned television station... their Jerusalem correspondent with a great reputation writes that his stringer was told to keep quiet about withholding evidence. The book is supposedly read by several critics and... I think I'm the only one who picked up that item. That's the sloppiness of it all. Going back to the forensic evidence... of course Nahum Shahaf was the first to investigate that. He is a physicist. He did us a great service, not only in investigating and explaining, but also because he got the raw footage shot that day and without it we would have had a much more difficult time explaining what went on. When you look at the video... it is six thin slices of film... it lasts about 55 seconds if you include the last bit where the child looks up at the camera and goes down. There is no raw footage of that scene. Even if there were no forensic evidence, it is clear that nothing happened. I describe it as a poster. It is not news... not journalism.... it is like advertising. It doesn't have the same configuration. Nobody would shoot a scene that way if it were journalism. It's a close up and it's a poster. It is clear that Israeli soldiers did not fire for 45 minutes trying to kill the child. One or two days after the incident Talal made a sworn statement to the Palestine Center for Human Rights. He swore the Israelis did it in cold blood, deliberately... they saw the man and the boy. He said as a war reporter he knows that is the only place the bullets could have come from. A cameraman shoots a scene and then runs over to some Palestinian NGO and makes a sworn affidavit saying what he saw? The thing is ridiculous from the very beginning. I have talked with so many people and presented it to so many people. If you say to them, Talal says the Israeli soldiers fired for 45 minutes, it wasn't a crossfire. He's the witness... people are inventing the crossfire. He said five minutes of crossfire then 45 minutes only from the Israeli position. Talal said "I filmed 27 minutes of it" and he has only 55 seconds. Now if someone lies to that extent... Then Jamal, says the same thing. "They fired for 45 minutes. They saw me. I tried to get them to stop. I saw my son. I looked at my son I saw the bullet and I saw he was dead." Well then look at that video. He never looked at his son in the video and there is no other footage. When did he look at his son? Every detail is that way. I don't know how any honest, sensible person can hear that and believe that this is journalism. I make a distinction between what is journalism and what happened. We don't know what happened and we don't know who that young man is. Journalism is telling things that happened that you can corroborate and verify. Look at Dominique Strauss-Kahn in the hotel room in New York. All kinds of lawyers, all kinds of lawsuits, the police, every kind of investigation... We don't know exactly what happened and there is no way to know. No one saw it, so you can't build a case on what happened. You can only build a case on what you know and that's journalism. Al-Dura is not journalism. It is not a news report and in any other situation it would have been off the air.

Gordon: Because the Al-Dura affair has persisted, it has involved a series of legal matters in the French courts. One of the principle accusers of the fraud is Philippe Karsenty. He appears to be a minor hero for taking on this myth that Mr. Enderlin and others including the Palestinian camera man have perpetuated in this regard. What can you tell us about that and more importantly how peculiar is the French juridical system?

Poller: I attended almost every hearing. I have known Philippe since he started working on the case. In the first trial I was close to Maître Amblard — the lawyer for France 2 and Enderlin. I wrote about looking at her pile of folders and thinking: "My goodness, she must have all of this evidence and here I am stupid, and thinking I'm a journalist, and writing about this." It turns out there was nothing in that stack of files. In all these years they've never produced a bit of evidence. It's nothing you could imagine compared to an American court where people are put on the spot. There was no cross-examination. Over the years, I've seen Philippe improve his presentation. He made a three dimensional mockup of the Netzarim Junction. At first, the three judge panel looked like they were thinking "What's this excited guy doing?" They were hostile to Karsenty. And then they started to really look at the evidence. Talking as a writer, not a journalist, I think they were saying, "Oh my goodness, how are we going to convict this guy? It is a fake." So they have postponed their verdict twice.

They can't settle this issue in court. You can't settle this issue if you only stay on the Al-Dura affair. That is why I moved on to "lethal narratives." You have to examine how the Al-Dura affair fits in to Enderlin's vision of the Mid-East conflict. All these mechanisms for making war against Israel by way of a peace process. By climbing further, all the way to the whole reality of Islamic jihad... we understand the so-called Intifada and what is called legitimate demands for territory. We understand today that they are fighting jihad against Israel... and now the West is drawn in. I think we can see it when just a short while ago a British soldier was hacked to death in South London. This is happening all of the time in Israel ... Because of Al-Dura, because of the blood libel, instead of it being seen as an atrocity, the reaction was, "You have to understand, you are killing their children, they have no other way to hit back..." So, first they made a fake child-killing. Then they sent the children to be killed. They've been doing it ever since... and they have committed atrocities and killed Israeli children... The world did not react as it should have. That is why this movement continues to spread... And it is beyond Israel and beyond the Jews... and it's the same mechanism. I think the more we can help to explain this... Then we can come back to al-Dura affair and unravel it. It is a linchpin for this whole affair. And when you look at the video with open eyes, you see that it is totally fake. Even people who are quite aware of the nature of Palestinian propaganda were taken in by the video. Blood libel works that way because blood libel speaks to those who think Jews are Christ killers, child killers. It's the same thing. But blood libel also speaks to Jews who haven't gotten over Jewish guilt feelings. Once you touch that... Jews always feel they might be guilty. There are nations, activists, groups that think killing children is great. Samir Kuntar was welcomed as a hero in Lebanon for brutally murdering an Israeli child. They can justify it. Jews can't. Some Jews, instead of thinking, "We didn't do it" react with: "Oh, that's terrible. How could we do such a thing?" Once a person reacts that way it's so deep-seated that you can't get out of it by any superficial technique. That is why I never give up working on the Al-Dura affair. Because it is one of the deepest problems that has confronted us in my lifetime.

Gordon: Nidra, how would you compare the Al-Dura affair to another French travesty, The Dreyfus Affair in *fin de siècle* France ?

Poller: When I published my first article for *Commentary — Betrayed by Europe: An Expatriate's Lament*—I told about this sea change in France... Jews were confronted with anti-Semitism... and how I felt, having left the United States to live here. There were two letters to the editor: one from the French ambassador to the United States, Jean-David Levitte, and the other from Alain Besançon. They said France is not anti-Semitic, they mentioned the Dreyfus Affair as an example of how France is good to the Jews. In other words, we kicked him into the ground, sent him into exile, disgraced him, led him practically to his death and then we said no, as a matter of fact he wasn't guilty. If you compare Al-Dura to the Dreyfus Affair, I would say that French intellectuals have been distinctly absent including, in the early stages, high powered Jewish French intellectuals. I met with many of them—together with Richard Landes and others—and showed them the evidence. Very few wanted to hear about it and none of them wanted to talk about it. They didn't mobilize. Intellectuals did mobilize, yes, for Enderlin. At the slightest danger that the hoax would be recognized they would sign petitions, write articles. It has been 13 years and they still haven't admitted it is a hoax. Blood libel is far more dangerous than commonplace anti-Semitic harassment. And the reaction has been very slow in coming, which is all the more disgraceful because we are in the 21st century... this is after the Shoah.

Gordon: Were there any American groups that were complicit in covering up the blood libel of the Al-Dura affair? What can you tell us about that and what effect did it have?

Poller: It was general, so I wouldn't like to mention any particular explosive case. There is too much conflict among people who should be working together. I don't want to pinpoint any individual or group. For years we have presented the evidence to American Jewish groups. They have so much more money than our French organizations... if they wanted to do something... At first, the Jewish umbrella organization, the CRIF, didn't want to talk about it at all. When Richard Prasquier became president, he took it on... and he was criticized for it. It's the same when you talk about jihad or Islamization. The mechanism is like a flashing light pinned on our lapel. It says, "This is bad." And then it's associated with bad things of the past: the Shoah, Nazis, Hitler, discrimination, killing people for their ideas and beliefs. Every time somebody tries to explain the danger— I could mention our friends, Bat Ye'or, Andy Bostom, yourself— I don't want to leave anyone out... When they put that flashing light on Philippe Karsenty, the Israeli Ambassador, heads of this or that Jewish organization, they have to balance things out, keep good relations with our friends and enemies, raise money... They have to keep their reputation clean and once that flashing light is pinned on a person they say, "Oh no don't go near him. Maybe the child was killed in a crossfire, we don't know and we're not going to get involved. Karsenty goes too far. He says it's a hoax." And another thing—people in the American Jewish organizations don't read the material, don't speak French.

Gordon: Nidra, you have been keeping an important watching brief on this blood libel of the 21st Century and for that we have to commend you. We appreciate this time you have spent with us and we look forward to the publication of your chronicle hopefully this coming fall.

Poller: Thank you, Jerry.

— *New English Review (video at vimeo.com/68104063)*

AL DURA SHOW TRIALS END BADLY
July 3, 2013

An apparent victory for state-owned France Télévisions network and Jerusalem correspondent Charles Enderlin in the long legal battle they initiated against French citizen Philippe Karsenty may turn out to be the last stage in a cascade of strategic errors... by the broadcaster. On June 26th the 11th Chamber of the Appellate Court convicted citizen Karsenty of slander and ordered him to pay €7000 in damages for publicly declaring that the al Dura news report broadcast from Netzarim Junction in the Gaza Strip on September 30, 2000 was a hoax.

The video at the heart of the controversy was said to depict in real time the killing of a Palestinian youth, identified as Mohamed al Dura, and the wounding of his father Jamal, "targets of gunfire from the Israeli position." None of this is visible in the video shot by cameraman Talal Abu Rahmah—less than one minute of an essentially static scene. The action and the accusation are superimposed by Enderlin's voiceover commentary and elaborated in an enveloping narrative constantly repeated over the years. The incendiary effects of the broadcast were instant and long-lasting while, in other quarters, doubts were immediately raised about its authenticity.

In 2004, ignoring a substantial body of critical analysis published worldwide, France 2 and Charles Enderlin pressed charges against three seemingly defenseless bloggers, with the announced intention of silencing all doubters once and for all. The persistent line of attack pursued in the courtroom as in the media has been to portray those who question the reliability of the al Dura broadcast as far-right crackpot conspiracy theorists with axes to grind. Additional adjectives are added according to circumstances.

By suing for libel, the plaintiffs avoided a serious probe of the controversial news report while playing on the ambiguity of libel law to claim, with each small legal victory, that its authenticity was validated. In fact, the Court was not called to judge the facts but, rather, to judge the competence and good faith of citizen Karsenty: did he, at the time he denounced the report as a hoax, perform due diligence, accumulate adequate proof, and express himself in measured terms without personal animosity against Charles Enderlin and France 2.

Utterly disregarding this distinction, al Jazeera's on the spot courthouse report opened with a banner: "French court rules intifada video was authentic." Briefly interviewed, Philippe Karsenty said he is confident that the truth will not be silenced. "What happened here was outrageous...obnoxious." Counsel for the plaintiffs, Maître Bénédicte Amblard, announced with a smile: "My client is satisfied with this condemnation that will bring an end to years and years of trials." As if Charles Enderlin had been dragged through the courts for 7 years by grumpy crackpots!

A France Télévisions communiqué reiterates her client's satisfaction that Philippe Karsenty was punished for "baseless accusations against the news report of the death of Mohamed Al Durah." In sanctioning a "grave insult to the honor of a journalist" the court recognizes the merits of all journalists who practice their vocation with professionalism.

Having attended 99% of the hearings in this case I can testify that citizen Karsenty became increasingly professional while France Télévisions and Charles Enderlin fumbled and mumbled, endlessly repeating the same weak arguments, producing no evidence to substantiate their case. Convicted in the court of first resort despite the *avocat général's* [public advocate] eloquent plea for acquittal, Karsenty won on appeal... because the court viewed raw footage shot at Netzarim Junction that day by Abu Rahmah.

The plaintiffs took the case to the highest court ["*Cassation*," which cannot be compared to the Supreme Court] where it was remanded to the appeals court on the grounds that the Appellate judge had improperly assisted the defendant by ordering France 2 to hand over the raw footage. In plain terms this means that the concrete evidence sustains Karsenty's claim that the scene was staged. But he didn't have the footage in 2004.

Given this bizarre judicial logic, the Appellate Court reached its guilty verdict on June 26th. Case closed? On the contrary, the accumulated evidence produced by the defense in the course of this stubborn litigation has visibly strengthened the case against the broadcaster. Elsewhere, Al Dura demythifiers have pursued and refined their investigations, reaching and convincing an ever wider public.

Forces determined to erase the al Dura blood libel are emboldened, not intimidated. In the space of a few short days since the verdict was pronounced, new information has been made public, new voices are raised. Several books—in French and in English— are slated for publication this fall.

And what will France Télévisions and Charles Enderlin do about it? If the al Dura news report met the standards of professional journalism, if the broadcaster had responded to challenges by providing corroboration instead of suing bloggers, the affair would have been honorably settled long ago. The problem is that the news report cannot be corroborated and the endless lamentation of its producer cannot substitute for concrete evidence.

The al Dura broadcast is not a mixed grill that can be served to each according to his taste; it is an indivisible whole. The France 2 cameraman who shot the alleged incident testified under oath: Israeli soldiers fired on their sitting target for 45 minutes until they "finally" killed the Palestinian "child" ... deliberately... in cold blood. The crossfire dear to hearsay commentary does not exist. The 45 minutes of uninterrupted gunfire "solely from the Israeli position" are necessary to establish the heartless cruelty of Israeli soldiers.

The blood libel triggered the 21st century version of pogroms in Israel—*shahid* operations misnamed as "suicide bombings" —and vicious attacks on Jews worldwide. Why would the targets of the blood libel stand by in silence today, when a French court managed to recognize legitimate doubts about its authenticity? Jews are not defenseless!

Overcoming deep-seated reluctance to impinge on press freedom or conduct what could look like a whitewash, the Israeli government formed a commission under the direction of General Yossi Kuperwasser, appointed by General Moshe Ya'alon, to investigate the affair. The findings are published in a 36-page document that is a model of clarity. After months of thorough examination of the evidence, the commission concludes that Jamal and Mohamed al Dura were not hit by Israeli gunfire and, moreover, as far as the video is concerned, were not hit or wounded at all. Countless discrepancies, anomalies, inaccuracies and outright falsehoods support the claim that the scene was staged.

Charles Enderlin, who is wont to dismiss critics who have never set foot in Gaza and know nothing about war, had to find other ways to deflect the findings of the top brass commission composed of a solid roster of specialists. He claims France Télévisions was not invited to participate. Our sources report that the invitation, relayed by the French ambassador to Israel, was declined.

Convicted but not beaten, Philippe Karsenty deplores the unhealthy collusion between the executive, the courts, and the media to stifle the truth. "If President Hollande is serious about his promise to combat anti-Semitism, he should demand that France Télévisions withdraw the falsified news report."

The al Dura affair is not a *mano a mano* between Charles Enderlin and Philippe Karsenty in the French judicial arena; it is a burning international issue that must be addressed— the perversion of Western journalism in the service of forces opposed to civilized values, including the very press freedom enjoyed by those journalists. The al Dura news broadcast with its enveloping narrative not only incites to murderous hatred, it undermines the rational thinking that is our safeguard against tyranny.

— *American Thinker*

Afterword

FROM THE STAGED "DEATH" OF A PALESTINIAN YOUTH TO THE REAL THREAT OF AN IRANIAN BOMB

June-December 2013

The 21st century that prides itself—in democratic countries—on its humane humanitarian humanism, its ultra-refined sensitivity to diversity, its invulnerable bulwarks against every sort of discrimination or persecution that has ever darkened the face of history, has produced a blood libel of global proportions. While the campaign to demolish the Jewish state by lethal narrative warfare moves ahead, the Arab-Muslim world is shaken by a paroxysm of internecine slaughter and wanton destruction that no amount of misinterpretation can transform into the advent of democracy. These two currents—the blood libel, commonly known as the al Dura affair, and the savagery that convulses Islamic nations—mix and flow, confusing the issues and drowning the truth, as our hard-won liberty breaks up like a rain-soaked hillside that engulfs the village at its feet.

The crudely faked killing of a Palestinian youth identified as Mohamed al Dura sent shock waves through the collective international soul that nothing has been able to dispel. The slaughter of civilians on a massive scale in Islamic nations, the destruction of world heritage sites, persecution of blacks and Christians, rapes, beheadings, cannibalism and other horrifying atrocities committed daily are met with vague pleas to "do something..." verging on indifference. In both cases the misinterpretation is abysmal: the Arab Spring never blossomed, the Palestinian "child" was never killed in front of a France 2 camera at Netzarim Junction on September 30, 2000.

ARAB SPRING HOAX

When Egyptians massed in Cairo's Tahrir Square in 2011, the revolt was clicked into the Arab Spring narrative and packaged with the appropriate angles to hide troublesome details such as anti-Semitic posters and heavy Muslim Brotherhood presence. Taking serious risks to report from the midst of excited and sometimes enraged crowds, journalists and cameramen tiptoed around facts that clashed with the Arab Spring narrative. Or, if they tried to be honest, they were "corrected" in the studio. Female journalists finally dared to admit they were victims of sexual assault in those triumphant public squares. Some described the brutal gang attacks in graphic details— "I thought they were going to kill me"— adding that it was, of course, out of the question to keep female journalists away from these perilous assignments and, of course, we don't see them so often in the bustling crowds. In spite of censorship and gleeful here-comes-democracy commentaries, images of brutality slipped through, from the gory murder of Muammar Gadhafi to the latest Syrian rebel beheading videos, while cries of *Allahu Akhbar* [Allah is the Greatest] ring out like an advertising jingle.

The discourse trotted along with the movement, putting a good face on things. When the newly liberated populations in Tunisia and Egypt elected sharia-friendly governments, instant revisionism came up with "moderate Islamists," another layer of hype on the term "Islamist," already coined to separate Islam from "terrorism." When crowds gathered two years later to get rid of Muslim Brotherhood President Mohamed Morsi, they were again colored in Facebook-Twitter pastels. This time, really truly, it's the secular democracy crowd that has prevailed. Then, in a sudden lurch, media sympathy tipped in favor of the Muslim Brotherhood. And the Arabian Night's Dream continues.

In fact, we've already met these "moderate Islamists" inching toward

Jeffersonian democracy ...in the Palestinian camp. When they get radical, it's Israel's fault for refusing to satisfy Palestinian demands. The same shift-the-blame logic attributes the radicalization of the Syrian rebellion to the failure of the West to come swiftly to the aid of the good guys who couldn't overthrow the dictator without our help.

Well, we didn't help the good guys in Iran in 2009. Shouldn't it be our fault that the Islamic Republic is rushing to produce nuclear weapons? No. Iran's ambition for regional hegemony is, in the terms of this shifting discourse, no less legitimate than the Palestinian need to chip away at Israeli sovereignty and security. We did go into Afghanistan and Iraq to kick out the bad guys and help the good guys achieve democracy, so at least someone got it right there? Wrong! Our invasion of these two Muslim states, goes the story, created a backlash. To this day it is inspiring young men all over the world to rush to the latest flashpoint and wage... jihad! How can we withhold aid to the Syrian rebels (or opposition or *résistance*), how can we stand by as the death toll passes 120,000, how can we quibble about a black flag of jihad here and a lack of due process there, when... When the same blame-shifting narrative claims we financed and armed Osama bin Laden to do our heavy lifting against the Soviets in Afghanistan, so we shouldn't be surprised that his guys attacked us on 9/11 in Manhattan.

Then we shouldn't be surprised that the mujahidin we armed, trained, protected, and financed in Libya attacked the American mission in Benghazi, slaughtering the ambassador and three servicemen? Apparently not. The "we created the extremists" narrative wasn't applied to the Benghazi attack, an act of war aggravated by treason or, at the least, dereliction of duty by President Obama, then campaigning for re-election.

Two years of horror stories packaged as the Arab Spring—graphic images of enraged mobs, terrifying footage of brutal men with their faces swathed in keffieh, heads sawed off with dull kitchen knives, ruins, rubble, and desolation— leaves the Arab Street of the Western world indifferent. This is the Arab Street that could not bear to see a Palestinian stone-thrower roughed up by an Israeli soldier, the Street that was so horrified by the "murder" of Palestinians that it had to cool its rage by attacking Jews in Europe.

Journalism brings us the daily news as separate incidents packaged for a distracted audience, thrown onto the screen, treated hastily, and whisked away. Frivolous commentators monopolize the attention of a scatterbrained public, while serious thinkers that build a coherent picture are dismissed as fomenters of alarmist conspiracy theory. We see this for the al Dura affair as for jihad conquest in general.

This dispersion/distraction is weaponized by a coherent movement with clearly stated aims and purposes, directed by masterminds and implemented by millions in such a wide variety of operations that no superficial flyover can capture its contours. The slapdash style of 21st century jihad facilitates its dismissal. No individual incident looks like conquest, the toll of damage and casualties is not high enough to cause appropriate concern. The connection between small scale attacks by a weak disorganized adversary and loss of freedom and sovereignty in our societies is blurred. Aggressive Islam hides behind a religious screen. No matter how many *mujahidin* emerge in full battle dress under the black flag of jihad, their Islamic orthodoxy is denied: they are hijacking Islam, Islam has nothing to do with violent jihad. No matter how many imams preach the same Islam as the *mujahidin*, no matter how many Islamic nations move from secular dictatorship to sharia oppression, the protective shield of religious tolerance remains in place... in the free world. Religious tolerance is perverted into the permission to commit atrocities. This did not begin with the al Dura fake news report but the current acute phase was triggered by it.

Why was it so easy to fool people of all sorts everywhere? Why is it so hard to help people relinquish their attachment to the al Dura narrative, why do those who produced and broadcast it obstinately refuse to abandon it, why can they bank on enduring support from colleagues, officials and courts? The editorial director of the nominally conservative *Figaro* daily Yves Thréard admitted, in a panel discussion organized by a Jewish organization, that his staff wouldn't even let him publish a soft-pedaled article about the al Dura affair by Richard Prasquier, then president of the CRIF.

The enigma is like a concrete object I hold in my hand and turn this way and that, looking for glimmers of light. The al Dura broadcast is a fake. The burden of proof of a news report lies totally with the journalist and the media that broadcast it. France Télévisions trusts Charles Enderlin who trusts Talal Abu Rahma and none of them have ever offered any proof that the news report is authentic. On the contrary, they have been distorting the facts, changing their story, and outright lying for thirteen years. If it were authentic, the plaintiffs would have produced evidence at the first hearing. They didn't. Objectively, they lost the case. Judicially they won. If they weren't confident that it would be a show trial they wouldn't have dared to file suit. Definitive proof that the al Dura death scene was a staged hoax is offered by Charles Enderlin himself: *L'Enfant est mort* is an interminable barrage of libel against all who have dared to question the authenticity of the news report. And now his faithful henchman, Guillaume Weill-Raynal, has published a companion piece, "to put an end to the al Dura affair." *[Pour en finir avec l'affaire al Dura*, éditions du Cygne, Paris, 2013]. Here in France, no informed criticism of these books ever reaches the general public. Elsewhere, they are barely noticed.

TO PUT AN END TO THE AL DURA AFFAIR

If no French official at any level will force them to admit or dismiss them because of their dishonesty and incompetence, if the courts will not do justice, the media will not plead guilty, the liars won't suddenly tell the truth, shall we, with Guillaume Weill-Raynal, finally put an end to the al Dura affair? His bizarre stretched-out essay melts like a piece of ice on the burning brick of my collected al Dura works focused on the al Dura report as journalism. Either there are no standards for reliable reporting or any news report can be questioned and the only legitimate response is factual evidence.

[I refer to Guillaume by his initials to avoid confusion with his twin brother Clément Weill-Raynal and his sister Aude Weill-Raynal Esq., both of whom stand on the opposite side from him in the al Dura controversy.] But for G. W-R, who practiced law from 1985-2007, the killing of Mohamed al Dura and critical wounding of his father by gunfire from the Israeli position is a reality. Not a representation, a reality. As if a cameraman or journalist could deliver reality intact, unadulterated by the process of transmission let alone selection, viewpoint, or bias.

The incident, he repeats, is a reality. You don't have to prove a reality, it's real. So what can explain the unprecedented scope of the controversy? Why have so many people been misled? Singling out Philippe Karsenty as the personification of the hoax theory, G. W-R promises to do what no one has ever done— demolish Karsenty's evidence point by point. He then devotes the first 77 pages of the 99-page "book" to slander. Prominent individuals, anonymous groups, various media, community organizations, intellectuals, academics, and elected officials are put through the grinder, slathered with contempt, diagnosed as demented, perverse, idiotic and, worst of all, Jewish and Zionist. Anyone familiar with the case will notice the arbitrary selection: some who have been active for years, such as Richard Landes, are never mentioned. Alain Finkielkraut, who has held the issue at arm's length, is repeatedly propped up and gunned down. Daniel Pipes is a "controversial neoconservative," Emmanuel Navon is an "Israeli academic who belongs to Netanyahu's Likud party," Philippe Karsenty is blindly followed by a "pack of mad dogs."

When G. W-R finally gets around to the promised refutation, he plays cat and mouse with the truth, not hesitating to contradict his own assertions; the point is not to clarify but to exhaust and confuse the reader. Like his comrade Charles Enderlin in *l'Enfant est mort*, he writes as if no well-informed person could ever get in his way.

It seems he also assumes that readers will skip lightly, forgetting as they go. Obviously embarrassed by the absence of raw footage of the al Dura scene, he describes (p. 28) Talal Abu Rahma lackadaisically filming commonplace scenes at Netzarim Junction on September 30, 2000. Palestinian demonstrators harass soldiers in the Israeli outpost and play to the camera, making a big deal about slight injuries. The cameraman, with nothing better to do, kills time and accumulates footage, the very raw footage, snarls G. W-R, that detractors will later tear apart.

The professional cameraman's battery is nearly exhausted when, suddenly, all hell breaks loose, people scatter in panic, Abu Rahma catches sight of the man and boy pinned down by gunfire. He captures the scene in fits and starts, the camera goes off and on [by itself?], he misses key moments, the image is shaky, but the reality is there, the boy is dead the man is critically wounded.

Fifty pages later (p.78) this uneventful footage turns into the video of the dramatic 45-minute firefight that ended with the death of Mohamed and the wounding of Jamal al Dura. Of course the gunfire was not aimed at the man and boy for 45 minutes, declares G. W-R. It was all over the place... "as can be seen in the raw footage." The eight bullets that hit the wall and seven nearby were more than enough to wound and kill.

This wild turnabout on the contents of the raw footage contradicts the testimony given by the sole witnesses, Jamal al Dura and Talal Abu Rahma, immediately after the alleged incident and to this day. Here is Jamal quoted in Al-Monitor on May 22, 2013:

"*Jamal told Al-Monitor what happened: 'On Sept. 30, 2000, I went with Muhammad to Gaza City. Upon our return, there was a lot of shooting and confrontation with Israeli soldiers near the Israeli settlement of Netzarim, so we had to get out of the taxi. I went behind the agricultural lands of the almond trees, east of Salahuddin Street, the location of the clashes between Palestinian youths and the Israeli army. Then we took a street that intersects with Salahuddin. At the intersection's other corner, there was an Israeli military watchtower from which they started shooting at us directly and continuously for approximately 45 minutes. Muhammad was hit in his right foot. I was scared and tried to comfort him, but he was in high spirits.'*"
al-monitor.com/pulse/originals/2013/05/

So much for that! G. W-R's haphazard refutation is all cut from the same cloth. But one would have to know the documents to recognize the truncated citations, glaring omissions, and twisted details that lead to monumental conclusions such as the following:

(p. 83) "*On a rational level it is difficult to doubt the reality shown by this image [the lifeless Mohamed]. Yes, it is blurred and the exact moment when the fatal shot was fired was not filmed, but the sequence of the death of the child is inscribed in the logical framework of a chain of events, all of them real, that runs from the general context of the Israeli-Palestinian conflict to the failure of the Oslo process on to the shootout at Netzarim and the confrontations filmed in the hours that preceded it. Incidents covered by media all over the world. Impossible, in such a context, for a twelve year-old child and his father to act in a staged scene.*"

He asks what can explain the demented obsessional refusal to accept the truth (p. 91). "…a twelve year-old child is killed before the cameras of the whole world [sic] in the course of a firefight whose reality cannot be seriously contested by anyone." An "inane" theory buttressed by "puerile evidence" is swallowed by "all the Jewish pro-Israeli intellectuals and community organizations." These Zionists can't face up to their evil deeds. They hide behind the white robes of victimhood [he cites the pet theory of Esther Benbassa]. Constantly imagining existential threats, always on the verge of another wave of extermination, incapable of recognizing the humanity of Palestinians, unable to accept the slightest criticism of the Jewish state, they immediately start whining about anti-Semitism and, instead of admitting the Israeli army killed a Palestinian child, they dig up old stories of blood libel.

Case closed.

If I may be allowed just one question, your honor, I would like to know if European Jews in the 1930s were, they too, whining about anti-Semitism, imagining they were on the eve of another pogrom, unable to recognize the humanity of their Gentile neighbors, and so hypersensitive to criticism that they had to dig up old stories about Amalek, Haman, and the Cossacks instead of simply admitting ... What is it, exactly, they should have admitted?

The late Gérard Huber was struck by the inability of viewers of the al Dura video to distinguish between the living and the dead. The difference between Mohamed al Dura and, for example, a crumpled body lying in a pool of blood in a Nairobi mall (September 2013), should be obvious. It is obvious and has been amply demonstrated. Why is it not recognized?

PEACE PROCESS HOAX

The al Dura blood libel, we will recall, was perpetrated in the wake of the July 2000 Camp David summit that was supposed to be the culmination of the Oslo agreement. The "Intifada" it triggered was the continuation, not the breakdown of the peace process: both are aimed ultimately at the destruction of the State of Israel. Five years after the al Dura hoax, Jewish residents of Netzarim were evacuated along with the rest of the Israelis in the Gaza Strip. Not only did Gaza become a launching pad for attacks on Israel, the very fact of withdrawal is not acknowledged. For free-Gaza activists it's an "open-air prison." And the same would hold for any piece of Israel turned over to a Palestinian authority...the so-called painful concessions. The reasons go deeper than geopolitical strategy. The allegedly "occupied" are inhabited by an absence that they project onto their surroundings, a negative force that demolishes and destroys. The Gaza they coveted was the one that belongs to Jews. When it belongs to them it becomes worthless. Demands uttered from within that gnawing absence cannot be satisfied by practical arrangements. Despite concrete proof that withdrawal is not the solution, the pressure for territorial concessions persists. Why? Because "territorial concessions" like "the death of Mohamed al Dura" is a belief that is not subject to rational verification.

The al Dura hoax is still seen as an Israeli-Jewish image problem—bad publicity, justified or unfair depending on the vantage point. Victims who have fallen on one side or another of the Arab-Israeli conflict are lumped together and, most often, chalked up to the stubborn pursuit of a quarrel that could have been settled decades ago. Outside the small circle of the convinced and devoted, there is no sense of an imperative need to grapple with the al Dura issue. Much energy is dissipated, within that circle, in repeatedly proving the "death in real time" was a staged scene. This is why I see no interest in the creation of a hypothetically neutral international commission—occasionally promised by French authorities and/or requested by one or another demythifier — that would theoretically look at the evidence and decide once and for all if the news broadcast was authentic. The challenge today is to explore how the permission to massacre civilians in Israel has been extended to Europe, the Americas, and beyond... wherever jihad sets its sights.

Acquiescence in the mass murder of Israelis is periodically renewed, under cover of sympathy for the Palestinian cause. *Shahids* were glorified this year in an exhibition of blown-up photos of their iconic posters at the Jeu de Paume museum in Paris. Deaf to protests, the Minister of Culture defended the curator who defended the photographer who defended the mass murderers and perhaps they all thought it was cute to glorify the killers on the site of the Tennis Court Oath, prelude to the French Revolution. Protestors were refused authorization to demonstrate against the exhibition. This level of indulgence is so far reserved for enemies of the Jewish state. Will it some day be granted to the London, Madrid, or Boston Marathon bombers?

GLOBAL JIHAD CONQUEST

The staged al Dura scene provoked a chain reaction that began with a sting of stunning emotion. The concerted attack that followed in its wake was promoted as a spontaneous popular uprising, an "Intifada," spurred by the unrequited fervor for self-determination. I am not alone in defining it, on the contrary, as an acute phase in an ongoing campaign to destroy the Jewish state. Further, this determination to destroy Israel is not a localized conflict; it is the spearhead of global jihad conquest.

There is a logical progression from deliberate indifference to the lives of Israeli Jews and today's helpless indifference to the fate of Christians in Muslim countries or communities— Egyptian Copts, Syrian and Iraqi Christians, Nigerians persecuted by Boko Haram, infidels executed in Nairobi...and, ultimately, Christians beleaguered in Europe and America. Generally speaking, Americans and Europeans did not feel threatened by the violence unleashed in Israel in the early 2000s. When attacks were perpetrated in Manhattan, Madrid, London and, more recently, at the Boston Marathon, near a military base in Woolwich London, at an upscale mall in Nairobi— a small taste of what Israel got—denial was proclaimed at each blow: this has nothing to do with Islam, Islam has nothing to do with this violence.

As acts, threats, and fear of this particular type of violence— sometimes identified by the generic term "terrorism"— increase and spread, Islamic image-boosting is poured into our hearts and minds, gushes through our cultural circuits, rains down on our educational systems, spills into our religious institutions... Day in and day out, we are subjected to a torrent of *da'wah* disguised as history, art, peace, and friendship. In the halcyon days of the "Al Aqsa Intifada" the flood of pro-Palestinian anti-Israeli narrative sparked a defensive movement that tracked and dissected "disinformation"; a thankless task. Today we are drowning in a deluge of neo-apologetics for Islam.

Can the loss of sympathy for the Zionist project honestly be attributed to Israeli "colonization of Palestinian territories" after the 6-Day war? Israel didn't become a colonial power in 1967 any more than the West resumed the Crusades. These false accusations are weapons in the hands of an adversary that cannot defeat Israel in particular or the West in general by military means. In a geopolitically sane world that pre-1967 sympathy for Israel would be restored, the values of liberty and justice would be reasserted, and the West would rediscover its capacity to defend itself.

The Arab Spring hoax sheds light on the Intifada fakery. Where is the hypersensitivity to Muslim deaths that brought hundreds of thousands into the streets in "spontaneous" pro-Palestinian demonstrations? And the outrage over destruction of property when Israel counter-attacked in Gaza? Where is international opinion when mayhem explodes in one

Islamic nation after another supposedly yearning, like the Palestinians, to be free? Where is iraqbodycount.org [in fact, they are still counting... but who's listening?], where is "they are going to bomb Afghanistan back to the Stone Age" when these countries lurch headlong into self-imposed horrors after the withdrawal of the American "invaders."

From the September 11, 2012 attack against the United States in Libya to the revolt against the Muslim Brotherhood in Egypt, and including the savagery of anti-Assad rebels and the mobilization of Hizbullah forces in the ranks of the Syrian dictator, the figure of warriors fighting under the black flag of jihad can no longer be hidden behind the niceties of "militant, activist, freedom-fighter, *résistant*." The Islamic disaster is ineluctably visible.

Myths tumble one after the other, revealing the profound disarray of contemporary Islam. The "democratically elected moderate Islamists" determined to impose *sharia* are so repugnant that Muslim populations revolt and oust them. What does this have to do with the al Dura myth? The savagery of the "Arab Spring," displayed on television screens, was rhetorically denied in an attempt to uphold the illusion of a democratic breakthrough; the nonexistent violence of the al Dura video was invented to uphold the narrative of Israeli cruelty; Muslim populations in Europe were glorified by association with the supposed proof that Islam is compatible with democracy; Jews worldwide are declared guilty of Israeli brutality. Then what happens when these narratives collapse under the weight of reality?

WEAPONIZING CIVILIAN DEATHS

In Europe, a Great Divide is opening between citizens and officialized discourse. Though commentators, governments, the UN and the EU persist in singling out Israel for crimes against Palestinian humanity, thousands of civilians are killed every month by *mujahidin* or embattled governments in the Muslim world, blood and gore flow in the rubble of UN heritage sites, mosques, schools, and hospitals are attacked by all sides to these inextricable conflicts, millions of refugees flee, economies are in a shambles, and the Palestinian cause has lost its luster. A form of warfare waged against Israel, the weaponizing of civilian deaths, is visibly practiced on a massive scale. This has nothing to do with "collateral damage" or human shields. It is a military strategy consistently employed by the Palestinians and their allies against Israel, now used by the rebels against Assad, by Egypt's Muslim Brotherhood against the provisional government, and in countless smaller scale conflicts.

The natural emotion provoked by the sight and numbers of civilian casualties cannot preclude a critical evaluation of the indiscriminate practice of using civilian neighborhoods as military bases and then displaying bloody corpses as an argument for outside intervention. The Brotherhood put women and children on the front lines in their phony peaceful sit-ins after the ouster of President Morsi. They played the victims for Western consumption, displaying bloodied corpses, shrieking mothers, trembling children...and did their usual thuggery behind that screen.

The similarity between Brotherhood tactics during the August 2013 standoff and the Palestinian "intifada" in the fall of 2000 helps us understand the initial reaction of the Israeli government to the al Dura report and its long term consequences. Arafat's forces produced the fake child martyr, Mohamed al Dura, while organizing the "spontaneous" revolt, deliberately exposing civilians, including children, to gunfire, then using the victims to justify further violence. Israeli authorities, desperately trying to end the uprising by negotiations, allowed the al Dura story to pick up steam. Arafat, like the Egyptian Brotherhood from which he originated, was totally uncompromising. Our people will not give up, he said, after 3—and then 5, 13, etc.— innocent civilians have been killed. The media brandished the disparity between Palestinian and Israeli fatalities as proof of the justice of the Palestinian cause.

In both cases, public opinion was shaped by selective narratives— peaceful demonstrations against the Occupation in Israel, peaceful sit-ins in defense of democracy in Cairo. The Egyptian army was exhorted to compromise, respect the law, refrain from using excessive force. "The solution is political!" As the showdown approached, the negotiated solution was supposedly just one step away. A compromise was proposed by U.S. senators John McCain and Lindsey Graham: Pro-Morsi forces would slightly reduce the sit-in population, the military would promise to hold its fire. Palestinian uprisings go the same route: ruthless at the start, begging the international community to demand negotiations when they fail to achieve their goals.

Here, the outcomes diverge. The Egyptian military issued an ultimatum. It was ignored. The pro-Morsi rebellion was crushed without mercy. Over 600 dead in one day. Israel endured years of *shahid* atrocities before going on the offensive and, subsequently, building a defensive barrier. The scorn heaped on the provisional Egyptian government collided with the Arab Spring mystique. The westernized pro-democracy contingent that rose up against Islamic tyranny was abandoned, civilized values were betrayed, the Muslim Brotherhood was given endless opportunities to spread lies and play the victim. Their will to power was hidden behind the masses of ordinary men, women, and children. Journalists reporting from the heart of the Brotherhood sit-in, like their colleagues in Intifada-Gaza, risked their necks if they did not stick to the party line.

Why do the self-appointed moralists constantly intervene to prevent Israel from protecting its citizens... from genocide? Time and again every measure that reduces casualties, Palestinian as well as Israeli, is condemned. Non-existent or ambiguous international law is convoked to justify meddling in the "Israel-Palestine" conflict while horrendous violence rages in Syria, brews in Lebanon, rumbles in Libya, and explodes in Iraq. Relentless pressure is put on Israel to engage in negotiations for the creation of a Palestinian State when the surrounding nations are embroiled in a conflagration that would immediately engulf that stillborn state and existentially endanger what would be left of Israel.

It wouldn't have taken cruise missiles, U.N. mandates, or boots on the ground to save civilian lives in the dark years of jihad/intifada when violent attacks against Jews worldwide and the ruthless killing of civilians in Israel were blamed on the spectacle of Palestinian deaths, unbearable for Muslims. We now have irrefutable proof that Muslims in Europe and the United States do not spontaneously mobilize to protest or even show solidarity with their fellow Syrians, Iraqis, Egyptians, Libyans, Bahrainis, Lebanese... They do not, unlike their nominally Christian neighbors, show concern for Christians persecuted in Muslim lands. This doesn't mean they are indifferent, or selectively sensitive, depending on the identity of the perpetrator. It is because they are not mobilized by the upper echelons of the movement that exploits them.

ISLAM IS BEAUTIFUL

For years the Muslim masses were enlisted in the combat against blasphemy. "Insulting" images sent them to the streets, burning flags, torching embassies, slitting throats, getting themselves killed. Today, without the passage of anti-blasphemy laws, self-censorship is established in our once free world. We have moved on to a new phase of this ongoing war, an onslaught of smooth, sophisticated, highbrow Islam- is-beautiful indoctrination. At this very moment when rubble piles up from one to another dismal Muslim nation and bodies are strewn on the stage in a mega-reenactment of a Shakespearian tragedy, there is an outpouring of a new lethal narrative in the media, in academia, in political and cultural circuits. The story is that Jews and Muslims got along fine for thirteen hundred years; this past century, rife with conflict, is an aberration; people of good faith on all sides could, if they only recognized this fact, heal the rift and usher in a new period of harmonious coexistence. This fits nicely with the tale of reconciliation with Iran, now that big bad Ahmadinejad has been replaced by soft-spoken Rouhani. The world holds its breath, speaks in whispers, looks to the heavens for confirmation of Great Hopes. The time is ripe for Iran to renounce its nuclear ambitions and join the international community as befits its glorious history and current intentions. Does anyone really believe it? It doesn't matter. Just say it.

In both cases—13 centuries of harmony, Great Hopes of peaceful conflict resolution—who is the spoiler? The Zionists! Heavy-handed in the creation of their state and now huffing and puffing, drawing red lines, threatening unilateral military action just when an agreement is within reach.

The absurdity of this discourse is almost mathematical. Supposedly distressed by the daily massacre of Syrian civilians, world leaders are eating out of the mullocracy's hands in a peace-negotiations hoax without even asking them to stop supporting Bashir al Assad. Hizbullah, so kindly tolerated when it attacks Israel, is now Assad's indispensable ally. Is anyone asking the putative Lebanese government, which has always been able to count on benevolent diplomatic intervention when Israel retaliates against aggression, to rein in its very own Hizbullah?

The peace process logic is raised to worldwide proportions as Iran gallops toward nuclear weapons capability. Under pressure from the Obama government, Israel is forced to go round and round the mulberry bush with the Palestinians who will not give up an iota of their extravagant demands. The purpose of this round of idle talks is to position Israel as guilty of their inevitable failure and, eventually, try to impose a drastic resolution while distracting attention from the ticking Iranian time bomb.

The al Dura hoax triggered the "al Aqsa Intifada"—by its very denomination a religious conflict—in one stage of the ongoing project for the destruction of the State of Israel, which is validated theologically, ideologically, historically, politically, Islamically. Undaunted by the miserable failure of repeated military invasions and endless small scale attacks, the *umma* pursues its two-pronged strategy of pinpoint operations (misdefined as terrorism or freedom fighting) and a massive operation of demolition by narrative.

TWO-STATE SOLUTION HOAX

The foundation of this narrative is the "two-state solution." Those who—in the interests of Israel— dare to reject the "solution" are excluded from the debate and positioned, along with the mass murderers in the opposite camp, as one of the two extremes tugging against the inevitable, admirable, obvious and unique solution to the conflict.

Friends of Israel declare their undying affection while in the same breath exhorting Israel to make concessions, make peace, and create the Palestinian state that is dedicated to its destruction. It's perverse, it's insane, it's torture and the instrument is semantic deception. The two-state solution is a scimitar raised to the power of mass destruction.

Whatever legitimate aspirations might be lodged in the hearts of individual Palestinians, they have no place in the real project and no power to resist it. The well-intentioned are pawns of the jihad and decoys masking the planned destruction of Israel. Pawns, like the freedom-loving minority in the Arab world, held up as the driving force of an Arab Spring hoax, crushed in the immediate aftermath of what was in reality a retrograde Islamic method of regime change, replacing an old despised tyrant with a new idolized tyrant.

Why is it impossible to dissolve those misleading words: "two-state solution"? How is it a solution when no Palestinian leader can agree to such an arrangement? Even if a majority of the Arab population of Judea-Samaria were in favor of it, which they are not, the minority that is opposed would immediately rise up and destroy it. How can it be a two-state solution when the hypothetical state , if against all odds it were actually established, would be instantly overrun with the very same jihad forces that are wreaking untold destruction of life and property in the rest of the Islamic world,? How can withdrawal of Jews from Judea-Samaria, the so-called occupied territories, be a solution when withdrawal from Gaza gave the mujahidin an underground arms supply network and, on the surface, a launching pad for attacks on Israeli civilians? What solution? Israel is vilified for not withdrawing and Israel is vilified, after withdrawal, for the miseries of those who use their limited sovereignty, as in Gaza, to launch attacks and provoke the inevitable riposte.

Opposition to the "two-state solution" is not ideological, greedy, heartless or evil. It is simply realistic. Jewish awareness of an ever-present danger of genocide is not exaggerated, paranoid, or outdated. No one in any situation—personal, collective or international—can reach a viable arrangement through a process based on false premises. How can the words "two-state solution" be stripped of subterfuge and revealed as the expression of genocidal intentions?

In September 2000, viewers identified with the alleged innocent victims, Jamal and Mohamed al Dura; they saw themselves as targets of Israeli gunfire. They identified with the cameraman who observed and filmed but was helpless to save the father and his child. Viewers were the martyred child, they were the father who could not protect his son, they were onlookers trying to jump onto the television screen and stand between the cringing Palestinians and the heartless gunfire aimed at them. This emotional investment indelibly engraved the tragedy in an emotional realm, removed from the field of verifiable information.

Today we can see that those viewers are in fact victims of heartless gunfire, helpless onlookers of the massacre of innocents, unable to protect their children, disarmed, cringing, abandoned to the savagery of bloodthirsty monsters. Now we can identify the source of the gunfire, measure the shooting angle, count the minutes to the fatal outcome... of a nuclear-armed genocidal Iran. In the space of thirteen years a blood libel against the Jews has spread and grown to justify a massive attack against the West. The finger pointed at Israel is poked in the eye of the free world.

At the eleventh hour...

It is hard to believe that our fate will be decided in the coming weeks or months. Even if one believes it, it seems too extravagant to express publicly. The reasons for this dramatic suspense are multiple and diffuse.

Even as I highlight the role of the al Dura hoax, the strategy of lethal narratives, the implacable reality of jihad, I am aware of countless forces, currents, and vicissitudes that come together like so many rivulets, brooks, streams, and rivers to push us to this brink. The balance of power will shift dramatically to our detriment if the Islamic Republic of Iran pursues, unchecked, its race to develop nuclear weapons.

In October 2000, Prime Minister Ehud Barak, who was frantically trying to stop the "intifada" in its tracks, was received like a criminal by President Jacques Chirac who left him standing and did not even offer him a glass of water because, he said, "You are killing Palestinian children." In November 2013, French President François Hollande, standing side by side with Prime Minister Benyamin Netanyahu in Jerusalem, promised to prevent the conclusion of a sweetheart deal that would rescue Iran from crippling sanctions and allow the regime to pursue its nuclear arms program. The Obama administration, we learned, has been engaged in back door negotiations for a year already and was determined to conclude an agreement. It had seemed for a fleeting moment that France was going to fulfill its dream of replacing the United States as a decisive power in the Middle East while honoring its oft-expressed humanitarian values.

As Western powers scampered into a fool's bargain with Iran, Ayatollah Khamenei, addressing a congress of the Basiji, promised the destruction of Israel. Why? Not, as some argue, to pave the way for acceptance of an agreement that might seem like surrender even though it was clearly a subterfuge. No, the statement is a gigantic wink of complicity. It should have provoked the rupture of negotiations. Just as the al Dura hoax and ensuing violence should have put an end to the Oslo process, just as today's incitement should end the current "peace talks" with the Palestinians. Genocidal intentions are in a separate category. They have no relation to normal conditions of negotiation where each side defends its interests, creates facts on the ground, jockeys for position, seeks a better deal, ultimately makes compromises.

The wink of complicity entices a free world that can't acknowledge its meaning: "You know what we are going to do, and you are willing accomplices. We are all in this together." How else can we explain the transparent duplicity of the Iranian negotiators in this information age where everything is public knowledge? They boast of former exploits while engaging in a new round of cheater-takes-all. Public opinion pivots from a healthy attitude of self-defense to perverse hostility to Israel/ the Jews, preemptively accused of spoiling the appeasement plan. In the United States this anger is lodged in the heart of the administration.

The al Dura effect is raised to the ultimate degree: at the turn of the century an accusation of child-killing served to turn a blind eye to years of atrocities, today a peace process illusion covers acceptance of the nuclear arms that could finally satisfy the need to annihilate the Jewish people.

Does this justify historical comparisons with the 1930s: *Mein Kampf*, Chamberlain in Munich, the sacrifice of Czechoslovakia, the Evian conference that closed the doors of the free world on Jews fleeing extermination, the British blockade of Jewish immigration into mandate Palestine? Yes, to the extent that it reminds us of unheeded warnings and abject Western surrender to a rising totalitarian power.

However, one factor of the equation has changed radically. Judaism is not hunched in central European ghettoes, it is flourishing in a healthy prosperous State of Israel. The combined effect of inevitable strategic errors by Israel and tons of hostility heaped on Israel has not prevented the development of a vibrant, inventive, productive attractive society full of hope, a sterling example of doing good for oneself and others. The Israeli economy is healthy, its defenses are solid. Everything is open to debate in Israel, opinion is divided into millions of parts on every issue except for the existential question of survival and the integrity of Jerusalem.

What is happening to Israel's enemies and those who encourage the enemies of Israel? The ring of rocket launchers fiendishly set in place by the Iranian puppet master is no more invulnerable than the Maginot Line. Iran's proxy shield is crumbling into the craters of internecine strife. Europe is mired in self-inflicted distress. The United States has lost its compass.

If the Israeli government, with the consent of the governed, does in fact recognize the exterminationist configuration on the horizon it does not carry the analogy all the way to a 21st century Shoah. Israel's leaders may be berated by some for being too cowardly to strike Iran, chided by others for failing to clinch the two-state peace deal that would pacify the entire region, it would be only fair to admit that the Jewish state has chosen the heroic mode. At a time when western democracies, with rare exceptions, treat military preparedness like an outmoded fashion statement, Israel does not drop its guard. We will not know, until and unless it happens, whether the Jewish state is capable of striking Iran alone... or with the help of unlikely allies...but the attitude is courageous determination.

The metaphor is Hanukah, not Auschwitz.

This is the threshold on which we—or at least some of us— stand. Others, living in the same world, having access to the same information, surf on a different wave length. Dismissing the very possibility of an al Dura hoax, confident in the healing qualities of a Palestinian state, they see no signs of a comprehensive jihad movement, are horrified at the thought of a unilateral Israeli strike just when negotiations will bring Iran into the warmth of a peace-loving international community, and think that talk of genocidal intentions is paranoid.

It seemed, briefly, as if the French Foreign Minister Laurent Fabius had maneuvered into the position left vacant by the United States. Now it looks more like a child stepping into his father's shoes and taking five shuffling steps before stumbling into a fall. A deal was allegedly signed. Iran gets sanctions relief in exchange for empty promises it has already denied making. And Israel is immediately designated as the bad guy, the only hold-out, the one that doesn't want peace. A French journalist commenting on the agreement with Iran [Gérard Leclerc on the parliamentary channel Publi-Sénat, November 25, 2013] dismissed Israel's concerns with outright disgust: They're always seeing enemies that want to exterminate them. And that's their excuse for what they do to the Palestinians. Now it's Iran. It's Israel's fault the negotiations with the Palestinians are blocked. If the Iranian threat is lifted... they won't have that excuse anymore.

HOPE

The deal—no one even knows the terms, there's no formal signed agreement—doesn't remove the danger of a nuclear Iran, it intensifies it. Even if it the agreement had been drafted formally, the devil would not be in the details but in the principle. You cannot make a deal with a power that is determined to eliminate you, and has been working on it for decades. For the same reason, Israel can't make a deal with the Palestinians.

Should we not be dumbstruck by this transparent hoax? In the month since the televised hugs of Baroness Ashton, Secretary of State Kerry, Mohammad Jahad Zarif, et al, Iranian authorities from the Ayatollah Khamenei to the head of the nuclear weapons program and including the soft-pawed Rouhani and Zarif himself still warm from the free world's embrace have shouted from the rooftops: we have made no concessions, our right to develop nuclear power as we see fit is intact, we are moving forward on all levels.

All the red lines are hung out to dry. Our world has radically changed, the demolition of American leadership promised by Barack Hussein Obama is effective... but underhanded American power is used to manipulate natural allies and shore up our enemies. Our freedom hangs in the balance. Whatever the outcome, it will be the result of our ability—or failure— to perceive and analyze reality. No matter how dire the current situation, democratic nations don't lose the combat against tyranny... in the long run. The question is how much damage will be done before the tide turns. When it turns, the Al Dura hoax will be swept away with all the rest.

I intended to conclude this chapter and go to press at the end of August. The cutoff point for a writer is where the last lines of one book lead into the first paragraph of the next one. But I found myself pulled into a running commentary on events that seemed to have been crafted purposely to bring my arguments to a logical conclusion. A sterling demonstration of the lethal narrative strategy that connects the deceptively circumstantial al Dura hoax with the counterfeit P5 + 1 agreement with Iran. Metula News Agency immediately revealed the absence of a written engagement, while media worldwide swallowed the hoax and are still parroting nonsense about a "Geneva Agreement" that no one has ever seen.

Since June I have been writing close to the bone of events and then paring away, following things as they happened and then recomposing in a more comprehensive less chronological order. It was not my intention to conclude with a chronicle, a resumption of *Notes from a Simple Citizen*. As the months went by the story developed to an uncanny conclusion. More like a well-orchestrated novel than the mess of current events. The clarity was nearly blinding. My inner voice would gasp. They're not going to get away with this one? And then they did. But if I say it loud and clear, will I lose my credibility? Your president, the president of my native land, wants to let Iran develop nuclear weapons. Our government, the government of the land of my birth, cuddles up to the Muslim Brotherhood. It's unbelievable!

When rage against the Jews is unleashed there are never enough Jews on this earth to satisfy its hunger. If one house on the block catches fire the whole city will burn unless that single house fire is extinguished. I am haunted by the scenes of mayhem in Syria, the blood-stained rubble, haggard women and children. How many children tortured to death, deliberately bombed in their schools, how many thousands of dead children that do not trouble the world's sleep, that weigh nothing against one al Dura hoax. I am chilled to the bone by the utter collapse of the Islamic world. How long will it take to reach us? I am not surprised that French troops sent to Mali last year and to the Central African Republic last month to perform neat operations and show the world how these things are done with style are caught in the gears of the grinding machine that rumbles and crushes in Iraq, in Afghanistan, in Libya, wherever our forces set foot without grasping the nature and extent of the war we must fight.

It all hinges on a shift in perception. And the courage to speak one's mind. Our primary source for judging current events is journalism but the ethics of journalism is based on an urbane pose of objectivity that is not without merit... when appropriate. In the case of the al Dura hoax it has failed miserably. And where has it gone as Iran puts the finishing touches on its mujahidin bomb?

The timing was diabolical. As the year 2013 was drawing to a close, the slapdash results of secret backdoor U.S.-Iranian diplomacy were pulled out of the hat and proclaimed to be The Agreement the World was Waiting for. The awesome threat of a nuclear Iran was stopped in its tracks? The gigantic monster who only wanted to be loved is shutting down its machine of mass destruction and getting ready for a life of dinner parties and costume balls?

The jingle of festivities drowned out the groans of overwhelming evidence that the agreement is a low down hoax. We entered the timeless zone where logic is suspended. The media indulged in their favorite game of retrospectives. And the window of opportunity, the last window of opportunity opened... or closed... or was already closed. If our hopes are pinned on Israel—who else has the guts and the stuff to do it—our hopes billow to, as they say, biblical proportions.

What if they won't? Won't because they can't? Or can't because Israel's leaders, too, are caught in the lethal narrative. One more round of negotiation to show we are really truly willing to give peace a chance. One more month of trust in the American ally that won't let us down, even though it looks like they already have, we'll wait just a bit to make sure.

How can we know what time it is on our watch? We who follow events day by day, hour by hour, drawing on a vast pool of sources, letting no detail escape our vigilance, checking and cross-checking, monitoring mass media to see what our fellow citizens are being told, writing, speaking, debating, forming and modifying our opinions and predictions... where are we now? Have we veered off the road and over a cliff? Did someone rip out a chapter in the book of contemporary history? Did something irreparable happen during a moment of inattention? Is it the eleventh hour? The stroke of midnight? The dark of a terrible night with no sign of dawn approaching? Are we going through the motions, already knocked out and dragged from the ring, muttering through swollen lips? We were, not long ago, on the way to a showdown. And now it seems that the confrontation took place, or didn't, and disappeared without a trace. It's over? We already lost?

No.

Even when it is too late it is not too late.

www.ingramcontent.com/pod-product-compliance
Lightning Source LLC
Chambersburg PA
CBHW031257110426
42743CB00040B/657